Geology of the Bury St Edmu

This memoir describes part of Suffolk and the extreme eastern part of Cambridgeshire extending from the south-eastern fringe of the Fens to the heavily drift-covered plateau to the south and east of Bury St Edmunds. The structure of the concealed Palaeozoic rocks that form part of the London Platform is considered with reference to boreholes and geophysical data in and around the district, and the stratigraphy of Jurassic and Lower Cretaceous rocks, also concealed, that lap onto the Platform is described from boreholes. Details of the outcrops of the Lower, Middle and Upper Chalk are presented, incorporating much new palaeontological data. The early Quaternary marine Crag sands, confined to the south-east, are detailed and set in their regional context. The succeeding Drift deposits are systematically described, commencing with pre-glacial river deposits and followed by a complex Anglian glacial suite of boulder clay, silt, sand and gravel that occurs both as extensive plateau deposits and as the fills of deeply incised channels. Local lacustrine deposits of Hoxnian age are reviewed, and the later drift deposits including the Cover Sand with its related patterned-ground phenomena are described. The memoir includes an account of the economic geology and water supply of the district.

BRITISH GEOLOGICAL SURVEY

C R BRISTOW

Geology of the country around Bury St Edmunds

Memoir for 1:50 000 geological sheet 189
(England and Wales)

CONTRIBUTORS

Stratigraphy
B S P Moorlock
T E Lawson
B C Worssam
E R Shephard-Thorn

Palaeontology
B M Cox
D K Graham
D M Gregory
H C Ivimey-Cook
A W Medd
S G Molyneux
A A Morter
B J Taylor
D E White
I P Wilkinson
C J Wood

Geophysics
J D Cornwell

Petrology
R J Merriman
G E Strong

Economic geology
P K Murti
P M Harris
S J Mathers

LONDON: HMSO 1990

© Crown copyright 1990

First published 1990

ISBN 0 11 884405 9

Bibliographical reference
BRISTOW, C R. 1990. Geology of the country around Bury St Edmunds. *Mem. Br. Geol. Surv.*, Sheet 189 (England and Wales).

Author
C R BRISTOW, BSc, PhD
British Geological Survey, Exeter EX4 6BX

Contributors
J D Cornwell, MSc, PhD; B M Cox, BSc, PhD; P M Harris, MA, CEng, MIMM; H C Ivimey-Cook, BSc, PhD; S J Mathers, BSc; R I Merriman, BSc; B S P Moorlock, BSc, PhD; S G Molyneux, BSc, PhD; E R Shephard-Thorn, BSc, PhD; G E Strong, BSc; B J Taylor, BSc, PhD and I P Wilkinson, MSc, PhD
British Geological Survey, Keyworth

D K Graham, BA
British Geological Survey, Edinburgh

D M Gregory, BSc; T E Lawson, BSc; A A Morter, BSc; A W Medd, BSc, PhD; P K Murti, MSc; D E White, MSc, PhD; C J Wood, BSc and B C Worssam, BSc
formerly of the British Geological Survey

Other publications of the Survey dealing with this district and adjoining districts

BOOKS

Memoirs
Geology of the country around Norwich, Sheet 161
Geology of the country around Ely, Sheet 173
Geology of the country around Cambridge, Sheet 188
Geology of the country around Braintree, Sheet 223

British Regional Geology
East Anglia and adjoining areas (4th edition)

Mineral Assessment Reports (sand and gravel resources)
No. 72   Bury St Edmunds (1981)
No. 110   North of Newmarket (1982)
No. 123   Mildenhall and Barrow (1983)
No. 127   Woolpit (1983)

Well Catalogue
Records of wells in the area of the New Series one-inch Geological Sheet 189 (Bury St Edmunds)

MAPS

1:625 000
Solid geology (south sheet)
Quaternary geology (south sheet)

1:50 000 and 1:63 360 (Solid and Drift)
Sheet 161   Norwich (1975)
Sheet 173   Ely (1980)
Sheet 188   Cambridge (1981)
Sheet 223   Braintree (1982)

1:250 000 East Anglia
Solid geology
Aeromagnetic anomaly
Bouguer gravity anomaly

1:125 000
Hydrogeology, northern East Anglia (1976)
Hydrogeology, southern East Anglia (1981)

Printed in the UK for HMSO
Dd 240409   C10   6.90

CONTENTS

1 **Chapter 1 Introduction**
   Geological history 1

4 **Chapter 2 Concealed strata—Precambrian to Lower Cretaceous**
   Precambrian 4
   Palaeozoic 4
   Triassic 7
   Jurassic 8
     Lias 8
     'Estuarine Series' and Blisworth Limestone 8
     Cornbrash 9
     Kellaways Beds 9
     Oxford Clay 9
     West Walton Beds 9
     Structures affecting Jurassic strata 9
   Lower Cretaceous 9
     Lower Greensand 9
       Woburn Sands 10
       Carstone 10
     Gault 10

16 **Chapter 3 Upper Cretaceous: Chalk**
   Lower Chalk 16
   Middle Chalk 20
   Upper Chalk 22

30 **Chapter 4 Quaternary Solid: Crag**

35 **Chapter 5 Quaternary Drift: Pre-Anglian and Anglian**
   History of research and nomenclature 35
   Kesgrave Sands and Gravels 36
   Ingham Sand and Gravel 38
   Drift-filled channels 38
   Lower Glacial Sand and Gravel 43
   Boulder Clay (Till) 47
   Upper Glacial Sand and Gravel 52
   Glacial Silt 54
   Woolpit Beds 57

60 **Chapter 6 Quaternary Drift: Hoxnian to Flandrian**
   Lacustrine Deposits 60
   Head and Head Gravel 61
   River Terrace Deposits 63
   Cover Sand 70
   Patterned ground 74
   Alluvium 74
   Peat 76

78 **Chapter 7 Economic geology**
   Sand and gravel 78
   Chalk 80

   Brick-clay 80
   Water supply 81

83 **References**

86 **Appendices**
   1 List of Geological Survey photographs 86
   2 Abridged log of Stowlangtoft Borehole 87

91 **Fossil index**

95 **General index**

FIGURES

1 Simplified solid geology of the Bury St Edmunds and surrounding districts 2
2 a) Bouguer anomaly map of the Bury St Edmunds district 5
   b) Bouguer anomaly profile AA' 6
3 Geophysical and borehole evidence for the nature of the pre-Mesozoic basement in and around the Bury St Edmunds district 7
4 Generalised vertical section of the Gault of East Anglia showing the main lithological and faunal features 11
5 Distribution of ostracoda in the Gault from Ely-Ouse Scheme boreholes 2 and 11 12
6 The Chalk outcrop showing localities mentioned in the text 17
7 Subdivision of the Chalk in the Bury St Edmunds district with particular reference to the Stowlangtoft Borehole 18
8 Section in Upper Chalk including the Brandon Flint Series in a flint mine near Brandon 1879 (after Skertchley in Ward and others, 1968) 23
9 Sections in Upper Chalk at Dalham, near Barrow Heath and at Higham 25
10 Section in Upper Chalk, Stowlangtoft Quarry 28
11 Grading curves and size distribution histograms for samples of Crag sand from the Woolpit Borehole 31
12 Conductivity map of part of the drift-filled system in the Ixworth-Woolpit area 39
13 Grading curves and size distribution histograms for samples of Cover Sand around Woolpit, Elmswell and Tostock 72
14 Incidence of 1:25 000 sand and gravel resource maps in and around the Bury St Edmunds district 78

TABLES

1 Physical properties of basement rocks in and around the Bury St Edmunds district 7
2 Classification of the Chalk 7
3 Physical properties derived from the geophysical logs of the Stowlangtoft Borehole 17
4 Classification of the Quaternary deposits (Drift) in the Bury St Edmunds district 35
5 Thicknesses of Second River Terrace Deposits between Fornham All Saints and Hengrave 67
6 Distribution of Pleistocene and Holocene freshwater molluscs in the Bury St Edmunds district 69
7 Analyses of groundwater (expressed in milligrams/litre) 82

PLATES

1 Kesgrave Sands and Gravels and Head, near Stanton 36
2 Ingham Sand and Gravel, Ingham 38
3 Chalky Boulder Clay overlying contorted Glacial Sand and Gravel, Fornham Park 43
4 Chalky Boulder Clay overlying Lower Glacial Sand and Gravel, Fornham Park 44
5 Finely laminated silty clay and fine-grained sand of the Woolpit Beds, Woolpit Brickworks 58
6 Ice-wedge cast within Second River Terrace Deposits, Cavenham 64
7 Cryoturbation of Cover Sand into Chalk, Kentford 71
8 Subsidence above old chalk mine workings, Jacqueline Close, Bury St Edmunds 80

PREFACE

This memoir describes the geology of the district covered by the 1:50 000 (Bury St Edmunds) New Series Sheet (189) of the Geological Map of England and Wales. The district was first geologically surveyed on the one-inch scale mostly by F J Bennett, with smaller tracts by J H Blake, S B J Skertchly, W H Penning and A J Jukes-Browne between 1879 and 1882, and published as Old Series Sheets 51 SE (1882), which covers most of the present district, 51 NE (1883), 50 NW (1882) and 50 SW (1881). Descriptive memoirs of these sheets were published in 1886 (Bennett and Blake), 1891 (Whitaker and others), 1884 (Bennett) and 1881 (Whitaker, Bennett and Blake) respectively.

Several of the Geological Survey 'Water Supply' memoirs have dealt in part with the district, namely: 'The water supply of Suffolk from underground sources (Whitaker, 1906); Wartime Pamphlet No. 20, Part III, compiled by Dr A W Woodland (1942); a Well Inventory compiled by Miss B I Harvey and others (1973). The Hydrogeological Map of southern East Anglia, published in 1981, covers the Bury St Edmunds district.

Several publications by the former Industrial Minerals Assessment Unit are relevant to the Bury St Edmunds area and include assessments of the sand and gravel resources of the following 100 km grid squares: TL 76 and 77 (and part of TL 87) (Clayton, 1983), TL 86 (Hawkins, 1981) and TL 96 (Clarke, 1983).

The primary six-inch geological survey of the Bury St Edmunds area was made by Drs C R Bristow and B S P Moorlock between 1976 and 1978 and by Mr T E Lawson in 1977 and 1978. A small tract on the western margin was surveyed by the late Prof. J H Taylor in 1938–39 and by Mr B C Worssam in 1953. The 1:50 000 geological map of the area was published in 1982.

As well as accounts by the field officers, the memoir contains contributions on the macropalaeontology of the Palaeozoic rocks by Dr D E White, the Lias by Dr H C Ivimey-Cook, the Upper Jurassic by Dr B M Cox, the Gault by Mr A A Morter, the Chalk by Mr C J Wood, and the Quaternary by Mr D K Graham. The micropalaeontology of the Palaeozoic is contributed by Dr S G Molyneux, the Gault by Dr A W Medd and Dr I P Wilkinson, and the Quaternary by Miss D M Gregory. Dr B J Taylor has reported on Quaternary coleoptera. Dr J D Cornwell has provided a geophysical account of the concealed formations of the district and Dr E R Shephard-Thorn a description of the Palaeozoic, together with an abridged log (Appendix 2) of the Stowlangtoft Borehole. Mr R J Merriman has undertaken analyses of glauconite in the Crag, and Mr G E Strong has carried out grain-size analyses on Crag sands and Cover Sand. Mr P K Murti drafted the account on the water supply of the district, Mr P M Harris the section on chalk and Mr S J Mathers that on sand and gravel.

We are grateful to Dr G R Coope (Department of Geological Sciences, University of Birmingham) for the identification of Quaternary coleoptera; to Mr J J Wymer for Quaternary vertebrates from the Lackford Pit; to Dr M J Tooley (Geography Department, University of Durham) for palynological examination of samples from Lackford; to the late Dr M Black for coccolith identifications from Gault samples; to Dr H W Bailey for foraminiferal determinations on Chalk samples; to Dr R N Mortimore for information about boreholes in Bury St Edmunds; and to Dr R E H Reid for identification of sponges from the Top Rock of the Chalk; also to Dr J B Richardson for identification of Siluro-Devonian miospores and Dr D J Siveter for identification of Palaeozoic ostracodes. Official photographs were taken by Messrs H Dewey and H J Evans. The areas surveyed by the respective field officers are shown in the list of six-inch maps on p.ix.

Thanks are given to Messrs Binnie and Partners and the Anglian Water Authority for making available the cores of the Ely-Ouse Transfer Scheme boreholes to the then Institute of Geological Sciences.

The surveyors are grateful for the ready cooperation of landowners and tenants in facilitating access to their properties. The memoir has been compiled by Dr C R Bristow and edited by Mr W B Evans, Dr B N Fletcher and Dr R G Thurrell.

F G Larminie OBE
Director

British Geological Survey
Keyworth
Nottingham NG12 5GG

3 August 1988

LIST OF SIX-INCH MAPS

NOTES

The following is a list of six-inch geological maps included wholly or in part within the 1:50 000 Bury St Edmunds (189) Geological Sheet, with the initials of the surveyors and the date of the survey for each map. The surveyors were C R Bristow, B S P Moorlock, T E Lawson, B C Worssam and J H Taylor.

Manuscript copies of these maps have been deposited for public reference in the libraries of the British Geological Survey. They contain more detail than appears on the published map. Open-file reports on the detailed geology are available for sheets marked by an asterisk.

TL 65 NE	Woodditton	JHT	1938–39
TL 66 SE	Chevely	JHT, BCW	1938, 1953
TL 66 NE	Kennett	BCW	1953
TL 67 SE	Freckenkam	BCW	1953
TL 67 NE	Mildenhall Airfield	BCW, CRB	1953, 1979
TL 75 NW	Lidgate	BSPM	1977
TL 75 NE	Chedburgh	BSPM	1976
TL 76 NW	Kentford	BSPM	1977
TL 76 NE	Risby	BSPM	1977
TL 76 SW	Dalham	BSPM	1977
TL 76 SE	Barrow	BSPM	1976, 1977
TL 77 NW	Eriswell	BSPM, CRB	1978, 1979
TL 77 NE	Eriswell High Warren	TEL	1978, 1979
TL 77 SW	Tuddenham	BSPM	1978
TL 77 SE	Icklingham	TEL	1978
TL 85 NW	Whepstead	CRB	1976
TL 85 NE	Bradfield Combust	CRB	1976
TL 86 NW	Fornham All Saints	BSPM	1976, 1977
TL 86 NE	Great Barton	CRB	1976
TL 86 SW	Horringer	BSPM	1976, 1977
TL 86 SE	Rushbrooke	CRB	1976
TL 87 NW	Elveden	TEL	1977
TL 87 NE	Barnham	TEL	1977, 1978
TL 87 SW	West Stow	BSPM, TEL	1976, 1977
TL 87 SE	Great Livermere	TEL	1977
TL 95 NW	Felsham*	CRB	1976
TL 95 NE	Rattlesden*	CRB	1976
TL 96 NW	Pakenham	CRB	1977
TL 96 NE	Stowlangtoft	CRB	1978
TL 96 SW	Beyton	CRB	1977, 1978
TL 96 SE	Woolpit	CRB	1978
TL 97 NW	Little Fakenham	TEL	1978, 1979
TL 97 NE	Barningham	CRB	1978
TL 97 SW	Ixworth	TEL	1978
TL 97 SE	Stanton	CRB	1978

The word 'district' used in this memoir means the area included in the 1:50 000 Geological Sheet 189 (Bury St Edmunds).

National Grid references are given in square brackets throughout the memoir. All lie within the 100 km square TL except where otherwise indicated.

Letters preceding numbers refer to Survey collections as follows:

X Powder films in the data bank
BGS Ze Palaeontological collection.

CHAPTER 1

Introduction

The district described in this Memoir lies entirely within the county of Suffolk but for a small tract in the south-west in Cambridgeshire. It takes its name from the ancient market and cathedral town Bury St Edmunds, so called from the martyred Saxon King, St Edmund, whose bones were brought to the Abbey (now in ruins) on the banks of the River Lark early in the 10th century. In the Middle Ages, Bury St Edmunds was a shrine and centre of learning, famed for producing illuminated manuscripts. In 1214, it is recorded that local noblemen resolved to force King John to accept the Magna Carta, an event recalled in the town motto 'Shrine of a King, cradle of the Law'. Apart from the 13th century Abbot's Bridge over the Lark and two fine gatehouses, the town boasts an impressive square, Angel Hill, surrounded by fine buildings which house museums, meeting rooms and hotels and which include St James' Cathedral. In recent years, the predominantly agricultural economy of the district has been augmented by light industrial developments and the population of Bury has grown to 30 000 or so. Mildenhall, in the north-west of the district, is the second largest settlement, depending for much of its trade and prosperity on the presence nearby of two major military airbases.

The boulder clay soils are extensively cultivated for cereals and sugar beet. Until recently, the lighter soils supported heath and open woodland. Modern farming methods have produced an increasing pressure to convert these areas of lighter soils to arable farm land. This process has been accompanied by the removal of many of the hedgerows and woodlands, and in places this has given rise to monotonous, featureless terrain. An extensive area of Forestry Commission coniferous woodland, the King's Forest, has been planted in the north.

The geological deposits preserved within the district are listed on the inside front cover of this Memoir. The district lies on the northern edge of the London Platform and is everywhere underlain by the Chalk; in the south and east, marine Pleistocene Crag deposits overlie the Chalk. At depth, except in the north-west, the Gault everywhere rests on folded Palaeozoic strata. In the north-west, Lower Greensand and various Jurassic formations have been proved in boreholes.

The oldest strata to crop out in the district, those of the Lower Chalk, occur over a limited area around Mildenhall in the north-west; younger strata appear successively south-eastwards. Middle Chalk occupies a broad band in the north-western quadrant of the district. Upper Chalk underlies much of the rest of the district, but has a fragmentary outcrop because of the drift cover.

Obscuring much of the solid geology at outcrop, especially in the south and east, is an extensive spread of glacial and postglacial drift deposits.

Glacial deposits dominate the drift and consist of Glacial Sand and Gravel, Boulder Clay (Till) and Glacial Silt. Locally, there are patches of older fluvial deposits—the 'Bunter'-rich Ingham Sand and Gravel, and the quartz/quartzite-rich Kesgrave Sands and Gravels. Glacial Sand and Gravel has a patchy distribution, occurring both above and below the Boulder Clay and, locally, within Boulder Clay. The upper deposits, commonly chalk-rich, are found principally in the south-east around Tostock. Boulder Clay occurs mostly over the higher ground of the south-eastern two-thirds of the district, and forms extensive featureless plateaux. Glacial Silt is mostly confined to the valley of the River Lark. Deep drift-filled valleys, extending to at least 63 m below OD, are followed by the present-day rivers, their fill consisting of Glacial Sand and Gravel, Boulder Clay and Glacial Silt.

Postglacial sediments include Lacustrine Deposits and River Terrace Deposits, which occur mostly along the River Lark and its tributaries, with minor spreads along the River Kennett in the west and The Black Bourn in the east. Alluvium, and locally Peat, are present along all the major valleys and many of the minor ones. Heterogeneous deposits of Head and Head Gravel mantle many of the valley sides and floors. Spreads of wind-blown sand, the Cover Sand, occur principally in northern and central parts. Before re-afforestation, severe problems associated with 'sand blows' occurred in the northern part of the district.

The highest ground is on Boulder Clay in the south-west extremity of the district, with the highest point, 125 m above OD, at Chedburgh. Most streams flow northwards from the Boulder Clay plateau, and drain via the River Lark into The Wash. The lowest point within the district is 7 m above OD near Mildenhall in the north-west. In the east, much of the drainage is northwards via The Black Bourn and its tributaries, which also flow into the Wash. A small tract in the south-east is drained by headwaters of the River Gipping which reaches the North Sea via the Stour Estuary.

The various solid and drift deposits give rise to three main soil types: light chalky soil on Chalk; heavy, clayey, poorly draining calcareous soil on boulder clay, and light, more acid soils on the sands and gravels. Cryoturbation structures, developed during the late Pleistocene, have locally produced areas of intricately patterned ground, with polygons and stripes of sand and Chalk. In such areas, commonly mapped as drift-free Chalk, the patterning is picked out by the younger crops or, in areas of heath, by the distribution of calcifuge and calcicole plants.

GEOLOGICAL HISTORY

Silurian/Devonian rocks on the northern side of the London Platform lie at depths of between 160 and 200 m below OD. It is probable that much of the region remained a land area throughout the later Palaeozoic and much of the Mesozoic era. Triassic and Jurassic strata occur in the north-west where they are banked against, or locally faulted into the London Platform. The Cretaceous Lower Greensand appears to have been the first Mesozoic formation to lap southwards and south-eastwards on to the platform, the most easterly occurrence having been proved in the Culford Borehole (Figure 1) where it rests directly on Palaeozoic strata. After the deposition of the Lower Greensand, the platform continued to subside (or the sea-level to rise) and the Gault sea spread across a surface of Palaeozoic rocks. The transgression was at first probably intermittent, for many of the Lower Gault beds thin out against the platform. Later the platform ceased to exert any significant influences on sedimentation, the Upper Gault being present everywhere within the region. During deposition of the Chalk, marine conditions persisted throughout the region, but intermittent shallowing of the sea took place. During such shallow-water periods, sedimentation was interrupted and scouring took place, with the result that condensed sequences (notably the Cambridge Greensand and Top Rock) and local breaks occur at several levels within the Chalk. At the close of the Mesozoic era, the district was gently uplifted and the higher zones of the Chalk were removed by erosion. In the early part of the Tertiary, marine conditions were re-established and the Thanet Beds were probably deposited across much of the district. However, erosion during the early Pleistocene removed most of them, such that only the basal glauconite-coated flints of the Bullhead Bed remain, incorporated as a *remanié* deposit in the basal bed of the Crag (Bristow, 1983).

On regional evidence it is inferred that some folding and faulting took place during the Miocene, and such tectonic activity was probably responsible for the establishment of the basins in which the Crag was deposited (Bristow, 1983). These basins occur mainly to the south-east of the district; the Crag being restricted to the east and south-east parts with its shore-line probably extending along a north-east–south-west line from Stanton to Chedburgh. Renewed movement along the faults bounding the Crag basins took place during the Pleistocene.

The Quaternary period was dominated by glacial and periglacial activity. The oldest nonmarine Pleistocene deposits are those of the fluviatile Ingham Sand and Gravel and the Kesgrave Sands and Gravels. These units may be contemporaneous, but they represent deposits from different catchment areas. The Ingham Sand and Gravel probably derives from the north-west, whereas the Kesgrave Sands and Gravels were laid down by a river (?proto-Thames) that flowed north-eastwards across Essex and East Anglia (Rose and Allen, 1977). The main glacial episode was the advance of the Anglian ice-sheet, which gave rise to patchy deposits of Glacial Sand and Gravel overlain by the more extensive chalky Boulder Clay (Till). An amelioration of climate at the end of the Anglian resulted in the accumulation of interglacial deposits of Hoxnian age, preserved at Sicklesmere (West, 1981) and probably at Icklingham (Kerney, 1976; Holyoak and others, 1983). Solifluction deposits (Head) occur in nearly all the valleys, but the evidence to substantiate more than one episode of periglacial activity is insufficient. The Haughley Sands and Gravels in the south-east are meltwater deposits of uncertain age, possibly in part

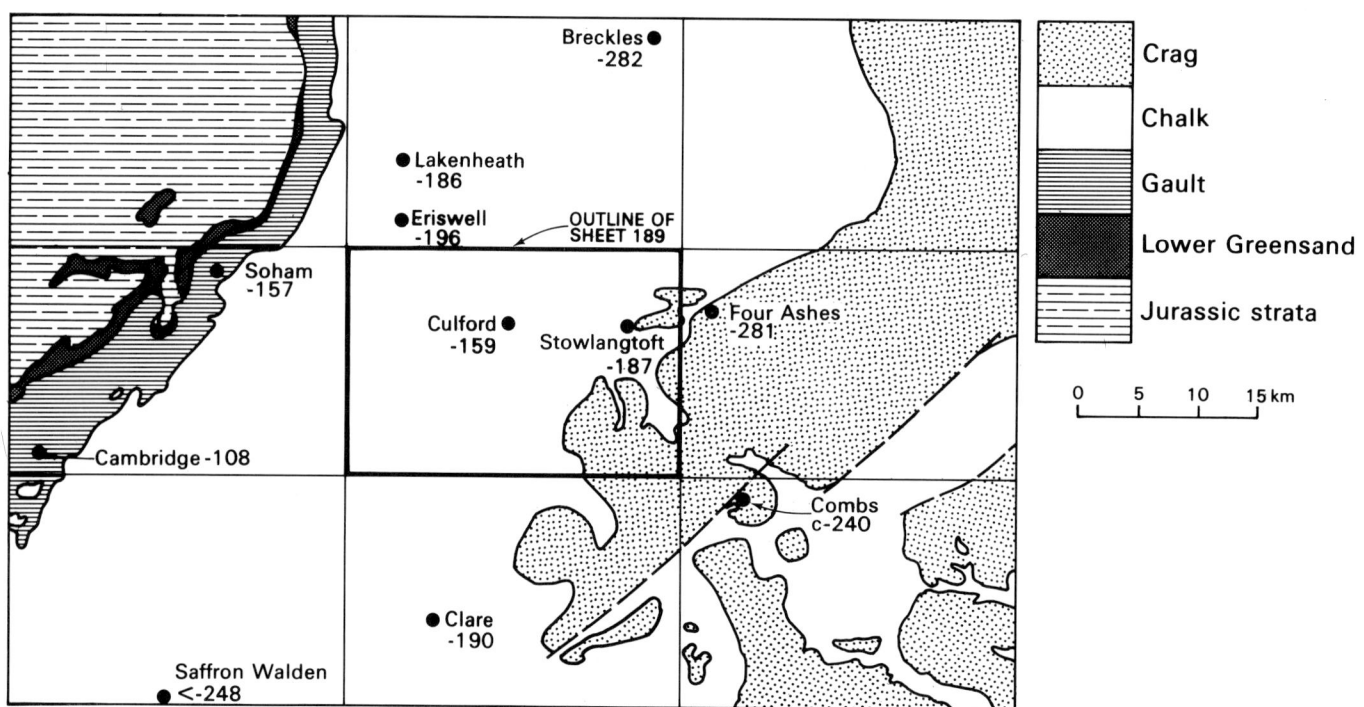

Figure 1 Simplified solid geology of the Bury St Edmunds and surrounding districts showing the location of the boreholes and depths in metres below OD to the Palaeozoic basement

Anglian and in part Devensian. Glacial Silt is widespread, occupying a deep channel along the Lark Valley and occurring over a restricted area at Woolpit (Bristow and Gregory, 1982). The Woolpit Beds are also of uncertain age, but may be Devensian. Fluvioglacial outwash of presumed Devensian age gave rise to sheets of sand and gravel (First to Fourth River Terrace Deposits). At the close of the Pleistocene, and continuing into the Holocene, much sand was blown into the district to lodge as Cover Sand.   CRB

CHAPTER 2

Concealed strata—Precambrian to Lower Cretaceous

PRECAMBRIAN

The few deep boreholes in and around the district (Figure 1) penetrate only a few tens of metres into the pre-Mesozoic basement rocks. It is probable, however, that the district is underlain at a considerable depth by magnetic rocks possibly of Precambrian age. Aeromagnetic data suggest that these rocks rise northwards to culminate in a pronounced east-south-east-trending ridge to the north of the district, at a depth of about 5 km. There is no evidence from the aeromagnetic map (Institute of Geological Sciences, 1982) that any magnetic material exists at the basement surface. Some weak aeromagnetic anomalies suggest the existence of magnetic rocks at depths of a few kilometres north of Bury St Edmunds in an area delimited to the south and west by Bouguer anomaly lows (Figure 2a).

A broad north-west-trending Bouguer anomaly low crosses the north-east extremity of the district near a seismic refraction site at Bridgham (Bullard and others, 1940) which revealed a high basement velocity of 5.98 km/s. Although Chroston and Sola (1982) expressed doubts as to the validity of this particular result, they considered that similar high velocities recorded in north Norfolk point to the presence of igneous or metamorphic rocks in the basement which could be Precambrian in age. The gravity evidence might, therefore, indicate a north-west-trending ridge of such rocks surrounded by the Siluro-Devonian sediments, although it is not associated with any distinct magnetic anomaly.   JDC

PALAEOZOIC

Boreholes in and around the district (Figure 1) have proved Siluro-Devonian rocks, peneplained to form part of the London Platform. The surface slopes down towards the north-east.   CRB

Palaeozoic rocks were encountered at a depth of 225 m (187 m below OD) in the Stowlangtoft Borehole [9475 6882] and were proved for 70.6 m. The sequence consists dominantly of siltstones and interbedded siltstones and mudstones, with sandstones common in the uppermost 27 m. The siltstones and mudstones are micaceous, patchily bioturbated and commonly laminated or interbanded to give a striped appearance. Loading structures and minor channelling occur, with graded bedding in the channels. The sandstones are fine to medium grained, silty, micaceous and locally laminated; minor channelling and bioturbation are present. The beds are mainly medium to dark grey, but the uppermost 26 m are red-stained with patchy greyish green reduction zones. Dips increase with depth from 20 to 80°; two fault-planes were noted in the core.   ERST

Below 234 m a shallow-water marine macrofauna of late Silurian aspect is scattered through the sequence. It consists mostly of molluscs including *Nuculites sp.*, *Orthonota rigida*. *Palaeopecten* cf. *danbyi*, *Ptychopteria (Actinopteria) sp.*, *Murchisonia sp.* and cf. *Tritonophon trilobata*, and numerous hyolithid fragments. Brachiopods are much less common, but species of *Craniops*, *Lingula*, *Orbiculoidea* and *Protochonetes* are present. Two fragments of trilobite cranidia are possible examples of *Acaste*. *Ceratiocaris sp.* and a few poorly preserved kloedeniine ostracodes are also present, with crinoid columnals concentrated at some levels. Dr D J Siveter of Leicester University has confirmed (personal communication) that the kloedeniines are probably examples of *Londinia*, a genus recorded from the upper part of the Ludlow Series (Ludfordian Stage) to the middle part of the Přídolí (formerly Downton) Series.   DEW

Palynological studies have been carried out on 18 samples of the Stowlangtoft Palaeozoic rocks. The uppermost reddened sandy strata, between 226.50 and 235.65 m, proved either to be barren or to yield nondiagnostic assemblages. Acritarch and miospore assemblages from samples between 239.14 and 295.60 m are comparable with Ludfordian (Upper Ludlow) assemblages from the Welsh Borderland. The sample at 239.14 m yielded the following acritarchs: *Leoniella carminae*, *Micrhystridium stellatum*, *Multiplicisphaeridium asturiae?*, *?Oppilatala eoplanktonica*, *Tunisphaeridium tentaculaferum*, *Visbysphaera* cf. *dilatispinosa* and *V. meson*. Dr J B Richardson of the British Museum (Natural History) reports (personal communication) that the miospores include *Ambitisporites dilutus*, *Archaeozonotriletes chulus*, *?A.* cf. *divellomedium*, a dyad cf. *A. dubius*, and spores resembling *Apiculiretusispora* sp. C of Richardson and Lister (1969), an assemblage that indicates a probable mid-Ludfordian age.   SGM

Palaeozoic rocks were encountered at a depth of 194.3 m (159 m below OD) in the Culford Borehole [8310 7107]. A sample from the interval 194.3 to 195.07 m consists of angular fragments of medium grey, finely micaceous, indurated mudstone. Between 195.07 and 200.33 m similar mudstone is intensely sheared (possibly by drilling). The lowest sample, at 200.33 m, consists of medium grey mudstone as above, but with a weak cleavage. A sample from the interval 195.07 to 200.33 m was examined for spores, but none was found. The lithologies are similar to those of the Silurian at Stowlangtoft and to ?Upper Silurian/Lower Devonian strata encountered in Four Ashes [TM 0223 7186] (Bristow, 1980), Lakenheath [748 830] and Clare [7834 4536] boreholes.

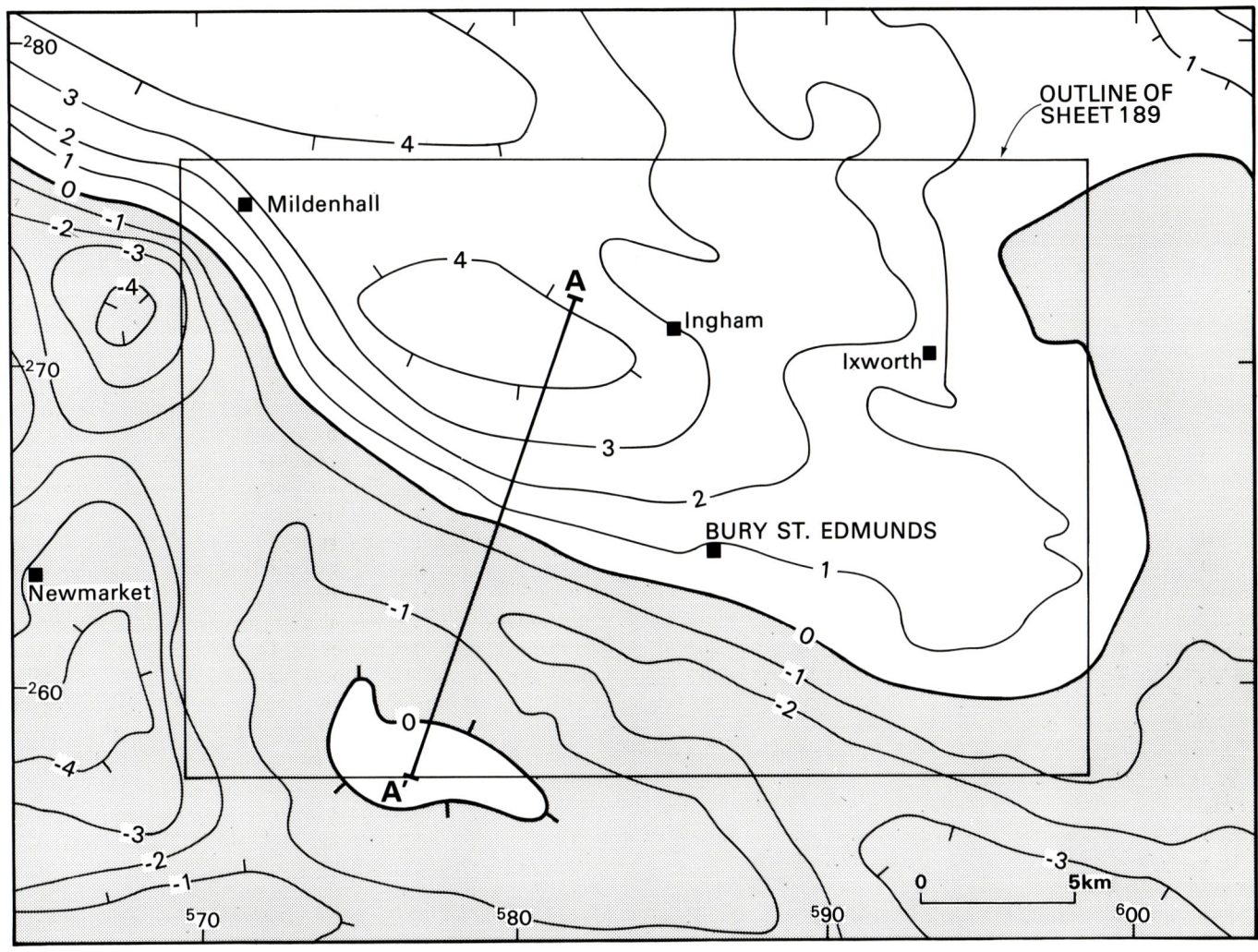

Figure 2a Bouguer anomaly map of the Bury St Edmunds district. Contours at 1 mGal intervals

In Eriswell Borehole [7423 7887], to the north of the district, the Palaeozoic rocks consist of 1.59 m of steeply dipping (c.45°), reddish brown to greenish grey, slightly micaceous, fine-grained sandstones and fine-grained sandy mudstones, similar to the reddened upper beds at Stowlangtoft. The beds are locally brecciated and cross-veined with quartz. Similar strata were encountered in the Cambridge and Soham boreholes (Worssam and Taylor, 1969) and were presumed to be of Devonian age. However, in the Soham Borehole, strata below 168 m contained a shallow-water marine macrofauna of late-Silurian or early-Devonian age, comparable with that recorded from the Lakenheath Borehole.   CRB

Regional aeromagnetic and gravity data (Institute of Geological Sciences, 1981; 1982 and Fig. 2a) and seismic refraction studies (Bullard and others, 1940 and unpublished BGS data) supplement information from the scattered boreholes. The Bouguer anomaly map (Figure 2a), in particular, shows variations which suggest structures within the basement rocks. The most obvious is a well-defined east-south-east-trending zone of steeper gradients passing south of Mildenhall and Bury St Edmunds, which forms the northern margin of an elongated Bouguer anomaly; the southern margin of this anomaly is less well defined. This difference is due partly to a regional northward increase in Bouguer anomaly values, which is also partly responsible for higher values north of the elongated low. No borehole is located near the centre of the low, and the gravity evidence can be interpreted in several ways, with the upper surface of low density bodies lying about 2 km below the surface (Figure 2b). Interpretations include antiform and synform bodies (models 1 and 2 in Figure 2b) and a dipping block (model 3). It seems most likely that the low-density body is formed by Palaeozoic, perhaps Lower Devonian, sediment, although model 2 could represent a ridge of ?Precambrian acid igneous rocks; an explanation in terms of an intrusive granite is thought to be unlikely because of the elongate form of anomaly. The limited density data available (Table 1) sug-

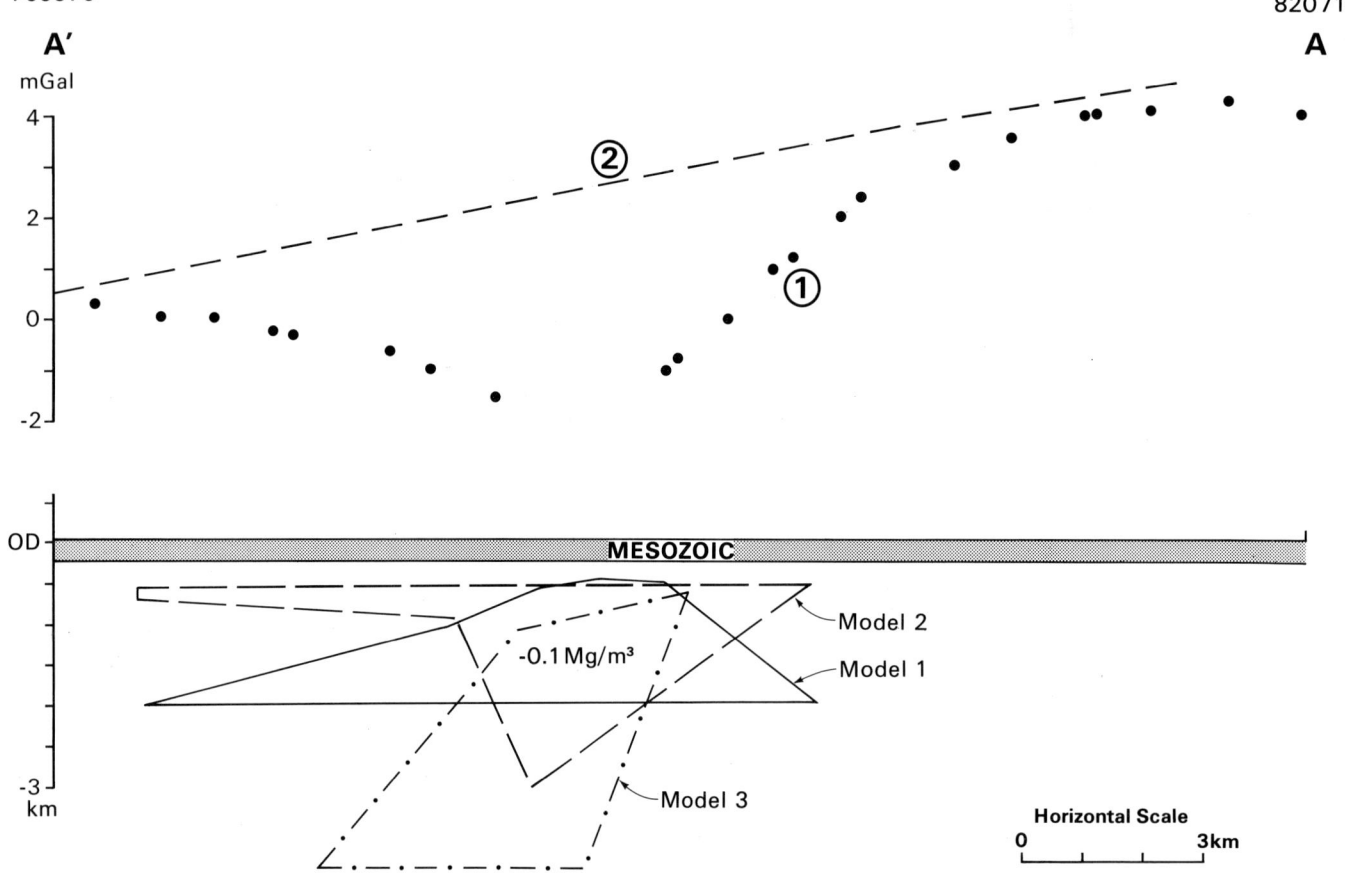

Figure 2b Bouguer anomaly profile AA′ and models producing theoretical curves similar to the observed profile shown by individual stations (1). The background anomaly is also shown (2)

gest that one possible source amongst the Palaeozoic rocks sampled could be Lower Devonian sediments as encountered in the Soham Borehole. Allsop (1985) has suggested on the basis of gravity and borehole evidence that a basin of Devonian sedimentary rocks (the 'Luton–Cambridge Basin') extends south-westwards from the western part of the Bury St Edmunds region. The few density values available from boreholes in the region (Table 1), however, are higher than those considered by Allsop (1985) and the gravity evidence does not therefore exclude the possibility that a more extensive basin of thick Devonian rocks exists in this part of East Anglia.

Two seismic refraction sites are located on gravity lows (Figure 3). The results from Freckenham [686 762] are unusual for the area in that the basement velocity is high (5.5 km/s) and is recorded from a greater depth than is typical for the area. The results are difficult to interpret because of the existence of another higher-velocity layer within the Mesozoic (probably Middle Jurassic limestones), but one possible explanation is that high-velocity basement is overlain by several hundred metres of Palaeozoic sediments, perhaps similar to those in adjacent boreholes, but not sufficiently thick to appear on the seismic records. This in-terpretation would be consistent with model 2 in Figure 2b. The seismic data, however, do not rule out the possibility that part of the Bouguer anomaly low is due to a local thickening of Triassic strata.

The seismic refraction results for the Kentford site [711 684] (Figure 3) (Bullard and others, 1940) have been revised in the light of recent evidence, so that the basement depth is comparable with that in nearby boreholes. This revision largely rules out the possibility that the Bouguer anomaly low is due to a topographic low in the basement surface.

Although its origin is uncertain, the Bury St Edmunds-Mildenhall Bouguer anomaly low represents a major structural element which extends for a distance of 60 km, and is possibly related to a similar feature which continues for a further 100 km across the south Midlands. Its linear character (Figure 2a) suggests fault control, and the east-south-east-trend is shown by several other geophysical anomalies in East Anglia (cf. Linsser, 1968).

South-west of Mildenhall, the east-south-east trend of the Bouguer anomaly low is deflected southwards where it intersects a northerly-trending low passing near Newmarket (Figure 2a). There, the low may result from a partially Trias-filled trough, as at Soham (Figure 1), where almost

Table 1 Physical properties of basement rocks in and around the Bury St Edmunds district

Borehole	Grid Ref	Basement depth m OD	Saturated	Density mg/m³ Grain	Porosity %	Sonic velocity km/s
Clare	783454	−190	—	—	—	—
Culford	831711	−161	—	—	—	—
Eriswell	742789	−195	2.7L	—	—	4.1L
Four Ashes	022718	−219	2.67 ± 0.03 (7)CS	—	—	—
Lakenheath	748830	−180	2.62 ± 0.04 (6)CS	—	—	4.42R
Stowlangtoft	948688	−187	2.71L	—	—	4,50L
Soham	593745	−158	2.59 ± 0.07	(4) 2.65 ± 0.03	5.4 ± 3.6	4.03R

L — result from geophysical borehole log
R — result from seismic refraction survey
CS — reported by Chroston and Sola (1982)

30 m of 'red beds of uncertain age' were proved (Worssam and Taylor, 1969).

Palaeozoic sediments similar to those proved in the basement commonly contain little or no magnetite, and all borehole core samples examined have low magnetic susceptibilities of about 1 to 10 × 10⁻⁵ SI units.   JDC

TRIASSIC

Almost 41 m of red mudstones, sandstones and conglomerates were encountered in the Eriswell Borehole (Figure 1), compared to 12 m in the Lakenheath Borehole to the north, and 30 m of 'red beds of uncertain age' in the

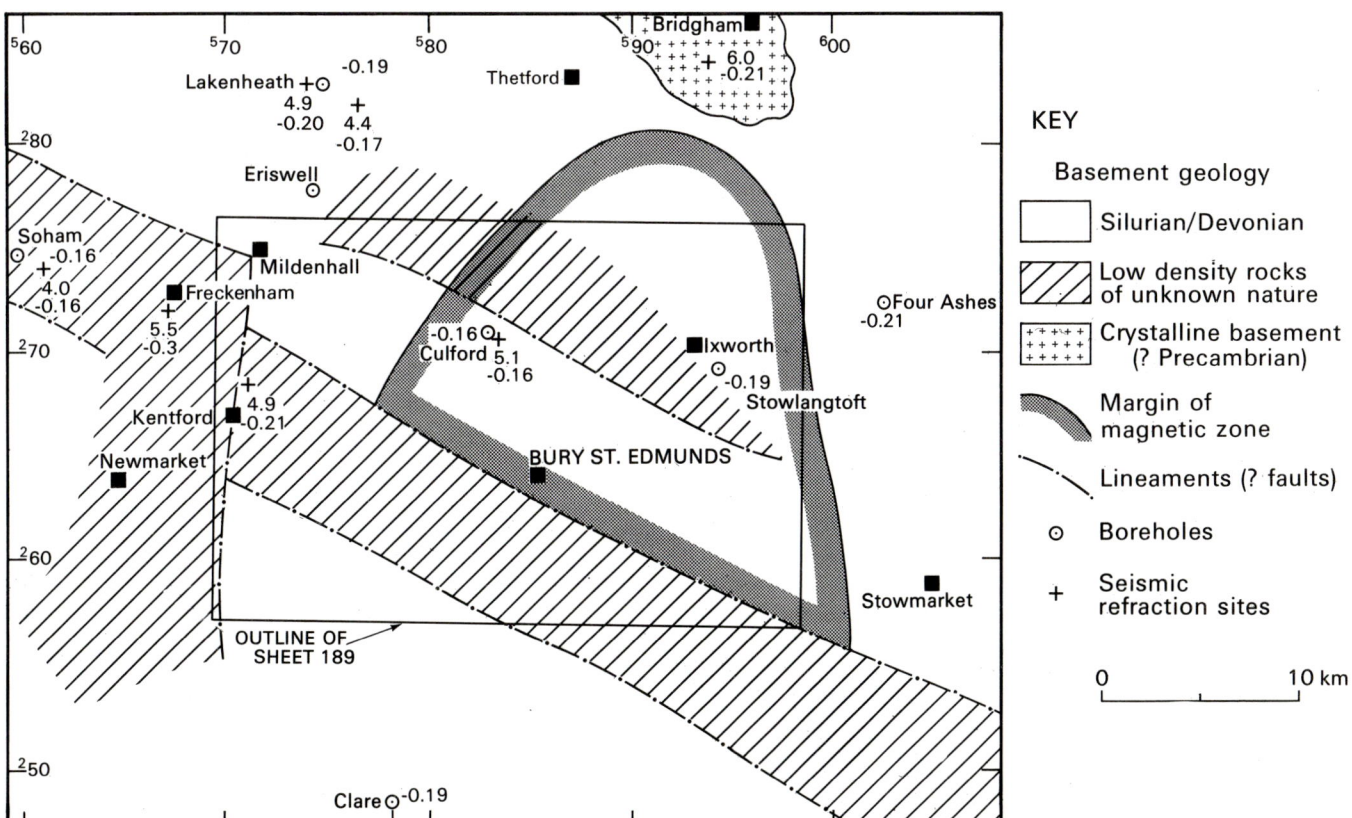

Figure 3 Geophysical and borehole evidence for the nature of the pre-Mesozoic basement in and around the Bury St Edmunds district. Depths to basement (in km below OD) are shown for borehole and seismic sites. Seismic velocities for basement rocks (in km/s) are indicated at seismic sites.

Soham Borehole [5928 7448] to the west-south-west (Worssam and Taylor, 1969). At Culford and Stowlangtoft to the south-east, Trias is absent. The existence of a weak Bouguer anomaly low north of Ingham [850 720] (Figure 2a) could be due to the preservation of thicker Triassic rocks in an east-south-east-trending fault-controlled trough. The southern bounding fault to the trough is placed between Eriswell and Mildenhall, north of Culford and south of Stowlangtoft.

At Eriswell, the lithology is dominantly of sandstone, varying from fine to coarse grained and pebbly, with interbeds of conglomerate, breccia and mudstone. The last lithology is commonest in the lowest 18 m. Dolomite and dolomitic beds are common, particularly towards the top. Dr D B Smith notes that there is slight to marked brecciation, with listric surfaces at most levels, which indicates that the rock has almost certainly been broken up by anastomosing gypsum and/or halite veins that have since been dissolved. The general depositional environment was probably a brine-soaked alluvial desert plain, subject to inundation by an expanding and contracting playa under alternating dry and wet season regimes, and with some phases of subaerial weathering and soil formation. CRB

JURASSIC

Lias

On the basis of data from the Eriswell Borehole which lies 3 km north of the district, and from the Soham Borehole which lies 10 km to the west-south-west (Figure 1), it is probable that up to 39 m of Lower Lias mudstones, with thin limestones, may be preserved in the extreme north-west, though thinning rapidly to the south-east; they probably belong to the Lower Pliensbachian Substage. The progressive onlap of the Lower Lias onto the north-west margin of the London Platform was discussed by Donovan and others (1979).

The log of Borehole 1a (Kentford) [7024 6838] of the Ely-Ouse Water Transfer Scheme (Figure 6) records grey and pale reddish brown silty mudstone, containing small ?selenite crystals and with bedding surfaces coated with small (less than 1 mm) grey, ?sulphurous nodules between 111.13 and 111.26 m; this mudstone might belong to the Lower Lias. A sample examined for foraminifera was barren. CRB

At Eriswell, the *luridum*, *valdani* and probably the *masseanum* subzones of the *ibex* Zone, and the *jamesoni* and *brevispina* subzones of the underlying *jamesoni* Zone have been proved. These rest unconformably on coarse arenaceous beds of probable Triassic age. At Soham, the *ibex* and *jamesoni* zones were also proved in the 42 m of Lower Lias which rest on arenaceous beds of probable Triassic age. In these two boreholes, as along much of this flank of the London Platform, the *davoei* Zone was not proved, although it may be present in the topmost silty mudstones which have a typical late Lower Pliensbachian bivalve fauna at Eriswell; no ammonite was found to indicate beds younger than the *luridum* Subzone.

No younger Liassic rocks are known from the area. If formerly present, they were eroded prior to the deposition of the 'Lower Estuarine Series'. HCIC

'Estuarine Series' and Blisworth Limestone

In the Ely-Ouse Borehole 1a (Figure 6), 4.65 m of strata have been assigned to the 'Estuarine Series'. The upper 0.2 m probably corresponds to the mid-Bathonian 'Upper Estuarine Series' and the lower 4.45 m to the Aalenian 'Lower Estuarine Series'. The overlying Blisworth Limestone is represented by 1.62 m of strata. In this borehole, Lower Cretaceous Woburn Sands rest unconformably on Blisworth Limestone. No younger Jurassic strata have been proved in the district, but the boreholes at Eriswell and Soham suggest that younger Jurassic formations probably occur at depth in the north-west between Borehole 1a and Eriswell as described below (Figures 1 and 6). No 'Estuarine Series' was present at Eriswell, but 11 m of sand and shelly clay at Soham belong to the 'Lower Estuarine Series' (?Grantham Formation).

Details

The sequence in Borehole 1a is as follows:

	Thickness m	Depth m
BLISWORTH LIMESTONE		
Limestone, densely cemented, shell-fragmental, clayey in part; pale grey below 104.85 m, but oxidised to pale yellowish brown above 104.85 m, and with dull purplish red-stained zone up to 2 cm thick immediately below the unconformity; irregular, fissile, clayey limestone bands at 104.93 and 105.03 m set in dense, bluish grey, shell-fragmental micrite with a complex burrow-fill network of pale brownish grey, smooth-textured, muddy micrite	0.30	105.16
(Core lost)	0.81	105.97
Limestone, shell-fragmental, with muddy burrow-fills as above; serpulids common, also bivalves, rhynchonellids and terebratulids	0.51	106.48
'UPPER ESTUARINE SERIES'		
Siltstone, pale grey, gritty, with comminuted shell debris; intensely foraminifera-spotted throughout; interburrowed with smooth dark grey clay; bivalve fragments common, including oysters, many with encrusting *Bullapora*	0.20	106.68
'LOWER ESTUARINE SERIES'		
Core lost (driller records 'silt' to 107.70 m, then 'purplish brown clay' clay to 109.73 m, on 'cementstone and dark grey clay')	3.05	109.73
(Engineering samples)	0.46	110.19
Mudstone, smooth, medium grey, unfossiliferous	0.22	110.41
Mudstone, grey, unfossiliferous, non-calcareous, becoming silty downwards. Outside of core, bedding surfaces and joints coated with lemon yellow sulphurous material. Small (1 mm) ?selenite crystals in		

	Thickness m	Depth m
the matrix. At 110.74 m, intensely burrowed by small (1 mm) burrows. One horizontal burrow filled with buff, silty, very fine-grained sand	0.59	111.00
Sandstone, fine-grained, pale purplish grey, hard, noncalcareous, silty, passing into very hard, purplish brown, fine-grained sandstone with greyish green streaks and patches	0.13	111.13

Samples from the intervals 110.21 to 110.39 m and 110.64 to 110.69 m were examined for foraminifera, but none was found.

Cornbrash

At Eriswell (Figure 1), the 1.37 m of Cornbrash consist dominantly of limestone, but include a 0.3 m bed of siltstone and thin (0.03 to 0.09 m) beds of sandstone. It rests unconformably on a bored and eroded surface of the Lower Lias. The sparse fauna includes *Camptonectes sp.*, *Chlamys* (*Radulopecten?*) *sp.*, *Meleagrinella sp.* and *Myophorella sp.*

Kellaways Beds

The Kellaways Beds at Eriswell comprise 0.18 m of sandy and silty, calcareous, bioturbated mudstones resting on the eroded and bored surface of the Cornbrash. Shell fragments and the belemnite *Hibolites* are present.

Oxford Clay

A total of 17.36 m of calcareous, silty, shelly mudstones belonging to the Lower and Middle Oxford Clay was proved at Eriswell, beneath West Walton Beds. Between there and Soham, where West Walton Beds rest on Upper Oxford Clay of the *mariae* Zone, the Upper Oxford Clay and some of the Middle Oxford Clay have been cut out.

At Eriswell, the Lower Oxford Clay consists of 10.44 m of medium to pale grey and slightly brownish grey, variably calcareous (with cementstones), silty and shelly mudstones. The *jason* Zone and possibly part of the *calloviense* Zone are represented in the basal 0.52 m. The *coronatum* Zone and *athleta* Zone, with the Acutistriatum Band at its base, are readily identifiable by their ammonite assemblages. The *athleta* Zone continues into the Middle Oxford Clay and is probably the youngest Oxford Clay zone present in the district. At Eriswell, the base of the Middle Oxford Clay is taken at a burrowed horizon, where pale and very pale grey calcareous mudstones with cementstones are interburrowed with pale brownish grey mudstone below. Some 6.92 m of Middle Oxford Clay of the *athleta* Zone are preserved.

West Walton Beds

The youngest Jurassic strata presumed to extend into the district are the West Walton Beds. At Eriswell (Figure 1), 14.9 m of strata belonging to Beds 7 to 16 of Gallois and Cox (1977) are present, resting unconformably on a bored surface of Middle Oxford Clay. They consist mostly of pale grey silty mudstones with cementstones. Ammonites indicate the *densiplicatum* and *tenuiserratum* zones of the Middle Oxfordian.

BMC, CRB

Structures affecting Jurassic strata

Little is known of the structures affecting the older Mesozoic rocks in the district, though there may have been some reactivation of basement faults. In the Cambridge district Worssam and Taylor (1969) described a group of north-north-east-trending fold axes affecting Jurassic strata (the Soham, Upware, Stretham and Haddenham axes), but the trend does not seem important in the Bury St Edmunds district.

JDC

LOWER CRETACEOUS

Lower Greensand

The Lower Greensand rests unconformably on Jurassic and older Cretaceous strata throughout East Anglia. It rests on the West Walton Beds at Eriswell and Lakenheath, on Blisworth Limestone at Ely-Ouse Borehole 1a (Kentford) and on Siluro-Devonian rocks at Culford (Figure 6).

The Lower Greensand comprises two formations (Woburn Sands and Carstone) which are the marginal facies of two separate basins of deposition; in the absence of fauna, the two formations cannot always be reliably distinguished.

The older Woburn Sands are thickest in the Leighton Buzzard–Woburn area, where they are locally in excess of 100 m, but thin to a feather-edge north-east of Ely. They are probably present at depth beneath much of the north-west of the Bury St Edmunds district, although possibly locally absent beneath the unconformable Carstone. They consist of patchily calcareous, fine-grained, glauconitic sandstones with rare limonitised ooliths. The following thicknesses have been recorded: 0.5 m at Culford, 1.5 m (base not reached) at Ely-Ouse Borehole 6 [7027 7307], 2.8 m at Eriswell, and 9.6 m at Ely-Ouse Borehole 1a. The only fossil recorded from the present district is the bivalve *Acesta sp.* from Ely-Ouse Borehole 6. Evidence from outside the area indicates that the Woburn Sands are of Upper Aptian age, but they may extend into the Lower Aptian (Casey, 1961). At Ely-Ouse Borehole 1a, a bed of pebbly, ferruginous sandstone, 15 cm thick, is lithologically similar to the Upper Aptian Seend Ironstone of Wiltshire.

The Carstone consists of coarse-grained, poorly sorted, oolitic sandstones, with ooliths of limonite and limonitised chamosite, and pebbles of quartz and chert. It forms a transgressive unit below the Gault, and extends from Bedford to Humberside. The formation grades upwards into sandy Gault (Gallois and Morter, 1982). In the Ely-Ouse boreholes its thickness is 0.76 m in Borehole 1a, more than 1.7 m in Borehole 6, 0.6 m in Borehole 9 [6975 7572]. It is 4 m thick at Eriswell and probably 11.4 m at Culford where, however, Whitaker and Jukes-Browne (1894) regarded the composite Lower Greensand as only 9.9 m thick, of which 9.45 m could be attributed to the Carstone. At Culford the above authors recorded unidentified fragments of echinoderms, brachio-

pods, bivalves and foraminifera. Ely-Ouse Borehole 6 yielded the annelid *Rotularia* cf. *polygonalis* and the bivalve *Camptonectes curvatus*.
AAM, CRB

Details

WOBURN SANDS The interval 95.17 to 104.78 m in Ely-Ouse Borehole 1a has been assigned to the Woburn Sands. The relevant part of the log is given below:

	Thickness m	Depth m
Sandstone, buff, greyish green, calcareously cemented, fine-grained	0.10	95.28
Sand, greyish green	1.19	96.47
Core loss	0.30	96.77
Sandstone, buff, greyish green, fine-grained, with rounded quartz pebbles; some reddish brown clayey sand burrow-fills	0.16	96.93
Sandstone, reddish brown with ironstone and abundant quartz and chert pebbles, very pebbly with oolitic iron ore at base [this example is very like the Seend Ironstone]	0.15	97.08
Core loss	1.52	98.60
Sandstone, hard, fine- to medium-grained, with well-polished quartz grains, larger clasts (2 to 3 mm) of limonitic siltstone, white quartzite and greenish silty clay; cemented by brown siliceous material; small (1 to 2 mm diam. × 15 mm long) burrows filled with greenish grey clay; fish remains at 98 m	1.07	99.67
Core loss	0.91	100.58
Sandstone, fine-, medium- and coarse-grained with a weakly calcitic matrix (much core loss)	1.53	102.11
Core loss	1.52	103.63
Sandstone, fine- and medium-grained, with small pebbles scattered throughout; intensely burrowed, with pinkish brown calcite cement in burrow-fills, some of which are plant-rich; pebbles of quartz and limonite/ironstone common in lower part. Base irregular, with dark very sandy and oolitic (limonitised) very pebbly clay resting in a steep-sided solution hollow in the underlying limestone; some chloritised clay at junction	1.15	104.78

Woburn Sands were recorded in Ely-Ouse Borehole 4 [7012 7169] between 78.94 and 80.92 m, but the base was not proved:

	Thickness m	Depth m
Sandstone, clayey, pale brownish grey, soft, with patchy calcite/phosphate cementation and some burrow-fills of darker brown, slightly pebbly, oolitic sand; becomes very soft, sparsely pebbly limonite sand with weakly cemented burrow-fills of paler clayey sand below 79.93 m	1.37	80.31
Clay, dark grey, plant-rich, appears in burrow-fills and becomes more common downward until it constitutes 50 per cent of the sample between 80.54 and 80.92 m; wood fragment at 80.62 m	0.61	80.92

A thickness of 1.5 m of Woburn Sands was encountered in Ely-Ouse Borehole 6 but the base not proved:

	Thickness m	Depth m
Sandstone, rusty brown and grey mottled, loose, with scattered pale phosphate patches; numerous quartz and black chert pebbles	0.15	73.00
(Engineering sample)	0.05	73.05
Bed continues from above, transitional to bed below, interburrowed	0.03	73.08
Sand, fine-grained, light greenish grey, with vertical burrows of rust brown, coarse-grained sandstone from above; some quartz pebbles in burrows; sand locally cemented; some dark grey clay-filled burrows; scattered calcareous concretions	0.10	73.18
Sandstone, rusty brown and dark brown, interburrowed with dark grey clay; numerous small quartz and chert pebbles; some burrows of fine-grained, light greenish grey sand from above; clay content of bed increasing downwards; *Acesta* at 74.22 m	1.14	74.32
Mudstone, dark-brownish grey, interburrowed with brown sands of bed above; small chert pebbles in burrows; scattered chlorite patches	0.20	74.52
(Engineering sample)	0.08	74.60

CARSTONE In Ely-Ouse Borehole 1a, the Carstone consists of an upper unit, 0.33 m thick, of clayey, reddish brown and dark greyish brown, ?calcareously cemented sandstone, with clayey burrow-fills; rounded pebbles of chert become more common and larger towards the base. The lower unit comprises 0.1 m of interlaminated dark grey mudstone and reddish brown pebbly sand.

In Borehole 2 [7008 6976], 0.36 m of reddish brown and grey sandstone with chert and quartz pebbles were encountered but the base was not proved. In Borehole 4 the Carstone, 0.69 m thick, consists of fine-grained, clayey and pebbly, calcareously and phosphatically cemented sandstone with common limonitised ooliths and wisps of dark grey clay, together with burrow-fills of very pale grey calcareous clay. A small ammonite was found in one of the burrow-fills. Borehole 5 [6998 7249] encountered 1 m of mottled yellow, brown and grey clayey, pebbly sandstone, but it terminated above the base. The pebbles, consisting of quartz and chert, become less common downwards; a 75 mm phosphate nodule was noted. The basal 0.23 m consist of a dark grey sandy mudstone with abundant *Chondrites*.

The Carstone in Borehole 6 is represented by 0.37 m of argillaceous sandstone, which becomes a greyish brown pebbly sandstone at depth. It yielded the fossils *Camptonectes curvatus* and *Rotularia* cf. *polygonalis*, indicative of the Lower Albian *mammillatum* Zone.

In Borehole 9, some 0.2 m of sandy, greyish brown mudstone overlie 0.1 m of brown, patchily calcareously cemented sandstone, which passes down into 0.29 m of brown sand, with vertical sandy burrow-fills at the top.
CRB, AAM

Gault

The Gault consists of soft grey mudstones and paler grey calcareous mudstones with many seams of calcium phosphate. The basal beds are sandy and glauconitic, and grade down into the Carstone.

The Gault everywhere underlies the Chalk of the district. In the west it has been proved in all the Ely-Ouse Water

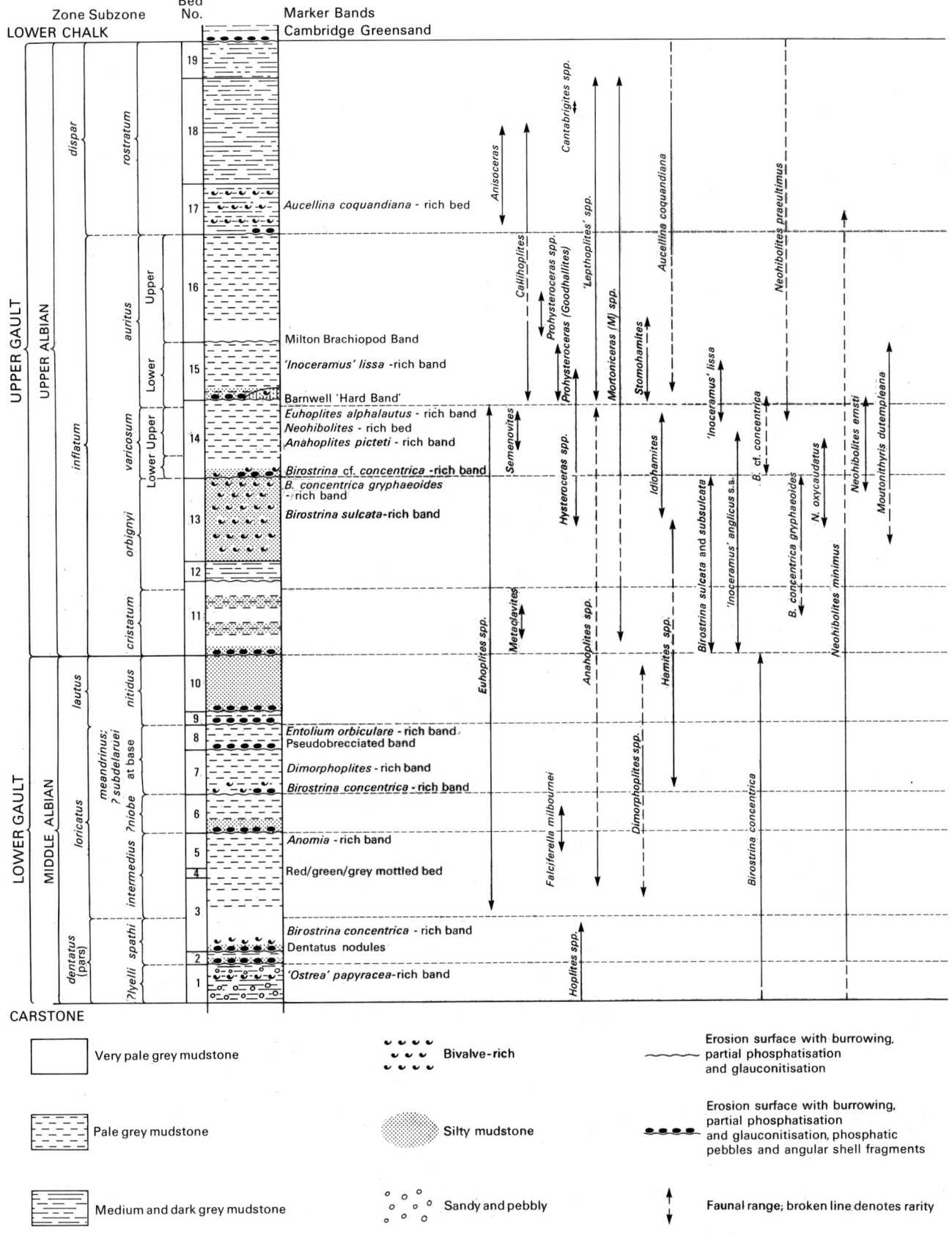

Figure 4 Generalised vertical section of the Gault of East Anglia showing the main lithological and faunal features (based on Gallois and Morter, 1982)

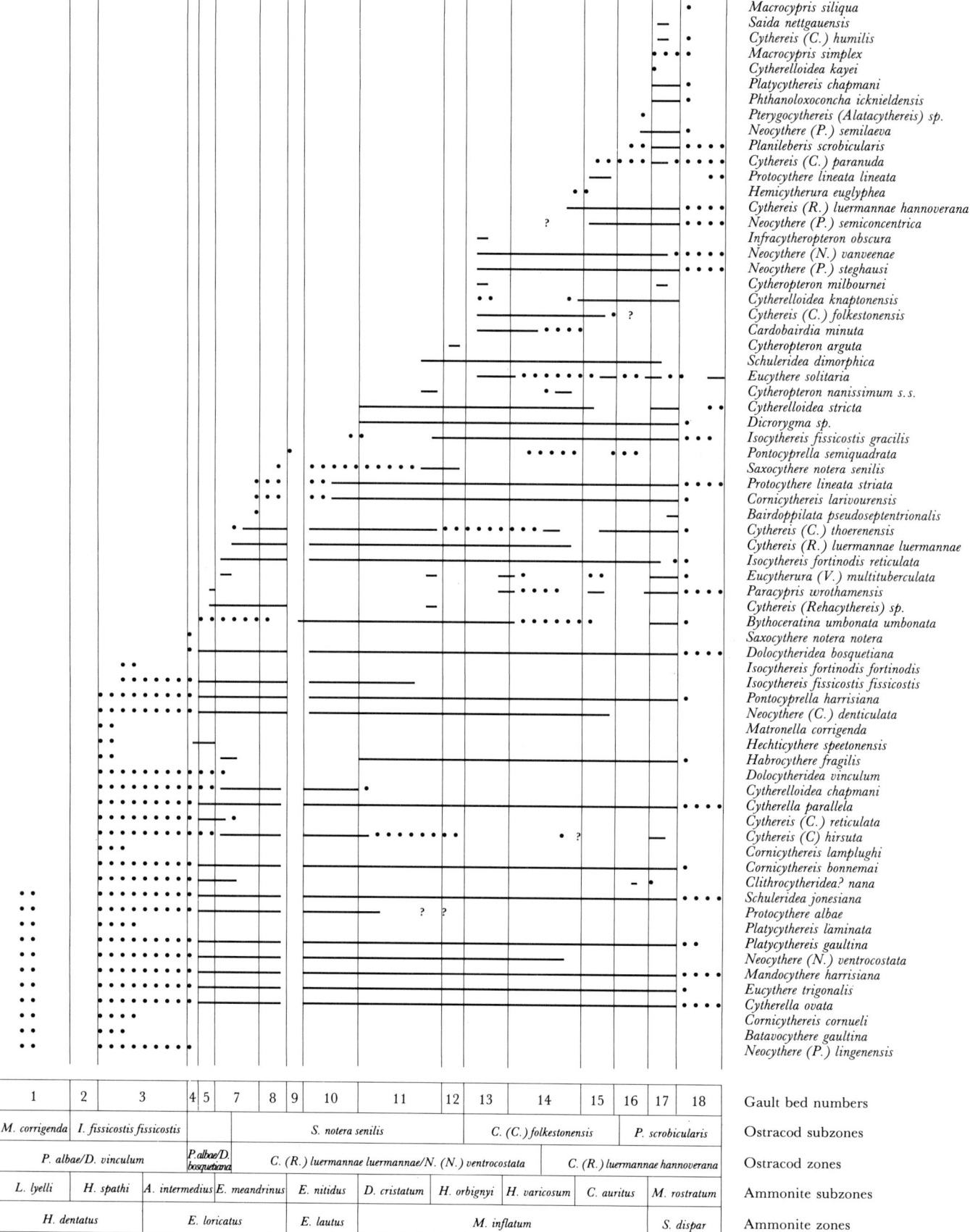

Figure 5 Distribution of Ostracoda in the Gault of the Ely-Ouse Borehole 2 (horizontal lines), supplemented by data from Borehole 11 (spots). Gault Beds 1–4 and 18 of Borehole 2 were not available for examination

Transfer Scheme boreholes (Figure 6), where it shows a gradual, but irregular, northward thinning from 22.4 m in Borehole 1a (Kentford) to 18.8 m north-west of Mildenhall. Eastwards and south-eastwards it thins towards the London Platform. The following thicknesses have been proved (Figure 1): 17.24 m at Eriswell; 10 m at Culford; 13.5 m at Stowlangtoft; 14.27 m at Four Ashes (Bristow, 1980), and 11 m at Clare. Most of the thinning occurs in the Lower Gault. At Four Ashes, the Lower Gault is only 2.5 m thick, and at Clare, the Lower Gault is virtually absent.

For almost 90 years the only information about the Gault of the district has come from the inadequately logged Culford Borehole (Whitaker and Jukes-Browne, 1894). Recently, all the fully cored Ely-Ouse boreholes have been examined; they provide a wealth of detail on the Gault of the western portion of the district. The detailed stratigraphy and palaeontology of these boreholes, published here for the first time, can be related to the lithological and faunal sequences established by Gallois and Morter (1982) throughout East Anglia (Figure 4). Additionally, material from two Ely-Ouse boreholes provided Black (1972–1975) with coccolith samples (mainly from Borehole 4 and Borehole 23 [6916 8817] in the adjoining Ely district). Jeans and others (1982) examined the clay mineralogy of the Gault from Borehole 23. The ostracods from boreholes 2 [7008 6976] and 11 [6973 7802], in the adjoining Thetford district, have been examined by Dr I P Wilkinson, and his findings are incorporated in the following account (Figure 5). The results follow studies of Wilkinson and Morter (1981) on three boreholes in the Gault of Norfolk.

For over a hundred years the Gault has been divided on gross lithology into Lower and Upper Gault (De Rance, 1868). The Lower Gault consists dominantly of medium and dark grey mudstones in which illite and kaolinite are the principal clay minerals; the Upper Gault consists mainly of pale grey calcareous mudstones in which smectite is the dominant clay mineral (Perrin, 1971). Jeans and others (1982), however, recognise only a mica-kaolinite clay mineral assemblage for the whole of the Gault of East Anglia.

Gallois and Morter (1982) have shown that the Gault of East Anglia can be divided into 18 (locally 19) rhythmic units (beds) that can be recognised throughout the region; many of the bed boundaries coincide with zonal or subzonal boundaries. On average, each bed is between 1 and 2 m thick, but considerable variation in thickness does occur; e.g. Bed 6 is 2.1 m thick in Borehole 1a and absent in Borehole 2. Each rhythm consists of several mudstone lithologies; at the base, there is a grey, shelly, pebbly, silty mudstone or muddy siltstone, which is commonly rich in inoceramid prisms, oysters, belemnites, exhumed phosphatised burrow-fills and phosphate pebbles, and which commonly rests on a partially phosphatised and glauconitised burrowed surface (Gallois and Morter, 1982). From the basal bed, there is an upward decrease in the coarser clastic and bioclastic fragments, and an upward passage into medium and pale grey mudstones, associated with an increased calcium carbonate content. There is also an upward decrease in faunal diversity. The rhythms are clearest in the Lower Gault and the lower part of the Upper Gault; locally, a bed may be cut out by an overlying rhythm. The main lithological and faunal features of the succession in the Bury St Edmunds district are shown in Figure 4; they are consistent with the regional picture of sedimentation and palaeogeography outlined by Gallois and Morter (1982).

Thickness changes of individual beds in the Ely-Ouse and Eriswell boreholes may be related to faults along the line of the valley of the River Lark and changing axes of sedimentation. Beds 1–6 of the Lower Gault show considerable variation in thickness, with Bed 6 being cut out northward beneath Bed 7a; beds 7a to 10 show a relatively more constant thickness. Rapid thickness changes near Borehole 8 [6957 7452] may be fault-controlled. In contrast, the Upper Gault has a relatively constant thickness, but individual beds (i.e. 14c, 15 and 16) show considerable, partly compensatory, variation. Bed 18 shows a general southwards thinning, probably as the result of erosion below the Cambridge Greensand.

Borehole 6 shows the most complete sequence overall, with fossiliferous Carstone at the base and is overlain by comparatively thick Cambridge Greensand. It may, therefore, lie along the axis of an Albian sedimentary trough.

The primary zonation of the Gault is by means of ammonites. A complementary ostracod zonation, together with the ranges of individual ostracods, is given in Figure 5.

AAM, CRB

Ostracoda are both numerous and diverse in the Gault, and the zonal scheme erected for northern Germany (Bertram and Kemper, 1971) has been used, in a modified way, for East Anglia (Wilkinson and Morter, 1981). The scheme can be applied to Ely-Ouse boreholes 2 and 11 as summarised below:

The *Protocythere albae/Dolocytheridea (P.) vinculum* ostracod Zone (Beds 1–3) is recognisable in Borehole 2 and can be subdivided into two subzones on the presence of *Matronella corrigenda* and the first occurrence of *Isocythereis fissicostis*. Within the zone, *Batavocythere gaultina*, *Cornicythereis cornueli*, *Matronella corrigenda*, *Dolocytheridea (P.) vinculum* and *Platycythereis laminata* disappear from the record.

The association of *Protocythere albae* and *Dolocytheridea (P.) bosquetiana* is found in Beds 4 and 7 (pars), the latter species having evolved from *D. (P.) vinculum*.

The *Cythereis (Rehacythereis) luermannae luermannae/Neocythere (Neocythere) ventrocostata* ostracod Zone extends from the upper part of Bed 7 to the middle of 14. The subzonal index *Saxocythere notera senilis* is rare and has a patchy distribution, but the succeeding subzone, defined by the presence of *Cythereis (Cythereis) folkestonensis*, is clearly seen in Bed 13 and the lower part of 14 in both boreholes. The last occurrence of *Protocythere albae* is within the *S. senilis* Subzone, at which level it evolves into *P. lineata*, and *Cytherelloidea stricta* appears for the first time at the base of Bed 11.

The highest ostracod zone in both boreholes is present in Beds 14 (pars) to 18 and is recognised by the first occurrence of *Cythereis (Rehacythereis) luermannae hannoverana*. In the lower part of the zone *C. (C.) folkestonensis* disappears from the record and *Planileberis scrobicularis* makes its first appearance. A little higher in the zone *Platycythereis chapmani* is added to the fauna.

The highest ostracod zone in Germany (Bertram and Kemper, 1971; modified by Kemper, 1984), recognised by the first occurrence of *Cythereis (Rehacythereis) bemerodensis*, has not been recognised in the Gault sequence in East Anglia because of the erosion which preceded the accumulation of the Cambridge Greensand and Chalk.   IPW

Details

Bed 1: This bed is dominantly a clayey, pebbly sandstone, although locally it is a sandy pebbly mudstone. It ranges from less than 5 cm in Borehole 8, where beds 1 and 2 cannot be separated, to 0.94 m in Borehole 1a. The bivalve '*Ostrea*' *papyracea* abounds. The bed is probably of *Lyelliceras lyelli* Subzone age, though the subzonal ammonite has not been recorded. The *Hoplites* species are associates of *L. lyelli* in the Weald, and the '*Ostrea*' occur in large numbers in the *lyelli* Subzone of the Aycliff Borehole, Kent (Owen, 1971a), alongside *Protanisoceras*, characteristic of the *lyelli* Subzone. Bed 1 falls within the *corrigenda* ostracod Subzone (Figure 5). The bed has also been recognised by Worssam and Taylor (1969) in the Cottenham Well near Cambridge within their Beds 6–8; similar beds have been recorded at Aylesbury (Owen, 1971a).

Bed 2: Pale and medium grey, sandy mudstones with *Chondrites* are the dominant lithologies; the 'dentatus nodule Bed' is commonly present at the top. Where separable from Bed 1, the thickness varies from a 0.03 m nodule bed in Borehole 1a, to 0.35 m in Borehole 6 and 0.46 m at Eriswell. The *Hoplites* species (Figure 4) are diagnostic of the *spathi* Subzone. The upper limit of '*O*.' *papyracea* probably coincides with the top of the *spathi* Subzone within Bed 3. *Birostrina* is especially common, occurring in shell plasters at the base of the bed. The *spathi* Subzone faunas have been discussed by Etie and others (1982), who concluded that 8 to 30 m was an appropriate depth of water for the deposition of this part of the Gault. The bed falls within the *fissicostis* ostracod Subzone (Figure 5).

Bed 3: This bed is absent in boreholes 2 to 8; it is best developed in the more northerly Ely-Ouse boreholes. The lithology is dominantly medium grey mudstones with *Chondrites*; these rest with a sharp break on the 'dentatus nodule Bed'. The thickness ranges from 0.3 m in Borehole 1a to 1.5 m at Eriswell. The greater part of Bed 3 contains typical *intermedius* Subzone faunas, such as *Anahoplites* and early *Euhoplites*. *Birostrina concentrica* and '*Ostrea*' *papyracea* are common in the basal part.

Bed 4: 'The Mottled Bed': Green, brown and grey mottled mudstones characterise Bed 4; they are present in boreholes 1a to 9 and at Eriswell, and vary in thickness from 0.2 m in Borehole 8 to 0.64 m in Borehole 9. Only a limited macrofauna, characteristic of the *intermedius* Subzone, the equivalent of the lower part of Bed II of Price (Owen, 1971a), occurs. The bed falls within the *albae/bosquetiana* ostracod Zone in Borehole 11.

Bed 5: 'Anomia Beds': This bed consists of basal brown mudstones, intensely burrowed by *Chondrites* and grading upwards into dark grey mudstone. Its distinctive lithology and abundance of the bivalve *Anomia* makes it a good marker. The bed is thickest in the south (1.07 m in Borehole 1a); at Eriswell it is 0.22 m thick. The diagnostic ammonites place it in the *Anahoplites intermedius* Subzone. Bed 5 of boreholes 2 and 11 falls within the *albae/bosquetiana* ostracod Zone (Wilkinson and Morter, 1981).

Bed 6: This consists of light to medium grey or buff mudstones, commonly with a concentration of *Birostrina concentrica* shells at the base. The maximum thickness is 1.68 m (Borehole 1a); however, it is commonly cut out beneath Bed 7a (Boreholes 2, 4 and Eriswell). Although the subzonal index species has not been recorded, the ammonites suggest the *niobe* Subzone. Bed 6 normally falls within the *albae-bosquetiana* ostracod Zone (Wilkinson and Morter, 1981).

Bed 7: This bed can be divided into a lower 7a and an upper 7b on faunal grounds. Bed 7a consists of medium or dark grey or brownish buff, mottled mudstones with *Chondrites*. The base is marked by a concentration of *B. concentrica* shells (Inoceramid Bed 1). The thickness ranges from 0.57 m at Eriswell to 2.51 m in Borehole 2. The bed is provisionally placed in the *subdelaruei* Subzone, though no diagnostic ammonite has been recorded. The base of Bed 7b is marked by Inoceramid Bed 2, at which there is a significant faunal and floral change. Above the base, medium grey mudstones are dominant. The thickness is fairly constant at about 1 m; in Borehole 9, however, it is only 0.2 m thick. A rich macrofauna has been recorded. The base of Bed 7b coincides with the base of the *luermannae-ventrocostata* ostracod Zone. The nannofossil *Parhabdolithus boletiformis* becomes extinct in Inoceramid Bed 2.

Bed 8: At the base, there is a distinctive breccia of brown and green mudstone containing angular pebbles of mudstone. It represents a widespread sedimentary event which is reflected in its sedentary and boring macrofauna. Above the breccia, medium brownish grey mudstones predominate. The thickness is fairly constant at about 1 m. The fauna is typical of the upper part of the *meandrinus* Subzone. The occurrence of '*O*'. aff. *papyracea* is of note as this species is normally found only in the shallow-water conditions of the *dentatus* Zone. Bed 8 falls within the *senilis* ostracod Subzone of the *luermannae-ventrocostata* Zone.

Bed 9: There is usually a well-developed phosphatic nodule bed and erosion surface at the base; pale and dark grey mudstones, intensely burrow-mottled with *Chondrites*, occur above. Its thickness varies from 0.2 m in Borehole 2 to 0.69 m in Borehole 4. A diverse, diagnostic fauna is present. The *Euhoplites* with channelled venters indicate the *lautus* Zone. Ostracod faunas fall within the *senilis* Subzone.

Bed 10: The mudstones of this bed are intensely bioturbated with *Chondrites*. Dark grey mudstones in the lower part rest on a phosphatic nodule bed overlying an erosion surface; lighter grey mottled mudstones above lie at the top of the Lower Gault. The type form of a small *Birostrina concentrica* is common in shell bands. The thickness varies from 0.41 m in Borehole 8 to 1.65 m in Borehole 2. Only a limited macrofauna occurs, but the bivalve *Birostrina concentrica*, the gastropod *Cirsocerithium subspinosum* and columnals of the crinoid *Isocrinus sp.* are common. The bed clearly belongs to the *nitidus* Subzone and falls within the *senilis* Subzone of the *luermannae-ventrocostata* ostracod Zone.

Bed 11: A basal phosphatic bed is usually present, marking the base of the Upper Gault and the late Albian. The beds above it consist of dark grey mudstones with intense bioturbation in the form of *Chondrites*. The thickness ranges from 0.85 m at Eriswell to 2 m in Borehole 6. A varied macrofauna is dominated in the top of the bed by *Birostrina sulcata*. The greater part of the bed can be placed in the *Dipoloceras cristatum* Subzone; the annelid *Ditrupa (Tetraditrupa)*, '*Inoceramus*' *anglicus* and *Cirsocerithium* are characteristic of this subzone. *Euhoplites* cf. *inornatus* implies that the top of Bed 11 is of *orbignyi* Subzone age. Bed 11 also lies within the *senilis* ostracod Subzone.

Bed 12: This bed varies in thickness from 0.2 m in Borehole 2 to 0.51 m in Borehole 9. It is intensely bioturbated with *Chondrites* and consists of mottled pale and dark grey mudstones. Only a limited macrofauna is present, with *Birostrina sulcata*, '*Inoceramus*' *anglicus* and *Nucula (Pectinucula) pectinata* the most common fossils. The ammonites place Bed 12 in the lower part of the *Hysteroceras orbignyi* Subzone, and it lies at the top of the *senilis* ostracod Subzone.

Bed 13: This bed of pale grey silty mudstone is highly bioturbated, especially by the trace fossil *Chondrites*. It contains an abundant macrofauna dominated by *Birostrina sulcata*, especially in the higher parts. The lower part is characterised by fragments of '*Inoceramus*' *anglicus* and a band of abundant *Neohibolites minimus minimus* in translucent preservation. The thickness varies from 1 m at Eriswell to 1.5 m in Borehole 4. The extensive fauna is characteristic of the *orbignyi* Subzone and presumably represents well oxygenated sea-floor conditions. Emergent phases, with several discontinuities, are represented by phosphate beds. The base of the bed coincides with the base of the *folkestonensis* Subzone of the *luermannae-ventrocostata* ostracod Zone.

Bed 14: This bed can be divided into three: a (lowest), b and c (highest). Beds 14a and b are treated together here, though only 14a contains representatives of the subzonal ammonite *Hysteroceras varicosum*. Bed 14c is only locally present (boreholes 5 and 7); it was thought to be of possible *auritus* Subzone age (Gallois and Morter, 1982), but new evidence suggests that it is probably of latest *varicosum* Subzone age, though it may represent a transition period between subzones. The thickness of Bed 14a varies from 0.28 m (Borehole 2) to 2 m (Borehole 9); Bed 14b is 1.1 m in Borehole 9 and 1.2 m in Borehole 2; Bed 14c is 0.8 m thick in boreholes 5 and 7 [6992 7381]. The lithology of 14a consists of dark grey mudstones with many dark phosphatic nodules; these grade upwards into medium grey mudstones of 14b, and medium to pale grey mudstones of 14c. The last are commonly gritty with inoceramid debris. Beds 14a and 14b contain an extensive fauna (Bed 14c is treated separately below) which is typical of the *varicosum* Subzone. The large numbers of *Neohibolites* suggest correlation with the 'Belemnite Beds' which extend northward into the Red Chalk sequence and across the North Sea into Germany, and thus provide a useful stratigraphic marker (see Spaeth, 1971; 1973). Much of beds 14a and 14b belongs to the *folkestonensis* Subzone of the *luermannae-ventrocostata* ostracod Zone, with the junction with the *luermannae-hannoverana* Zone lying in the highest part of 14b or at the junction of beds 14b and 14c, wherever the latter is present. The base of Bed 14 has been mistaken for the base of the Upper Gault (e.g. Black, 1972–1975, after Jeans).

Bed 14c is known only from Ely-Ouse boreholes 5 and 7, and the Milton borrow-pit in the adjacent Cambridge (188) district. The bed has commonly been removed by erosion below the Barnwell Hard Band (base Bed 15). Only a limited fauna has been recovered due to the bed's patchy distribution. Bed 14c represents the transition from the *Hysteroceras varicosum* Subzone to the *Callihoplites auritus* Subzone, with the bottom and top respectively belonging to these subzones. At the top, a very early eiffellithid nannofossil (A W Medd, personal communication) appears. This is an important marker throughout north-west Europe, and coincides approximately with a great change of macrofaunas, especially with the hoplitid ammonite *Callihoplites* becoming dominant. The bed lies within the *hannoverana* ostracod Zone.

Bed 15: The base of this bed is characterised by an abundance of the thick-shelled bivalve '*Inoceramus*' *lissa* which occurs as shell drifts, locally forming limestones such as the Barnwell Hard Band. Abundant phosphates and phosphatised thalassinoid burrow-fills are also present, indicating a period of winnowing and reduced sedimentation. The correlation of this event, which is recognised throughout Britain (Jeans, 1973; 1980; Gallois and Morter, 1982; Kelly, 1971; Casey, 1959; Owen, 1971b; 1976; Morter and Wood, 1983), may be extended eastwards into Germany, and even as far as Bulgaria (Dimitrova, 1974). The shell bed is succeeded by pale olive-grey mudstones.

Bed 15 is one of the thicker beds of the Gault, with a maximum of 3.8 m (Borehole 7), and a minimum of 0.81 m (Borehole 9). It contains an extensive macrofauna typical of the *Callihoplites auritus* Subzone (lower part) (Gallois and Morter, 1982), though some elements may be derived from Bed 14c. The primitive eiffellithid, '*proto-Eiffellithus*' (A W Medd, personal communication), is characteristic and marks the nannofossil version of the base of the Upper Albian. The bed lies within the *hannoverana* ostracod Zone. The transgressive event at the base is at least as important as the basal Upper Albian transgression (Owen, 1971a) and marks the incoming of 'Upper Albian faunas' (Owen, 1973; Jeletzky, 1980).

Bed 16: This generally consists of poorly fossiliferous, smooth, pale to medium grey mudstones, with few diagnostic fossils. The faunal assemblage is provisionally placed in the upper part of the *Callihoplites auritus* Subzone, but may represent a new subzone. Marked variations in thickness occur from 0.17 m (Borehole 7) to 1.8 m (Borehole 9). Bed 16 is characterised by oysters and a few richly fossiliferous bands with sponges and abundant crinoid ossicles. Towards the base lies the Milton Brachiopod Band, in which small brachiopods such as *Terebratulina* are common. The base of the Milton Brachiopod Bed probably marks the extinction of *Biplicatoria* spp., including '*Moutonithyris dutempleana* Auctt'. The abundance of oysters and crinoids, and the occurrence of the brachiopod *Dereta*, suggest warmer water, pointing to a probable correlation with the Ostrea vesiculosa Beds of south-west England and the Exogyra Beds at the top of the Foxmould of East Devon, both now provisionally placed in the *auritus* Subzone (Owen, 1976). Bed 16 lies within the *hannoverana* ostracod Zone; within the lower part of this bed, *Cythereis (C.) folkestonensis* disappears from the record and *Planileberis scrobicularis* first occurs. The incoming of the coccolith *Eiffellithus turriseiffelli* correlates the bed with the higher part of Bed XI at Folkestone (A W Medd, personal communication).

Bed 17: Bed 17 forms the base of the *Stoliczkaia dispar* Zone in East Anglia (Gallois and Morter, 1982). An erosion surface with phosphatic pebbles is commonly present at the base, and represents a widespread transgressive event. Above the base occur shelly mudstones with abundant smooth-shelled *Aucellina*, which correlate with those in Bed XII at Folkestone (Morter and Wood, 1983). This bed is thought to represent a colder water phase, coinciding with the acme of *Globigerinelloides bentonensis*, a significant European-wide event (Price, 1976). The thickness of Bed 17 varies from 0.5 m at Eriswell to 2.74 m in Borehole 2, but the latter thickness may be excessive due to core reversal. The general thickness is about 1.2 m. The ammonite assemblage indicates the lower part of the *Stoliczkaia dispar* Zone, *Mortoniceras rostratum* Subzone, though no *Stoliczkaia* has so far been recorded. The ostracod faunas still belong to the *hannoverana* Zone. The nannofossil assemblage is dominated by *E. turriseiffelli* with some remnant early eiffellithids.

Bed 18: The pale grey mudstones that characterise this bed contain very little fauna apart from *Aucellina*. The ammonite assemblage, like that of the underlying bed, can be placed in the *Mortoniceras rostratum* Subzone. This bed is the youngest Upper Gault in Suffolk.

Cambridge Greensand: Bed 18 is overlain disconformably by the Cambridge Greensand, which forms the basal bed of the Chalk and is of possible latest Albian or earliest Cenomanian age. The Cambridge Greensand is described in the next chapter.   AAM

CHAPTER 3

Upper Cretaceous: Chalk

The Chalk crops out over about one third of the district, principally in the north-west, but with large windows through the Drift around Bury St Edmunds and between Thurston [92 65] and Stanton [97 74] (Figure 6). It underlies the whole of the rest of the district, beneath a cover of Crag and/or Drift.

The Chalk is divided into Lower, Middle and Upper subdivisions, partly on lithology and partly on fauna. In addition, several regionally developed bands form useful markers. Of these, the Totternhoe Stone, Melbourn Rock, Chalk Rock and Top Rock have been recognised in boreholes and in scattered outcrops. There are also several local hard bands. These markers, along with the subdivisions, zones and stages of the Chalk recognised in the district are set out in Figure 7.

LOWER CHALK

Cambridge Greensand

The Cambridge Greensand, at the base of the Lower Chalk, rests discordantly on Bed 18 of the Gault (p.15). It is a thin (up to 1.8 m), grey, glauconitic, micaceous, silty marl with scattered black and brown, phosphatised pebbles up to

Table 2 Classification of the Chalk

Stratigraphical division		Zone	Stage
Upper Chalk	unnamed	*Marsupites testudinarius*	Santonian
		Uintacrinus socialis	
		Micraster coranguinum	Coniacian
		Micraster cortestudinarium	
	Top Rock		———?———
	unnamed		
	'Chalk Rock'	*Sternotaxis planus*	
	Brandon Flint Series		Turonian
Middle Chalk	unnamed	*Terebratulina lata*	
		Mytiloides labiatus s.l.	
	———?———		
	Melbourn Rock	*Neocardioceras juddii*	
	Plenus Marls	*Metoicoceras geslinianum*	
Lower Chalk	unnamed	*Calycoceras guerangeri*	Cenomanian
		Acanthoceras jukesbrownei	
		Acanthoceras rhotomagense	
	Totternhoe Stone		
	Chalk Marl	*Mantelliceras dixoni*	
		Mantelliceras mantelli	
	Cambridge Greensand		Albian

Table 3 Physical properties derived from the geophysical logs of the Stowlangtoft Borehole

	Density mg/m³	Velocity km/s	Resistivity* Ωm	Gamma-ray API units
Upper Chalk	2.08	2.30	35	7
Middle Chalk	2.11	2.35	25	7
Lower Chalk	2.20	2.45	17	15
Gault	2.10	1.65	7	95
Palaeozoic (cf. Table 1)	2.71	4.50	100	130

* Focussed electric log — approximate relative values

30 mm across. Some of these pebbles are *remanié* and indicate a late-Albian (*Stoliczkaia dispar* Zone) age for most of the derived material. There is a rich indigenous fauna, predominantly *Aucellina* (*A. gryphaeoides* and *A. uerpmanni*), which occurs both as shells and as phosphatised moulds; other fossils include *Actactosia obtusa*, *Biplicatoria spp.*, (including '*Moutonithyris dutempleana* Auctt.'), *Monticlarella carteri*, a small quadrate *Anomia sp.* and *Plagiostoma globosum*. Locally, for example in Ely-Ouse Borehole 6, a thin basal unit of silty micaceous marls with sparse glauconite and phosphate is preserved beneath the typical Cambridge Greensand. This bed is rich in *Chondrites* and contains abundant *Neohibolites praeultimus*, together with well-preserved oysters (*Ceratostreon rauliniana*, *Ostrea cunabula* and *Aucellina*).

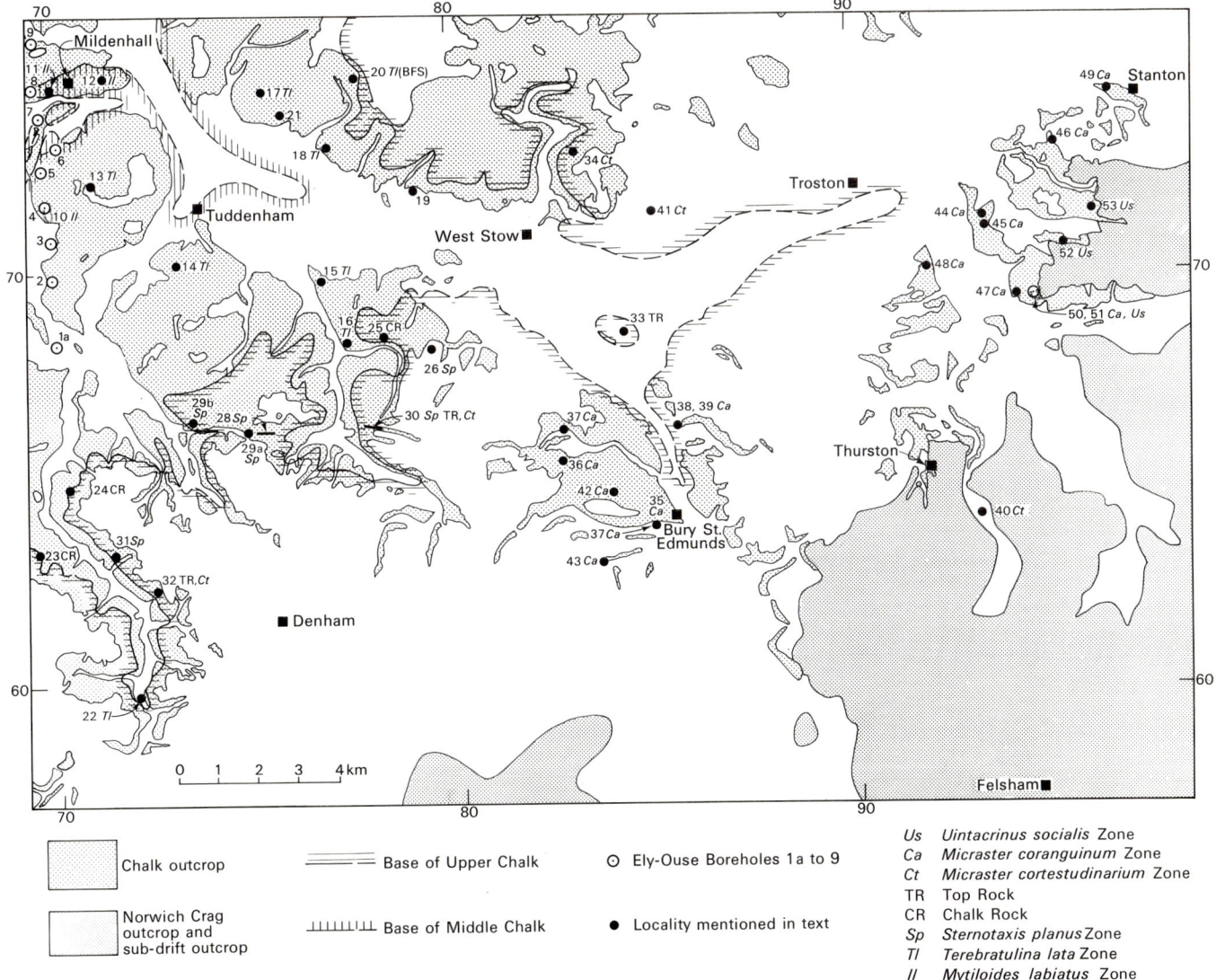

Figure 6 The Chalk outcrop showing localities mentioned in the text

Figure 7 Subdivisions of the Chalk in the Bury St Edmunds district with particular reference to the Stowlangtoft Borehole

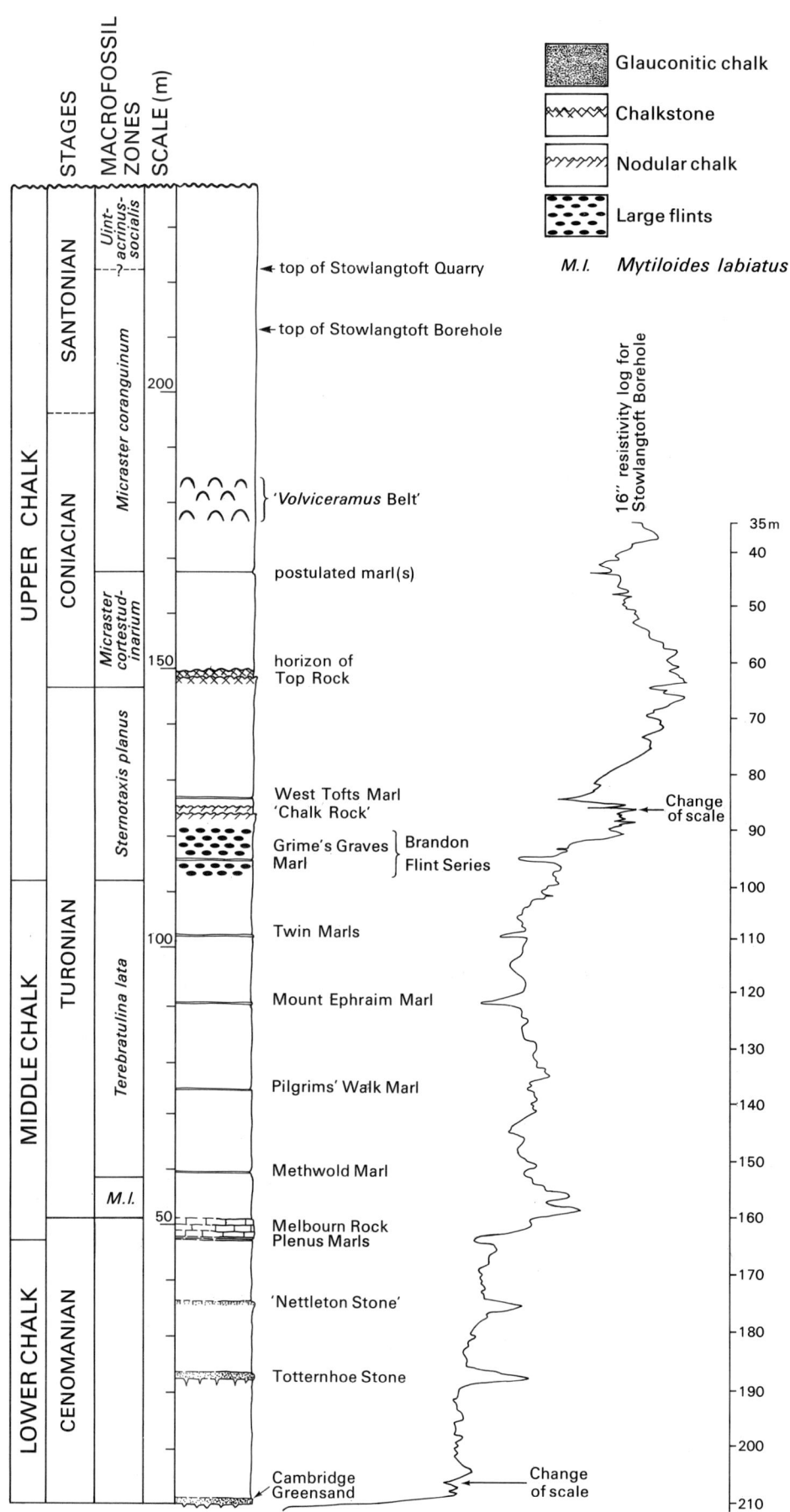

There is no outcrop of the Cambridge Greensand in the district, but it has been proved in all the Ely-Ouse boreholes, as well as in the Stowlangtoft and Eriswell boreholes (Figure 1). In the most complete sequence (Ely-Ouse Borehole 6), the succession above the basal unit can be divided into two (Morter and Wood, 1983). The lower part constitutes the typical Cambridge Greensand lithology and is rich in phosphatised pebbles, which occur both scattered and as lag accumulations on erosion surfaces. The higher part also comprises glauconitic silty marl, rich in *Aucellina*, but without phosphatised pebbles, except at the top where the contact with the overlying beds is indicated by a concentration of pale brown phosphates on an erosion surface.

The Cambridge Greensand has previously been considered to represent basal Cenomanian sediment containing derived Albian fossils, but detailed work on the ostracod faunas from Ely-Ouse Borehole 6 (Wilkinson, 1988) strongly suggests that the Albian–Cenomanian boundary coincides with one of the phosphate-strewn erosion surfaces within the phosphate-rich lower part of the member. Wilkinson found that ostracods below this erosion surface, including those from the thin basal unit with the belemnite *Neohibolites praeultimus*, belong to the *Cythereis luermannae hannoverana* ostracod Zone, indicating a late-Albian *Stoliczkaia dispar* ammonite Zone (*Mortoniceras rostratum* Subzone) age. Above this surface, *Cythereis bemerodensis* appears, together with an association characteristic of the basal Cenomanian, comprising *Platella icknieldensis* and numerous *Bythoceratina spp*. There is no evidence for the highest Albian *Mortoniceras perinflatum* Subzone, suggesting that there may be a significant nonsequence at this erosion surface.

Chalk Marl

The Lower Chalk below the Totternhoe Stone is known as the Chalk Marl, and comprises a succession of relatively fossiliferous marls, coarse bioclastic shell-detrital chalks, and fine-grained chalks. The Chalk Marl does not crop out in the district, but much detail on it is available from boreholes, particularly those of the Ely-Ouse Transfer Scheme. The thickness varies considerably over short distances. In the Ely-Ouse boreholes it is only 15.1 m thick in Borehole 7, about 24 m in Borehole 2 and as much as 36.6 m in Borehole 6; at Eriswell it is 27 m and in the Stowlangtoft Borehole 22 m. This variation is largely attributable to erosion prior to the deposition of the Totternhoe Stone, but is partly due to regional northward thinning.

Within the Chalk Marl, several distinctive, but poorly delimited beds can be recognised and used for correlation. At the base are the Porcellaneous Beds (Morter and Wood, 1983) which represent an expanded equivalent of the 'Paradoxica Bed' of the condensed sequences to the north. In the northern part of the district, for example in Ely-Ouse Borehole 8, these beds comprise pale, sparsely fossiliferous, chalky limestones with a porcellaneous texture. Farther south, clay-rich beds of bluish grey calcareous marl are intercalated between the limestones, and are dominant in Ely-Ouse Borehole 2. These marls superficially resemble the Gault and have commonly been recorded as such by drillers, for example in the Eriswell Borehole. Recognition of the base of the Porcellaneous Beds is not everywhere easy, though in Ely-Ouse Borehole 6, the Porcellaneous Beds contain no glauconitic grains, and the contrast with the micaceous and glauconitic silts of the underlying Cambridge Greensand is thus marked. Elsewhere, for example in the Stowlangtoft Borehole, glauconite extends up into the Porcellaneous Beds and even into the overlying inoceramid-rich beds.

The Porcellaneous Beds are characterised by a low-diversity fauna comprising *Actactosia sp.*, *Monticlarella carteri*, *Aucellina gryphaeoides*, *A. uerpmanni*, '*Inoceramus*' ex gr. *crippsi* and '*I.*' aff. *comancheanus*; the *Aucellina* are apparently restricted to the lower two-thirds. Poorly preserved ammonites, including *Idiohamites* aff. *alternatus*, *Mantelliceras sp.* and *Schloenbachia sp.*, indicate the lower part of the basal Cenomanian *Neostlingoceras carcitanense* subzonal assemblage of the *Mantelliceras mantelli* Zone. A flood occurrence of *Sciponoceras sp.* was found in Ely-Ouse Borehole 2, but was not encountered in any of the other boreholes.

The Porcellaneous Beds are overlain by dark grey, coarse, shell-detrital chalks rich in large pieces of *Inoceramus* shell, representing the expanded equivalent of the Inoceramus Beds of the Northern Province and belonging to the higher part of the *carcitanense* and overlying *Mantelliceras saxbii* subzones of the *Mantelliceras mantelli* Zone. The base of these is normally sharp, with coarse-grained sediment 'piped down' below the contact in a *Thalassinoides* burrow-system. The beds are characterised by common '*Inoceramus*' *crippsi* and '*I.*' cf. *crippsi reachensis* in ascending order, associated with *Grasirhynchia grasiana*, *Monticlarella? rectifrons*, *Ornatothyris spp.*, *Plagiostoma globosum* and *Pseudolimea sp.* Ammonites are represented by poorly preserved moulds of *Mantelliceras sp.* and *Schloenbachia sp.*

The expanded Inoceramus Beds pass upwards into pale-coloured, fine-grained chalks with *M? rectifrons* and abundant, inflated and relatively thick-shelled *Inoceramus* ex gr. *virgatus* (the *I. etheridgei* of earlier literature). These are overlain in turn by beds with thin-shelled inoceramids, including '*I.*' cf. *crippsi hoppenstedtensis* and *I.* cf. *crippsi reachensis*. By analogy with southern England successions, it is probable that the expanded Inoceramus Beds and the beds with *I.* ex gr. *virgatus* can be attributed to the *Mantelliceras dixoni* Zone, the overlying beds being questionably assignable to the higher part of that zone.

In successions where there is little pre-Totternhoe Stone erosion, as in Ely-Ouse Borehole 2 and in the Stowlangtoft Borehole, a band rich in *Orbirhynchia* cf. *mantelliana* is found some metres beneath the Totternhoe Stone, and is the equivalent of the Lower Orbirhynchia Band of the Northern Province. The age of these highest beds of the Chalk Marl is uncertain in the absence of diagnostic ammonites.

Totternhoe Stone

The Totternhoe Stone, known as the Burwell Rock[1] in the adjacent Cambridge district, overlies the Chalk Marl. It comprises up to 1.4 m of compact, greyish brown, clayey,

---

1 The relationship between the Burwell Rock of the Cambridge district and the Totternhoe Stone is not simple and requires further investigation. The Burwell Rock in its type locality appears to comprise several discrete beds of gritty and blocky chalk, and is considerably more than 1.4 m thick.

shell-fragmental silt, with small (5 to 15 mm), commonly green-coated, grey pebbles and scattered irregular phosphatic pebbles. Its characteristic 'gritty' texture is caused by comminuted inoceramid shells. In some localities, large glauconitised pebbles are concentrated in the basal part of the Totternhoe Stone, constituting the so-called 'Brassil' of quarrymen.

The Totternhoe Stone rests with discordant and strongly erosive contact on the Chalk Marl; commonly it is piped down into the upper 1 to 2 m of the Chalk Marl in anastomosing *Thalassinoides* burrows. The discordant nature of the contact is clearly demonstrated in the Ely-Ouse boreholes (Section 2 on 1:50 000 Sheet 189), and even more downcutting is now known to occur in other areas, particularly at Totternhoe itself, where the Totternhoe Stone apparently cuts down to only a few metres above the Gault. Current research suggests that the Totternhoe Stone was probably deposited rapidly on an irregular and locally deeply scoured and channelled surface.

Lithologically similar units occur at other levels, for example a bed of greyish white, shell-fragmental chalk with glauconitised pebbles between the depths of 45.47 and 46.08 m in the expanded 'Inoceramus Beds' of Ely-Ouse Borehole 2. However, the fauna of the Totternhoe Stone is quite distinctive. It is characterised particularly by the bivalves *Entolium laminosum* [= *E. orbiculare* Auctt.] and *Oxytoma seminudum*, in association with small brachiopods such as *Grasirhynchia martini*, *Kingena concinna*, *Modestella geinitzi*, *Capillithyris squamosa* and *Terebratulina nodulosa*. The belemnite *Actinocamax primus* occurs sporadically in the basal part of the bed in other districts.

Totternhoe Stone to Plenus Marls

These beds, and the overlying Plenus Marls, are the only part of the Lower Chalk to crop out within the district, though there is no exposure. They are generally pale grey and marly in their lower part, and off-white to white and hard in their upper part. Their thickness varies from 21 to 22 m in Ely-Ouse boreholes 1a, 2 and 4; they are 27 m and 26 m thick in the Eriswell and Stowlangtoft boreholes respectively. The beds encompass the higher part of the *Acanthoceras rhotomagense* Zone, the *A. jukesbrownei* Zone, and the Upper Cenomanian *Calycoceras guerangeri* Zone. Collectively these zones are equivalent to the *Holaster subglobosus* Zone of earlier classifications.

The most easily interpretable succession is in the Stowlangtoft Borehole. Immediately overlying the Totternhoe Stone there is 0.5 m of hard chalky limestone with *Orbirhynchia mantelliana*. This equates with the Upper *Orbirhynchia mantelliana* Band of southern England and marks the position of the mid-Cenomanian nonsequence of microfossil workers, as well as the top of the *Turrilites costatus* ammonite Subzone. Succeeding marly beds, 2 m thick, yield *Concinnithyris subundata* and *Kingena concinna*. An overlying rhythmic succession of marls and chalks, some 9 m thick, is poorly fossiliferous, apart from sparse occurrences of '*Inoceramus*' *atlanticus*. These beds are succeeded by 2 m of hard, coarse-grained, 'gritty' chalk which correlate with the Nettleton Stone of the Northern Province (Gaunt and others, in prep.) and 'Jukes-Browne Bed 7' of southern England. This bed, which has so far not been recognised in any of the Ely-Ouse boreholes, marks the *Acanthoceras jukesbrownei* Zone at the top of the Middle Cenomanian and also an upward change to some 10 m of massively bedded pale coloured chalks with thin marls. The latter sequence is poorly fossiliferous, apart from two horizons with small exogyrine oysters (*Amphidonte sp.*) near the base and occurrences of *Inoceramus pictus* in the overlying beds, notably in a shell-bed some 0.7 m beneath the Plenus Marls.

Much information is available from the Ely-Ouse boreholes, but these have proved difficult to correlate with the Stowlangtoft Borehole. In particular, the succession in Borehole 2 is quite different towards the top from that in Stowlangtoft or the other Ely-Ouse boreholes. It includes 1.37 m of distinctive very hard, pink, silty, unfossiliferous chalk; the lower part of this bed is mottled pink and greyish green and contains irregular nodules up to 25 mm across. A similar bed was noted at outcrop between Freckenham and West Row in the adjacent Cambridge district (Worssam and Taylor, 1969).

Plenus Marls

At the top of the Lower Chalk is the Plenus Marls, comprising alternating greenish marls and chalks less than 1 m thick. In the Ely-Ouse boreholes they have been proved only in Borehole 1a, where they consisted of 0.18 m of greyish green marl, overlain by 0.74 m of greenish buff, marly, hard, unfossiliferous chalk, terminating in 20 mm of khaki marl. In the highly anomalous succession of Borehole 2, they may be represented by a bed, 0.8 m thick, containing white phosphatised pebbles. Stowlangtoft Borehole proved 0.98 m of Plenus Marls, the succession being essentially similar to that of Ely-Ouse Borehole 1a, except at the top where a thin chalk bed was intercalated between two marls. The relationship between the condensed Plenus Marls in the present district and the standard sequence of southern England has not been investigated. The Plenus Marls are coextensive with the Upper Cenomanian *Metoicoceras geslinianum* Zone. The only fossils known from the district are crushed *Inoceramus pictus* from the Stowlangtoft Borehole.

Details

The Lower Chalk comes to crop only in the extreme north-west of the district around Mildenhall and even here it is largely covered by Quaternary deposits. There is no surface exposure of significance, but much detail has been provided by the Stowlangtoft and Ely-Ouse boreholes 1 to 9.

MIDDLE CHALK

On the published 1:50 000 Geological Sheet and on its accompanying script, the Middle Chalk has been taken to comprise the strata between the base of the Melbourn Rock and the base of the Chalk Rock. This interpretation follows the practice of Jukes-Browne (1903; 1904). However, it is valid only in areas with condensed sequences, where the Chalk Rock is a feature-forming member comprising several closely associated hardgrounds. In more expanded sequences, these split apart and pass laterally into bands of nodular chalk which eventually fail. The nodular chalks are rarely feature-forming and, in the North Downs, Geological Survey practice has been to take the base of the Upper Chalk at the base of an underlying sequence of chalks with large nodular flints and marl seams that is generally feature-forming.

The sequence in the present district (Figure 7) is even more expanded than in the North Downs, but the basal flinty belt of the North Downs is recognisable and is represented by a feature-forming unit of giant nodular and tabular flints known as the 'Brandon Flint Series' (Hewitt, 1935); the 'Chalk Rock' is reduced to one or more thin beds of nodular chalk which do not form a feature and which can be recognised only at exposure. The 'Brandon Flint Series' also equates with the succession of giant tabular flints at the base of the Burnham Chalk Formation in northern England (Mortimore and Wood, 1986). In the interests of regional consistency, the position of the base of the Upper Chalk has been changed in this account and has been taken at the base of the 'Brandon Flint Series'. Using this definition, the Middle Chalk is about 65 m thick in the Stowlangtoft Borehole and about 71 m thick in the Four Ashes Borehole just east of the present district (Figure 1) (see Bristow, 1980).

Melbourn Rock

The base of the Middle Chalk is taken at the base of the Melbourn Rock, a bed of hard, buff, yellow or off-white chalk up to 2 m thick, with common green-stained clayey bedding surfaces and buff or greyish green-coated chalk pebbles up to 30 mm in diameter. It gives rise to a low feature that can be traced from south of Worlington to Mildenhall; the latter town stands on a low rise formed by the Melbourn Rock. It has also been proved in Ely-Ouse boreholes 1a and 2, and in the Stowlangtoft Borehole. The Melbourn Rock is poorly fossiliferous apart from inoceramids, but it is probable that the boundary between the topmost Cenomanian *Neocardioceras juddii* Zone and the basal Turonian *Mytiloides (Inoceramus) labiatus* Zone sensu lato falls either within it or at its top.

The presence of the basal Turonian *Watinoceras coloradoense* ammonite Zone cannot be proved in the condensed sequences in eastern England. Consequently, the basal Turonian strata lie within a zone of *Mytiloides labiatus* sensu lato, corresponding to the *Inoceramus labiatus* Zone of earlier classifications.

Melbourn Rock to base of Upper Chalk

The Melbourn Rock is overlain by c.8 m of white, bioturbated, pebbly and/or nodular shelly chalk, rich in fragmented and complete valves of *Mytiloides*, together with *Orbirhynchia compta*, *O. cuvieri* and *Conulus subrotundus*, and falling largely within the *M. labiatus* sensu lato Zone. The nodules are grey or greenish grey coated and are up to 50 mm across; green-coated listric surfaces are common. In the Stowlangtoft Borehole, the lowest flints appear some 22 m above the top of these shelly chalks, but in Ely-Ouse Borehole 2, the appearance of flints marks their upper limit, confirming the suggestion (Worssam and Taylor, 1969) that flints first appear near the base of the *Terebratulina lata* Zone in the Cambridge district to the west.

The greatest part of the Middle Chalk belongs to the *T. lata* Zone and comprises firm to hard, white, nodular, shelly chalk with numerous irregular green-coated surfaces in the lower part, succeeded by more marly and less shell-rich chalks. In the Stowlangtoft Borehole these beds total 57 m. Pale green and buff-coated nodules occur throughout the lowest 20 m in Ely-Ouse Borehole 2. The succession includes several persistent seams of marl, up to 0.1 m thick, composed of montmorillonitic clay, that have been named in the adjacent Thetford district (Ward and others, 1968; and Figure 7). These seams, which give 'spikes' on resistivity logs, allow correlation throughout the Chalk of England and extend into France and Germany (Mortimore and Wood, 1986; Murray, 1986). Their lateral persistence strongly suggests that many may be argillised volcanic fall-out. In addition, courses of small nodular and finger-like burrow-form flints occur at several levels, particularly beneath the thickest of the marl seams (Mount Ephraim Marl) and towards the top of the succession. In the Stowlangtoft Borehole the *T. lata* Zone is significantly less flinty than around Mundford in the adjacent Thetford district, and flints enter much higher in the succession, as they do in much of southern England. Chalk-marl sedimentary rhythms are also more strongly marked; they are made obvious by burrowed, hardened omission surfaces overlain by dark marly chalk with concentrations of chalk pebbles.

The *T. lata* Zone fauna is generally of low diversity, characterised by *Concinnithyris sp.*, *Orbirhynchia heberti*, *Terebratulina lata*, inoceramid bivalves grouped around *I. cuvierii* and *I. lamarcki*, thin-tested *Micraster corbovis* of *T. lata* Zone type and *Sternotaxis planus*. The Mount Ephraim Marl contains a flood occurrence of the giant complex-chambered foraminifer *Coscinophragma*; flint-filled echinoids and inoceramids, notably *I. lamarcki* s.s., occur in the underlying chalk.

Details

Jukes-Browne and Hill (*in* Whitaker and others, 1891, p.44) noted a section [c.7005 7170] in the north-east corner of the Newmarket Road quarry (10)[1], and considered that the lowest bed was the upper part of the Melbourn Rock. Their section reads:

	Thickness m
Gravelly soil and rubble	1.2
Hard nodular whitish rock in thin beds, full of *Inoceramus mytiloides* and *Rhynchonella cuvieri*	1.2
Hard nodular rock chalk, white, with greenish marl between the lumps (no fossils)	0.9
Talus	1.2

[1] Numbers have been given to Chalk localities mentioned in the text. These are shown on Figure 6.

Worssam and Taylor (1969, pp.67–68, fig. 5) saw a similar section, with nodular chalk below a marl seam and with less nodular chalk above. Ely-Ouse Borehole 4 [7012 7169], drilled at the northern end of the pit, proved the base of the Melbourn Rock at 3.94 m. Its lowest 0.08 m was a buff, slightly greenish, locally pink-stained marl containing nodules up to 20 cm across; this was succeeded by 0.66 m of off-white hard chalk with buff-coated nodules. No higher strata were seen, but Borehole 2 [7008 6976], a little to the south, shows that at least 30 m of the succeeding Middle Chalk is nodular.

Hewitt (1935) noted a section (11) [7012 7440] on the north bank of the River Lark, Mildenhall, which yielded *Inoceramus labiatus*. The section is no longer accessible and its precise position in the sequence is uncertain. It has been shown as lying within the Lower Chalk on the published map, but may be above the Melbourn Rock.

A disused pit (12) [7144 7476] at Mildenhall probably lies just above the Melbourn Rock. The following fossils were collected: *Orbirhynchia sp.*, *Inoceramus apicalis*, *Mytiloides* cf. *labiatus*.

The Chalk in Howe's pit (13) [711 721] at Chalk Hill is much disturbed. A composite 22 m discontinuous section, beneath 1.5 m of drift, was recorded by Mr T Lawson in 1978, and is held in BGS records. The bottom 7 m of the section exposes flintless chalk with thin marl plexi, notably a conspicuous 0.15 m plexus 5 m above the base. The succeeding 8 m of section were not measured. The highest 7 m include two conspicuous marker horizons: a band of burrow-form and 'finger' flints overlying chalk with echinoids and inoceramids; and a 0.1 m band of brown-stained weakly indurated nodular chalk some 1.5 m above the flint band.

A temporary section (14) [7327 7050] at Mitchel Head, Tuddenham, yielded low *lata* Zone fossils: *Inoceramus cuvierii*, *I.* aff. *cuvierii* and *I.* ex gr. *inaequivalvis*.

A pit (15) [7680 6965] east of Cavenham was briefly described by Hewitt (1935, loc. 25). The section was measured by Mr T Lawson in 1978 (BGS records). The lower part of the pit exposes 2 m of flintless, marly, massively bedded chalk with weakly developed sponge beds forming patches up to 0.5 m across. *Inoceramus cuvierii* was collected from the basal 0.4 m. The central 2 m of the section is obscured. The top 3 m includes several flint bands, notably a band of 10 cm nodular flints with *Chondrites* in surface relief which overlies a sponge bed. Large, vertical, grey-skinned, black flints occur just below the 'Deadlime'. Fossils from the *Chondrites* flints horizon and in the underlying 0.9 m of chalk include: *Porosphaera sp.*, *Orbirhynchia* aff. *dispansa*, *Inoceramus* ex gr. *cuvierii*, *Bourgueticrinus sp.*, *Isocrinus? granosus* and *Sternotaxis planus*. Additional fossils collected by Hewitt (1935) include: *Serpula plana*, *Terebratulina lata*, *T. striatula*, *Inoceramus lamarcki*, *Metopaster exsculptus?*, '*Cidaris*' aff. *perornata*, *Echinocorys sp.*, *Micraster corbovis* of *lata* Zone type and *Cretolamna appendiculata*. The fauna indicates a high *lata* or basal *planus* Zone position. It is possible that the Twin Marls occur in the unexposed 1 m, in which case the flints in the upper part of the section could be at, or just below the horizon of the Rough and Smooth Blacks at the base of the 'Brandon Flint Series' (Figure 8).

At a pit referred to as Risby Heath by Hewitt (1935, loc. 24), but better known today as Robert's Bridge (16), Hewitt (1935) noted 1.2 m of Chalk with two lines of flint nodules, the lower ones large and almost tabular. The following section of a trial pit [7750 6807] in the old pit was recorded by Dr B S P Moorlock:

	Thickness m
Flint Band	
Chalk, gritty, fragments	0.6
Flint band, almost continuous, horizontal, grey-coated, nodular, partly burrow-form	0.1
Chalk, shelly, less fragmented than bed above; at base a yellow-stained bed with sponges	0.6
Flint, long, nodular with irregular bases, up to 0.33 m long; black interiors	0.1
Chalk, with grey burrow-fills, marly wisps, blocky weathering, seen for	0.3

Fossils from the middle bed of chalk include several *Gibbithyris* (including *G. subrotunda*), *Orbirhynchia sp.*, *Hyotissa semiplana*, *Cremnoceramus?* aff. *rotundatus* and *I.* ex gr. *websteri* sensu Woods *non* Mantell, *Plicatula barroisi*, *Sternotaxis planus* and *S. placenta*. *S. placenta* and *Echinocorys sp.* also occurred in the top bed. Hewitt (1935) also recorded the *lata* Zone form of *Micraster corbovis* (BGS Ze 3239) preserved in flint. The fauna is unusual in that it has close affinities with high *planus* Zone assemblages, for example the occurrence of *Sternotaxis placenta*, but the *Micraster* suggests a lower stratigraphical level, in or below the basal part of the 'Brandon Flint Series', a suggestion supported by the location of the pit relative to the one at Cavenham, and by its position below a marked feature ascribed to the 'Brandon Flint Series'.

The soil from a trench (17) [7544 7443] at Avenue Farm, Icklingham, included common fragments of *Inoceramus* ex gr. *cuvierii*, indicative of the *lata* Zone.

An extensive pitted area (21) [759 739] lies 1.3 km north-west of Icklingham, and may be the site of old flint workings. These lie at least 30 m topographically below the 'Brandon Flint Series' and are probably stratigraphically about 40 below that level.

Hewitt (1935, locality 37) recorded 3.6 to 4.5 m of chalk with rare small flints at the base, at a locality (18) [770 730] near Icklingham. He identified *Terebratulina lata*, but a re-examination of the specimen suggests that it is a juvenile *Terebratulina* ex gr. *striatula* of no zonal significance.

A trial pit (19) [7911 7197] east of Weatherhill Farm, Icklingham, exposed 3.3 m of shattered, blocky, white, locally iron-stained chalk containing fragments of bivalves, bryozoa, and *Chondrites*-like burrows.

An isolated exposure of chalk with *Spondylus spinosus* and a (?holasterid) echinoid test fragment that occurs beneath gravel [721 598] at Lidgate (22) in the extreme south-west, probably belongs to the uppermost Middle Chalk, but it could be low Upper Chalk.

UPPER CHALK

Much of the outcrop of the Upper Chalk is obscured by drift, while there is also a cover of Crag down-dip to the east. The greater part of the complete sequence has been removed by erosion: only the *Sternotaxis planus*, *Micraster cortestudinarium*, *M. coranguinum* and *Uintacrinus socialis* zones are present at surface, though the *Marsupites testudinarius* Zone may be preserved beneath drift in the extreme south and east. The fullest provings are in boreholes and these establish a number of marker bands (Figure 7). The Stowlangtoft Borehole proved 98 m of Upper Chalk, to which can be added the overlying 11 m exposed in the chalk pit within which the borehole was sunk. By comparison, Four Ashes Borehole (Figure 1), farther east and commencing in the *Uintacrinus socialis* or possibly the *Marsupites testudinarius* Zone, proved 125 m of Upper Chalk (Bristow, 1980). Within the Stowlangtoft sequence, the best markers are the 'Brandon Flint Series' and the Chalk Rock, both in the *Sternotaxis planus* Zone (Figure 7).

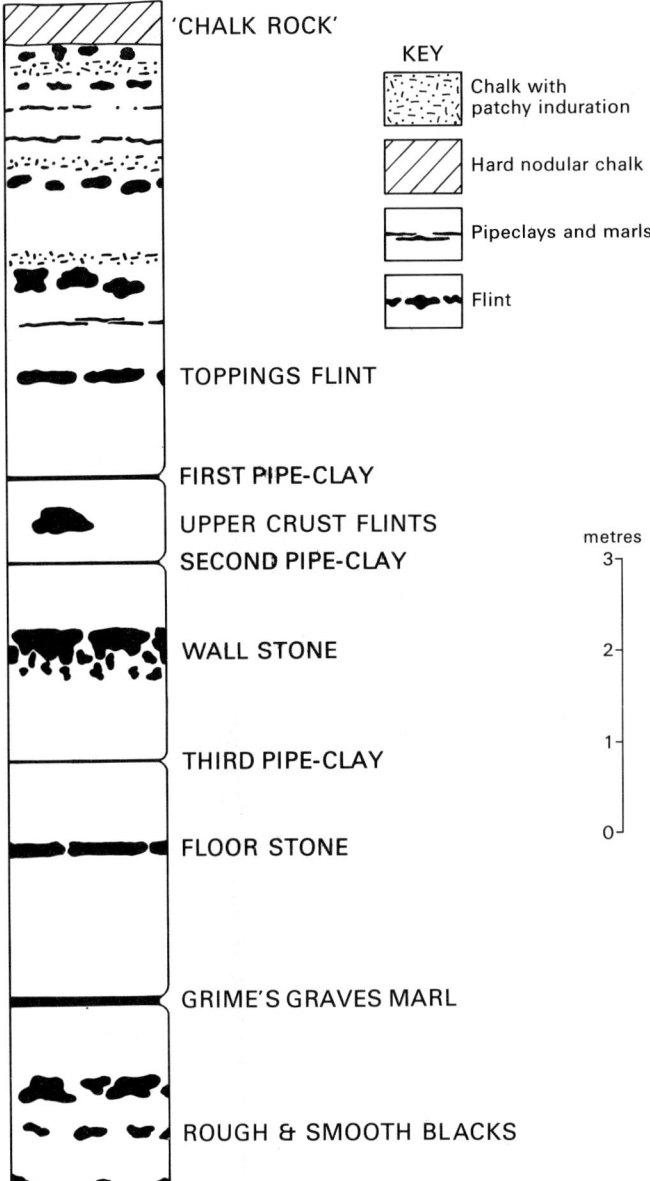

Figure 8 Section in Upper Chalk including the Brandon Flint Series in a flint mine near Brandon 1879 (after Skertchley in Ward and others, 1968)

'Brandon Flint Series'

The 'Brandon Flint Series', at the base of the Upper Chalk, comprises up to 15 m of relatively massively bedded chalks with marl seams and widely separated courses of giant (0.2 to over 0.4 m) tabular and nodular flints that were extensively exploited in the mines near Brandon, Norfolk, known as Grime's Graves (Figure 8), first by prehistoric Man for the manufacture of tools and weapons, and later for the manufacture of gun-flints. Taking the names of flints and marl seams (pipe clays) used by the miners, Skertchly (1879, fig. 2) published a generalised section based on the mines at Lingheath, and an essentially comparable section in the mines worked near Icklingham (see p.24). Skertchly drew attention to the persistence of three thin (5 to 10 cm) pipe-clays towards the top of the sequence and to the presence of a bed of hard, subcrystalline, chalky limestone beneath the uppermost of these (First Pipe-Clay). This hard bed was termed the 'False Chalk Rock' by Hewitt (1924), and was taken to mark the base of the *planus* Zone and the Upper Chalk. He thus placed the greater part of the 'Brandon Flint Series' in the Middle Chalk. Near Brandon, Ward and others (1968) additionally recognised a thick (0.1 m) marl-seam (Grime's Graves Marl) beneath the lowest flint (Floorstone) normally mined. This marl is represented by a marked low-resistivity 'spike' on geophysical logs and, together with the Floorstone flint, shows the 'Brandon Flint Series' to be the local expression of a flint optimum that everywhere marks the base of the *planus* Zone (Mortimore and Wood, 1986).

The Chalk Rock

The 'Brandon Flint Series' is overlain by the 'Chalk Rock', which here comprises one or more thin (up to 0.3 m) beds of hard, yellow, nodular chalk. It is richly fossiliferous and contains moulds of aragonite-shelled molluscs (scaphopods, gastropods, bivalves and ammonites), together with sponges, corals, brachiopods and echinoids (particular *Micraster leskei*). The ammonites are indicative of the Upper Turonian *Subprionocyclus neptuni* Zone of the standard ammonite zonal scheme.

Chalk Rock to Top Rock

A marl seam, 0.1 m thick, termed the West Tofts Marl, lies 0.3 m above the top of the Chalk Rock at the Winery on Risby Poor's Heath, and 0.2 m above it in the Stowlangtoft Borehole. In the Thetford district to the north, the separation increases to c.4 m of coarse-grained bioclastic chalk with weakly developed nodular chalk.

The succeeding part of the *planus* Zone comprises up to 10 m of somewhat mealy-textured, off-white to buff chalk, with numerous courses of flints including thin *Zoophycos* flints, finger-like thalassinoidean burrow-form flints and irregular nodular flints. Good exposures of these beds are found in a railway cutting near Higham and an excellent temporary section was available during the construction of the A45 dual-carriageway, west of Bury St Edmunds. The fauna is rich in bivalves, notably *Gryphaeostrea canaliculata*, *Hyotissa semiplana* and *Spondylus spinosus*, as well as echinoids such as *Echinocorys* cf. *gravesi*, *Micraster corbovis*, large *M. leskei*, *M. normanniae* and *Sternotaxis placenta*. Giant *M. corbovis* and *M. leskei* are particularly common towards the top of the succession.

Top Rock

The sequence grades up locally into the Top Rock, a bed up to 0.4 m thick of intensely indurated, yellow-stained chalk ('chalkstone' sensu Bromley and Gale, 1982), penetrated by an open *Thalassinoides* burrow system and possibly comprising several welded hardgrounds. Its upper surface is a glauconitised convolute hardground overlain by glauconitised and phosphatised pebbles; some of these pebbles are corroded steinkerns of fossils, particularly echinoids. The Top Rock represents a condensation of the lower part of the *Micraster cortestudinarium* Zone. It is highly fossiliferous, particularly in the top 0.1 m, and rich faunas were collected from a pit at Dalham, the A45 road-cutting, and from the base of a gravel pit at Fornham St Genevieve (p.26).

In addition to sparse moulds of gastropods and bivalves comparable to those from the Chalk Rock, the fauna contains abundant hexactinellid sponges, small corals, rhynchonellid and terebratulid brachiopods (*Orbirhynchia sp.* and *Concinnithyris sp.*), a diverse assemblage of inoceramid bivalves, and the echinoids *Echinocorys* cf. *gravesi* and *Micraster cortestudinarium*. The sponges are preserved as glauconitised pebble-fossils, though in most cases the preservation is inadequate for identification even at generic level. The inoceramids are preserved variously as lightly phosphatised shells, more strongly phosphatised steinkerns, and phosphatised steinkerns with a skin of glauconite. This variation in preservation is suggestive of derivation and reworking from several sources, so more than one assemblage may be represented. Apart from species of *Mytiloides*, including *M.* cf. *dresdensis* which could be of latest Turonian age, most of the inoceramids are earliest Coniacian species, such as *Cremnoceramus? rotundatus*, *C.? waltersdorfensis hannovrensis* and *C. w. waltersdorfensis*. Glauconitised pebble-fossils immediately overlying the hardground include *Cremnoceramus erectus* and common *Micraster cortestudinarium*, the former suggesting a higher horizon within the Lower Coniacian than that indicated by the Top Rock assemblage.

The Top Rock occurs only in the western part of the district, extending east as far as the Fornham St Genevieve gravel pit and the A45 section. In cored boreholes at Bury St Edmunds (39) [843 683] and in the Stowlangtoft Borehole (50), where there are greatly expanded *planus* and *cortestudinarium* zones, the Top Rock is absent, but may be represented by a group of closely-spaced, iron-stained, spongiferous, nodular chalk beds. The change is abrupt, only about 3 km separating provings in the two facies, possibly because sedimentation has been structurally controlled.

Above the Top Rock

The higher part of the *cortestudinarium* Zone, the *coranguinum* Zone and the *socialis* Zone consist of white chalk with numerous courses and scattered nodules of flint. It is significantly finer grained and whiter than the underlying beds and the faunas are generally of low diversity. There are no hardgrounds or rock-beds, though there is some nodular chalk in the basal few metres. Conspicuous flints form marker horizons at several levels within the *coranguinum* Zone and a conspicuous yellow sponge-rich bed lies in its higher part. Marl seams are absent from the exposed succession, but there may be one or more at the base of the *coranguinum* Zone by analogy with other areas. At some levels, particularly near the base and top of the latter zone, the chalk is rich in fragments and isolated valves of large inoceramids, notably *Platyceramus* and *Volviceramus*. The highest part of the exposed succession contains small, inconspicuous and widely scattered flints.

Apart from a chalk pit at Dalham (32) (Figure 9), which exposes 8 m of the higher part of the *cortestudinarium* Zone with *Cremnoceramus schloenbachi* and *Tethyoceramus humboldti*, and a small pit at Wyken Wood (p.29) in the *socialis* Zone, most exposures are in the *coranguinum* Zone. The boundary between the *cortestudinarium* and the *coranguinum* zones is not exposed within the district, and falls in an interval of core-loss in the Stowlangtoft Borehole. The lower part of the *coranguinum* Zone (best seen in a chalk pit at Willowmere Spinney [895 776], near Euston in the adjoining Thetford district) is characterised by beds rich in *Volviceramus* ex gr. *involutus* and subordinate *Platyceramus mantelli*, overlain by beds in which the relative proportions of these taxa are reversed. This '*Volviceramus*-Belt' was encountered at several localities near Bury St Edmunds. Higher beds within the zone crop out in several discontinuous exposures, notably in chalk pits at Horringer Court, south-east of Bury St Edmunds (p.27), and near Ixworth (p.27). The relative stratigraphical positions of the exposures in these pits are uncertain, as is the exact position of the Coniacian–Santonian boundary, though this must fall within this part of the succession. The top beds of the *coranguinum* Zone are exposed in Stowlangtoft Quarry and can be correlated with sections in the Isle of Thanet, taken as the standard for southern England. Foraminiferal zonation (Bailey and others, 1983) has been used to interpret isolated *coranguinum* Zone exposures in the district that have poor macrofossil control, and has proved of particular use in identifying possible *socialis* Zone localities in the absence of *Uintacrinus*.

Details

The 'Brandon Flint Series' is about 15 m thick near Desnage Lodge [740 675] and Risby Poor's Heath [775 675], appreciably thicker than around Brandon (about 8 m), and forms a good feature. Flints were once extensively mined [779 748] at Icklingham (20), Skertchly (1879) gives a general section for this locality:

	Thickness m
Sand	0.45 to 0.91
'Dead-Lime'	1.83
Soft, white chalk	0.91
Toppings Flint	0.13 to 0.30
Soft chalk	0.03
First Pipe-Clay	0.03
Hard chalk	6.10
Upper-Crust Flint	0.15 to 0.46
Soft white chalk	0.04 to 0.46
Second Pipe-Clay	0.04
White chalk, rather hard	0.91
Wall Stone	0.30 to 0.46
Soft chalk, full of horns	0.91
Hard chalk	0.91 to 1.52
Third Pipe-Clay	0.03
Floorstone	0.08 to 0.30
Moderately hard chalk	0.61 to 0.91
Very hard chalk	2.44 to 2.74
Rough and Smooth Blacks	0.30
Average for the pit	13.72

He also noted that there were up to 500 closely spaced pits in the neighbourhood, with an average separation of about 8 m. He does not record the presence of the Grime's Graves Marl (Ward and others, 1968), which lies between the Rough and Smooth Blacks and the Floorstone near Brandon.

Figure 9 Sections in Upper Chalk at Dalham, near Barrow Heath and at Higham

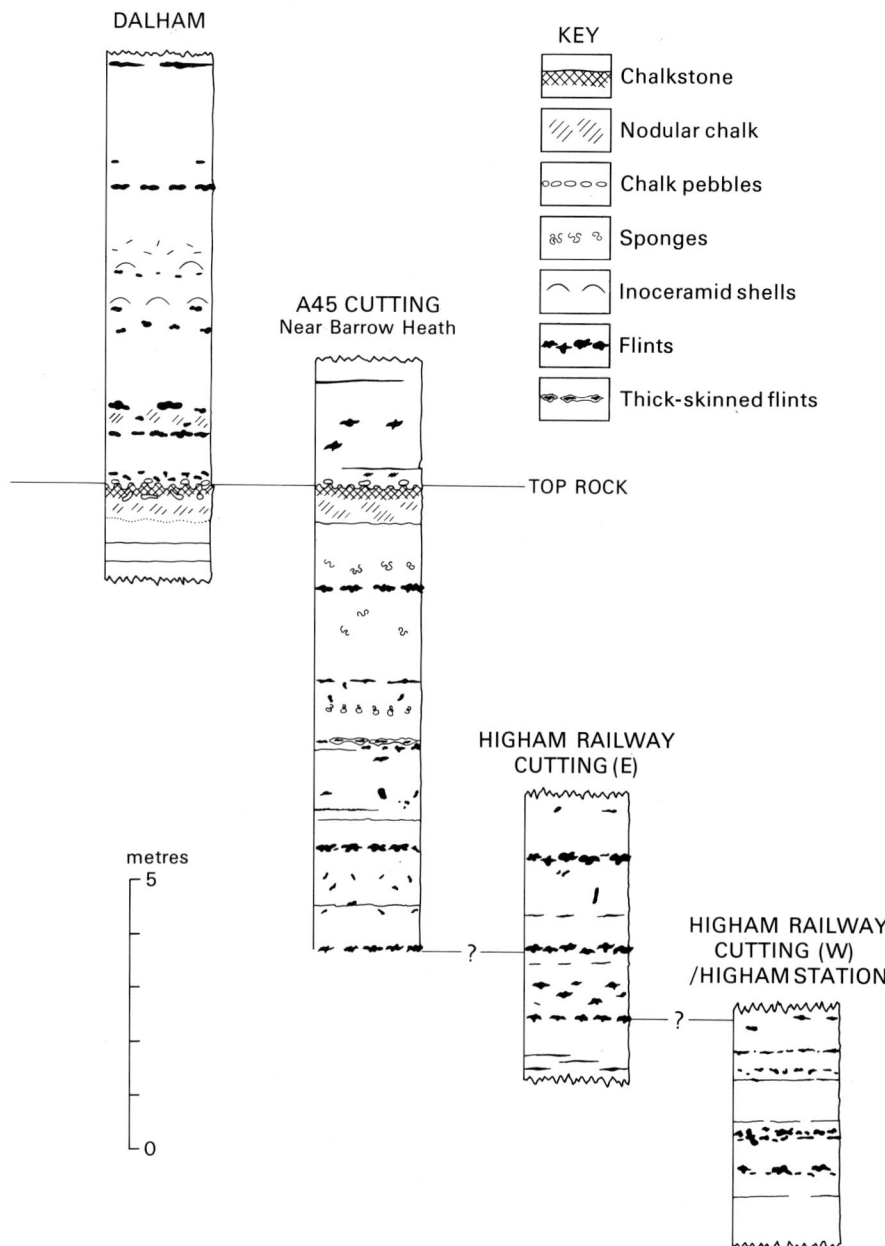

Part of the succession, including the Wall Stone and the two lower Pipe Clays, was not seen in the Stowlangtoft Borehole due to core loss, and the Rough and Smooth Blacks were very weakly developed. A hard nodular bed at 90.15 m depth, which may be the equivalent of the 'False Chalk Rock' of Hewitt (1924), i.e. the hard band beneath the First Pipe Clay, yielded well-preserved ammonites including *Scaphites geinitzii*, *Sciponoceras bohemicum* and *Yezoites* [*Otoscaphites*] *bladenensis*.

The local 'Chalk Rock' has been identified at few localities. Worssam and Taylor (1969) recorded its characteristic fauna from two localities (23 and 24) [697 632 and 703 648] near Moulton, near the western border of the district. The latter locality yielded an undescribed trochid gastropod, *Scaphites geinitzii*, *Suprionocyclus sp.* and *Sternotaxis planus*.

A section (25) at the Winery on Risby Poor's Heath [783 683] was in a lithology typical of the Chalk Rock, but it may lie higher in the sequence. A section measured by Dr B S P Moorlock in 1977 showed:

	Thickness m
Boulder clay	0.50
Flints; small, nodular	0.05
Chalk, firm, white with common terebratulids	0.60
Flints, large, nodular	0.15
Chalk, firm, white	1.20
Flints, large, nodular, 0.5 to 0.7 m across	0.15
Chalk, firm, white	0.70

Another section, slightly lower stratigraphically, showed:

	Thickness m
Chalk, with small nodular flints	0.3
Chalk, firm, white	1.0
Marl	0.1 to 0.2
Chalk, firm, white with yellow-stained nodules	0.3
Chalk, hard, yellow-stained, fossiliferous	0.3 +

The marl seam, if in situ, may be the West Tofts Marl, but it may be an injection of boulder clay along a weakness. Fossils from the bed immediately beneath the 'marl' include: *Ventriculites sp.*, *Gibbithyris subrotunda*, *Periaulax heberti*, *Chlamys sp.*, *Gryphaeostrea canaliculata*, *Hyotissa semiplana*, *Cremnoceramus?* aff. *rotundatus*, *Mytiloides dresdensis*, *M. striatoconcentricus* aff. *carpathicus* and *Micraster leskei*. A rich fauna obtained from yellow lumpy chalk on the spoil heap probably came from the same level. It included *Cameroptychium campanulatum*, *Sporadoscinia* cf. *stellifera*, *Gibbithyris subrotunda*, *Periaulax heberti*, 'Cirsocerithium' reussi, *Inoceramus longealatus*, *Mytiloides labiatoidiformis*, *M. striatoconcentricus*, *Micraster leskei* and *Sternotaxis placenta*. Fossils from just below the higher of the large nodular flint bands in the upper section include *Gibbithyris sp.*; *Micraster sp.* was found just above the flint band.

Some 0.6 m of very rubbly chalk, resting on 0.5 m of firmer chalk, which in turn rests on chalk with large nodular flints up to 0.3 m across, was exposed near Bullock's Lodge, Risby (26) [7940 6801]. It yielded *Paraplocia labyrinthica*, *Spirorbis sp.*, *Cyclothyris sp.*, *Gibbithyris subrotunda*, *Orbirhynchia reedensis*, *Inoceramus sp.*, *Mytiloides fiegei* [? = *M. incertus*] and *M.* aff. *lusatiae*. This site probably lies at, or just above, the 'Chalk Rock'.

In two boreholes at the Sugar Beet Factory (39), Bury St Edmunds, the 'Chalk Rock' occurs at a depth of between 54 and 57 m (R Mortimore, personal communication), and in the Stowlangtoft Borehole it lies at a depth of 85.2 m. At this latter locality, the West Tofts Marl is separated from the top of the Chalk Rock by only 0.2 m of chalk; this separation increases to 3 m in the other boreholes.

Chalk at a slightly higher horizon was exposed in the base of a small gravel pit (27) [810 695] near Flempton Hall. The rubbly chalk yielded a mixture of (presumably) derived *coranguinium* Zone fossils (*Volviceramus* and *Platyceramus* fragments) and in-situ fossils from the *planus* Zone. Amongst the latter are *Terebratulina* ex gr. *striatula*, *Mytiloides spp.* and pycnodonteine oysters.

Sections in Higham railway cutting, along the A45 at Barrow Heath, and in a chalk pit at Dalham show partially overlapping sequences from just above the 'Chalk Rock' to 8 m above the Top Rock. Only at Dalham and Barrow Heath does the presence of the Top Rock allow definite correlations to be made, but there are sufficient lithological similarities and faunal controls to link the sections adequately: there are, however, minor uncertainties in some details (Figure 9). The base of the Higham railway cutting (28) [749 661] probably lies between the Chalk Rock and the West Tofts Marl.

In the railway cutting, the tabular flint in the middle of the western section may correlate with one in the eastern section, but this is not certain. Fossils in the lowest exposed bed include *Cretirhynchia cuneiformis*, *Gibbithyris sp.*, sheets of *Inoceramus sp.*, *Spondylus spinosus*, *Micraster* cf. *leskei* and *M. corbovis*. The 0.5 m of chalk above the lowest flint in the section yielded: *Hyotissa semiplana*, *Ostrea incurva*, *Spondylus spinosus*, *Hirudocidaris hirudo* and *Sternotaxis* cf. *placenta*. *Micraster leskei* and *M. normanniae* occur in 0.3 m of chalk above the tabular flint. This is a high *planus* Zone assemblage. A course of conspicuous large nodular flints towards the top of the eastern cutting (29) [750 661] is at the level of an horizon rich in *Micraster normanniae*, many of which are superbly preserved and infilled with flint. The chalk immediately overlying this flint contains *Sternotaxis placenta*. Another cutting [736 663], at Seven Mile Bridge, yielded a poorly preserved sponge, *Inoceramus* ex gr. *websteri?*, juvenile *Spondylus spinosus*, and a marginal of *Metopaster uncatus*.

Dualling of the A45 near Barrow (30) [777 661 to 783 661] exposed 10 m of the uppermost *planus* Zone, the Top Rock, and 2.5 m of the overlying *cortestudinarium* Zone (Figure 9). The base of the section probably overlaps with the section in the eastern part of the cutting at Higham. The *planus* Zone, about 7 m thick, yielded the following rich fauna, particularly from the uppermost 3–4 m: limonitised sponges, *Gibbithyris sp.*, questionable juvenile *Cremnoceramus? waltersdorfensis*, *Hyotissa semiplana*, *Bourgueticrinus sp.*, ophiuroid debris, asteroids including *Metopaster sp.*, *Echinocorys* cf. *gravesi*, *Micraster corbovis*, large *M. leskei*, *M. normanniae*, *Temnocidaris (Stereocidaris) sceptrifera* and *Sternotaxis placenta*. The *Micraster corbovis* and *M. leskei* are giant forms, as large as any *Micraster* from the English Chalk. The Top Rock was also richly fossiliferous; in addition to the sponges *Hillendia* or *Guettardiscyphia sp.*, *Phymosinion sp.*, *Sporadoscinia* or *Coscinopora sp.*, determined by Dr R E H Reid, and ventriculids, the fauna included a small 'button' coral, *Concinnithyris* or *Gibbithyris sp.*, *Cretirhynchia subplicata* (rare), *Orbirhynchia sp.*, *Periaulex* aff. *heberti*, *Planolateralus dievarum*, phosphatised inoceramid moulds (including *Cremnoceramus? rotundatus*, *C.?* ex gr. *waltersdorfensis hannovrensis*, *Mytiloides* cf. *dresdensis* and *M. sp.*), *Spondylus spinosus*, *Tenea sp.*, *Micraster cortestudinarium* and *Ptychodus mammillaris*. Glauconitised pebble-preservation *Micraster cortestudinarium* occur on the top of the hardground.

Sections at Dalham duplicate the A45 sequence, but also expose higher strata. Echinoids collected from a temporary section (31) [7160 6305] at Dalham indicate an horizon within the *planus* Zone, slightly below that of the A45 section. The old chalk pit (32) [7255 6243], measured by Messrs T E Lawson and C J Wood in 1979, showed about 1.7 m of strata with *Micraster corbovis* below the Top Rock and 8 m of *cortestudinarium* Zone beds above (Figure 9). The Top Rock was very fossiliferous, particularly the uppermost 0.1 m, with phosphatised *Cremnoceramus? waltersdorfensis hannovrensis*, *C.? w. waltersdorfensis* and glauconitised *Cremnoceramus* near *C. erectus*. *Cremnoceramus schloenbachi* and *Tethyoceramus humboldti* were collected from immediately above the Top Rock, and fragmented material, presumably belonging to the same taxa, occurred in several higher beds.

The Top Rock was also exposed in the floor of the Fornham St Genevieve gravel pit (33) [843 683]. Fossils include: *Cameroptychium campanulatum*, *C. planus*, *Craticularia fittoni?*, *Coscinopora* or *Sporadoscinia sp.*, *Eurete spp.* including *E.* cf. *formosum*, *Ophrystoma?*, *Phymosinion muricatum*, *Rhizopoterion sp.*, *Sporadoscinia alcyonoides*, *Synolynthia subrotunda*, *Parsimonia* aff. *antiquata*, *Parasmilia?*, *Concinnithyris sp.*, *Orbirhynchia sp.*, *Bathrotomaria sp.*, *Freiastarte sp.*, *Mytiloides sp.*, 'Hirudocidaris' *hirudo*, *Echinocorys* cf. *gravesi* and *Micraster cortestudinarium*.

A sequence of inoceramid shell beds with *Volviceramus* aff. *involutus* and *Platyceramus mantelli*, constituting the '*Volviceramus* Belt', occurs within the lower part of the *coranguinum* Zone. In the Stowlangtoft Borehole these beds probably occur about 18 m above the base of the Zone, in a part of the core where recovery was poor. The '*Volviceramus* Belt' was also exposed in an old chalk pit (35) [8499 6385] at Bury St Edmunds, where the following section was measured by Dr C R Bristow in 1976:

	Thickness m
Chalk, white, with scattered nodular flints, *Platyceramus* common	0.80
Irregular layer of nodular flints, maximum 20 cm long	
Chalk, white, with *Volviceramus* and *Ostrea*	0.30
Irregular layer of nodular flints, maximum 20 cm long	
Chalk, white, with scattered nodular flints	1.50

Large, irregular, nodular flints up to 0.5 m across by
0.2 m high
Chalk, soft, white, with *Volviceramus*   1.20

The underground galleries at Jacqueline Close [8478 6398] (Plate 8) and at Bury St Edmunds Hospital (Pearman, 1976) may have been in the same belt. So, too, may be a temporary section (37) [8293 6603] at the Golf Course which has yielded many *Platyceramus mantelli* and *Volviceramus* aff. *involutus*. The railway cutting (36) [828 653] north-east of Westley is probably at this same level or a very slightly higher one, since fragments of *Platyceramus* are common, together with small *Phymosoma* radioles and a fragmentary radiole of '*Cidaris*' *perornata?*, but no *Volviceramus* has been recorded. Temporary exposures (38) [855 661] at or about this horizon have yielded fragments of *Volviceramus sp.* and *Platyceramus mantelli*, together with *Orbirhynchia sp.*, pycnodonteine oysters and a radiole of '*Cidaris*' *perornata*. A fifth locality also at or about this level is at Beyton (40) [9315 6380], where bridge foundations yielded white blocky chalk with common *Ostrea incurva* and fragments of *Platyceramus mantelli*.

North of Bury St Edmunds, the Ingham gravel pit (41) [8504 7135] is probably floored by chalk of this '*Volviceramus* Belt'. Rolled and fresh fragments of inoceramids (*Platyceramus mantelli* and *Volviceramus* aff. *involutus*), *Spondylus spinosus* and *Micraster sp.* have been found, and adnate *Spirorbis sp.* and *Crania sp.* occur on the inoceramid shell fragments. An exposure at the Barber Green Factory (42) [8400 6461], Bury St Edmunds, yielded large fragments of *Platyceramus sp.* and is probably slightly above the '*Volviceramus* Belt'.

Hewitt (1935, locality 56) recorded 5 m of chalk, of which the upper 1.4 m was rubbly, in a pit (47) [9410 6917] near Baileypool Bridge. Fossils in the BGS collection and in Thetford Museum include: *Porosphaera globularis*, *Cretirhynchia* aff. *subplicata*, *Spondylus dutempleanus*, *Echinocorys sp.* and *Temnocidaris (Stereocidaris) sceptrifera*. Hewitt regarded this pit as falling within the *coranguinum* Zone, but the *Cretirhynchia* is suggestive of the lower part of the *cortestudinarium* Zone.

The Santonian (upper) part of the *coranguinum* Zone is exposed at Horringer Court (43) [837 628]. There, the chalk was worked in galleries which extend for at least 150 m underground (Pearman, 1976). Access to the galleries was from entrances cut in the face of the old chalk pit. The chalk in the main pit is only sparsely fossiliferous and all the fossils collected during the survey were more or less fragmentary. *Spondylus* (spat.), *Conulus albogalerus* with adnate *Stomatopora sp.*, *Echinocorys sp.* and *Micraster sp.* were found 1.20 to 1.45 m below a tabular flint near the top of the section, and *Kingena sp.* from 1 m below the topmost flint. Work by Dr H W Bailey on foraminifera from samples from this pit places the boundary between the foraminiferal *Stensioeina exsculpta* and *S. granulata polonica* biozones towards the top of the section between the tabular and topmost flint. On foraminiferal evidence, therefore, this section straddles the Coniacian–Santonian boundary. A well-preserved *Micraster bucailli* (BGS Ze 2963) with adnate *Praelacazella wetherelli* and *Atreta nilssoni* collected by Hewitt from the underground galleries indicates a position near the top of the Coniacian. Hewitt also collected a *Gibbithyris sp.* from an unspecified horizon at this locality.

At Dairy Farm (44) [933 710], Ixworth, 3 m of Upper Chalk are exposed. The fauna includes: *Rhizopoterion sp.*, *Onchotrochus serpentinus*, *Cretirhynchia sp.*, *Gibbithyris ellipsoidalis*, *Kingena lima*, *Orbirhynchia* cf. *pisiformis*, *Praelacazella wetherelli*, *Ostrea incurva*, *Platyceramus sp.*, *Sphenoceramus* ex gr. *cardissoides/pachti*, *Micraster sp.* and *Temnocidaris (Stereocidaris) sceptrifera*. The *Sphenoceramus* places this fauna at or near the base of the Santonian portion of the *coranguinum* Zone. This is supported by a microsample assigned by Dr H W Bailey to the *Stensioeina granulata polonica* foraminiferal Biozone.

Another old pit (45) [934 707] at Ixworth probably lies slightly higher in the Santonian. Macrofossils include: *Spondylus* ex gr. *latusdutempleanus*, *Hirudocidaris hirudo*, *Platyceramus*, and the trace fossil *Teichnichnus* preserved magnificently in flint. Microfauna include *Cibicides ribbingi* and *Stensioeina granulata polonica*, indicating an horizon within the *Cibicides* ex gr. *beaumontianus* Assemblage Biozone. On this basis, the section should overlap with the basal part of Stowlangtoft Quarry, but the lithostratigraphy and macropalaeontology contradict such a correlation.

A pit (48) [9185 6983] at Great Queach formerly exposed 1.8 m of soft, friable chalk with a line of flints about 0.3 m above the base (Hewitt, 1935, locality 53). Fossils collected by Hewitt and now in BGS include: *Porosphaera sessilis*, *Terebratulina striatula*, *Gryphaeostrea canaliculata* (spat.), *Pseudoperna?*, *Bourgueticrinus sp.* and *Crateraster quinqueloba*. The *Actinocamax* recorded by Hewitt appears to be a malformed *Bourgueticrinus* columnal.

An old pit (46) [951 729], 1 km south-east of Bardwell, yielded fragments of *Bourgueticrinus sp.*, *Conulus sp.* and *Tylocidaris clavigera* indicative of the Santonian part of the *coranguinum* Zone.

A 6 m section with sparse small, thin-crusted flints, lying in the upper part of the *coranguinum* Zone, was recorded by Hewitt (1935, locality 48) at a pit (49) [9650 7415] behind the George Inn, Stanton: only poor exposures were visible in 1978. Hewitt noted that fossils were very scarce. His record of *Echinocorys scutatus* approaching var. *elevatus* Brydone (Hewitt, 1935) refers to a large *Conulus albogalerus* (BGS Ze 3240) preserved in flint containing a piece of inoceramid shell (*Platyceramus?*) with *Rogerella* borings; other fossils in the flint include *Nodosaria sp.* and oyster spat (*Pseudoperna*) with adnate *Neomicrorbis crenatostriatus*. The *Conulus* has a rich epizoan fauna including three species of bryozoans, the serpulid *Filograna cincta* and the thecidean brachiopod *Praelacazella wetherelli*. Other fossils collected from this locality by Hewitt and curated by BGS are *Glomerula gordialis*, *Kingena lima*, *Actinocamax verus* (10 ft (3 m) from base), *Bourgueticrinus sp.*, *Crateraster quinqueloba*, *Metopaster parkinsoni* and *Tylocidaris clavigera*.

Stowlangtoft Quarry (50) [9475 6882] exposes about 11 m of the highest part of the *coranguinum* Zone and extends up to an horizon at, or just below the boundary with the overlying *Uintacrinus socialis* Zone. The section recorded by Mr C J Wood is shown in Figure 10. The flints at the base of the section (a of Figure 10) yielded a giant inoceramid tentatively assigned to *Platyceramus sp.* The semi-continuous, irregular, nodular flint (b of Figure 10) forms a conspicuous datum plane. The 0.2 m of chalk immediately beneath it is rich in pieces of inoceramid shell, including *Cordiceramus* aff. *cordiformis* and *Platyceramus*. There is a significant change in the foraminiferal assemblage between a sample taken from this level and from 0.8 m above the flint. This change, which marks the boundary between the *Loxostomum eleyi* and *Cibicides* ex gr. *beaumontianus* foraminiferal assemblage zones (see Bailey and others, 1983), occurs in Kent immediately above Whitaker's 3-inch Flint Band, which is also underlain by an acme occurrence of *Cordiceramus* and *Platyceramus*, and which may equate with flint B. It is similarly tempting to equate a conspicuous yellow sponge bed with oxidised pyrite nodules (c of Figure 10) with Barrois' Sponge Bed of Kent. A bed rich in large pieces of *Platyceramus* (d of Figure 10) overlies the sponge bed. A rich fauna has been obtained from beds 1.0–2.2 m above the latter (e of Figure 10), and these include *Porosphaera globularis*, *Parasmilia sp.*, *Chlamys cretosa*, *Platyceramus* fragments (one with adnate *Proliserpula ampullacea*), *Plagiostoma hoperi*, and echinoids including *Conulus albogalerus*, *Echinocorys sp.* and *Micraster* aff. *gibbus*. It is possible that these beds equate with the *Conulus*-rich horizon about 1 m above Barrois' Sponge Bed, though *Conulus* is only a subordinate component of the Stowlangtoft assemblage. The higher part of the section is relatively poorly fossiliferous, apart from discontinuous concentrates of inoceramid shell pieces (*Platyceramus*), notably at 5.15 m above the sponge bed (f of Figure 10). The belemnite *Actinocamax verus* was found at two levels; just below this latter horizon and 1.25 m above the *Platyceramus* horizon in a conspicuous

28 CHAPTER 3 UPPER CRETACEOUS: CHALK

Figure 10 Section in Upper Chalk, Stowlangtoft Quarry

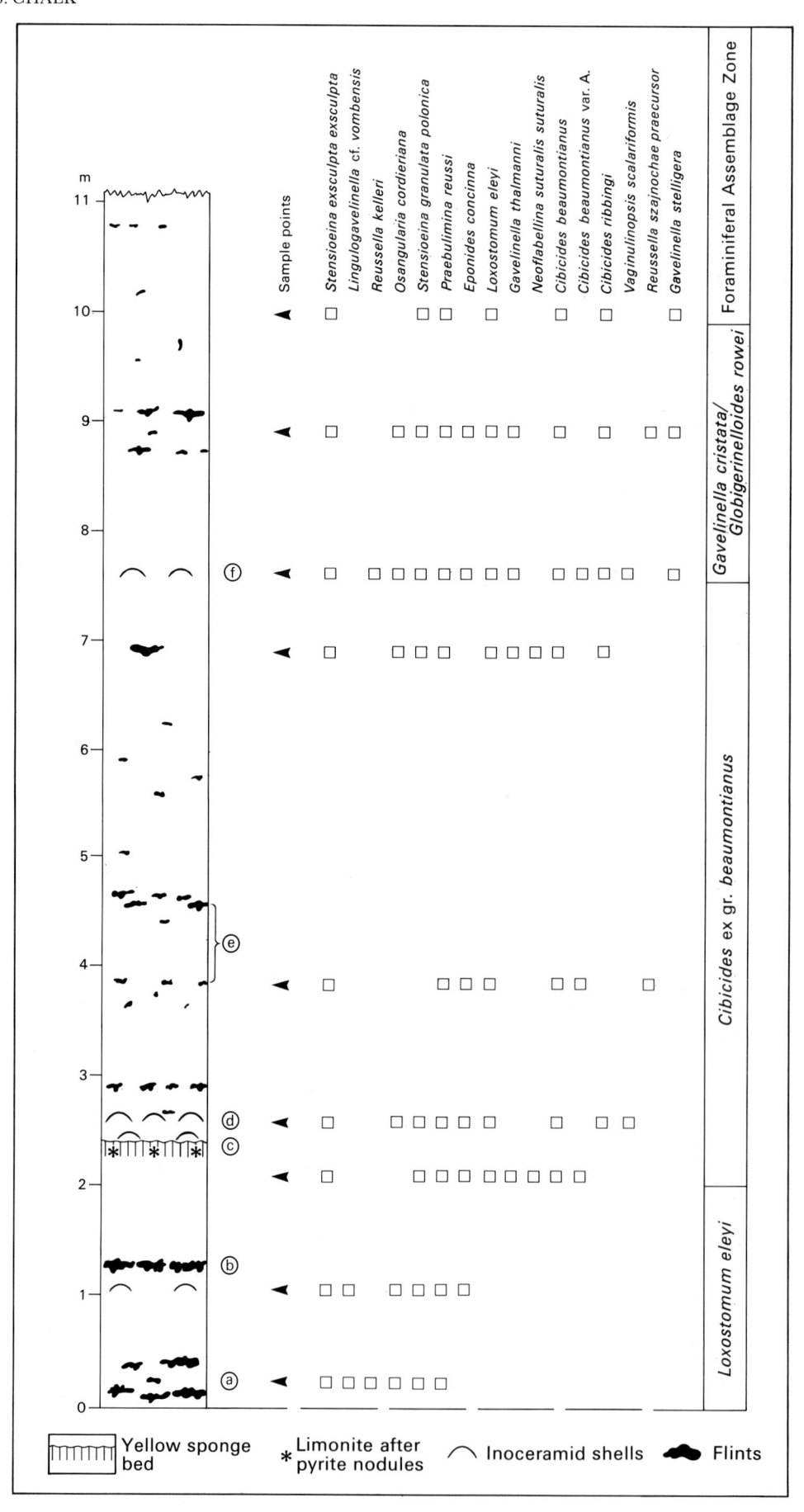

band of nodular flints. The best means of correlation is the microfauna. *Gavelinella* cf. *stelligera*, indicating the base of the *Gavelinella cristata/Globigerinelloides rowei* foraminiferal Assemblage Zone, appears at the *Platyceramus* horizon, suggesting, by analogy with the Kent section (Bailey and others, 1983), that this lies close to the top of the *corangiunum* Zone. The presence of *Stensioeina granulata polonica* in two higher samples indicates that the topmost beds still fall within the *corangiunum* Zone. Even higher beds, with finger-flints and sheets of inoceramid shell and *Actinocamax verus*, were exposed at the west end of the pit, but their zonal position is uncertain.

A pit (52) [9530 7035] with *Actinocamax verus* at Woodstreet Farm, about 1 km north-north-east, was probably dug in the top part of the *corangiunum* Zone, or the lowest part of the *socialis* Zone.

Hewitt (1935, loc. 49) noted 3 m of 'very soft and shattered' chalk in an old pit (53) [9613 7112] west of Wyken Wood. Material collected by Hewitt and the authors includes *Cretirhynchia plicatilis*, *Kingena lima*, *Orbirhynchia sp.*, *Actinocamax verus*, *Gonioteuthis westfalicagranulata*, *Gryphaeostrea canaliculata*, *Bourgueticrinus hureae*, *Nymphaster sp.* and *Conulus albogalerus*. The macrofossil evidence is equivocal, indicating a high *coranguinum* or *socialis* Zone position. The occurrence of *C. plicatilis* and *C. albogalerus* suggests that part at least of this section belongs in the uppermost part of the *coranguinum* Zone. A microsample from this pit examined by Dr H W Bailey was assigned to the *Stensioeina granulata perfecta* Assemblage Zone, despite the absence of the zonal index. The assignment was based on the presence of *Cibicides beaumontianus*, *C. ribbingi*, *Gavelinella stelligera* and *Reussella szajnochae praecursor* and the absence of *Stensioeina granulata polonica* and *Bolivinoides strigillatus*. The microfaunal evidence indicates that the pit falls within the *socialis* Zone, although *Uintacrinus* has not been found in it.

CJW, CRB

CHAPTER 4

Quaternary Solid: Crag

GENERAL ACCOUNT

Shelly marine Crag sands have been encountered beneath drift in many boreholes in the south-east of the district; they are locally green, and green-coated flints commonly occur at their base. Similar glauconite-coated flints have been found beneath unfossiliferous, locally green, sands, silts and silty clays in the Stowlangtoft [947 694] and Stanton [96 72] areas. These latter deposits, together with fine-grained sand at the surface in the Beyton area [92 64] and north [89 63] and south-west [880 605] of Rushbrooke, are regarded as Crag.

The subdrift occurrences of Crag, including outliers [e.g. 885 585] locally associated with shelly deposits, extend across the south-eastern part of the district from Chedburgh [790 575] to near Stanton [97 72]. North-eastwards the Crag is in continuity with the Norwich Crag. Southwards the Crag extends as far as the north-easterly-trending Kettlebaston Fault in the adjacent Sudbury (206) and Ipswich (207) districts (Bristow, 1983). The deposits south of the Kettlebaston Fault are known as Red Crag.

Within the present district the Crag rests unconformably on Upper Chalk. The basal bed is characteristically composed of glauconite-coated flints, probably derived from the Bullhead Bed at the base of the Thanet Beds (Bristow, 1983). Beyond the present district, where Crag overlies Lower London Tertiaries or London Clay, the basal bed of the Crag contains many phosphatic pebbles derived from Eocene strata (Balson, 1980). A few such phosphatic pebbles were noted in the basal beds in the Woolpit Borehole.

The pebble bed is succeeded by a dominantly arenaceous sequence, which, at the surface, mostly consists of fine-grained sands, commonly micaceous and locally with derived glauconite (Bristow, 1983; Merriman, 1983 but see Humphreys and Balson, 1985). Thin clay beds, or clasts of clay in a sandy matrix, have also been noted. In the Woolpit Borehole sand is again dominant, but is much coarser grained and contains much shell material, both whole and comminuted. CRB

The sands are poorly sorted with a weakly bimodal grain-size distribution (Figure 11); the dominant mode is medium- to coarse-grained, with a secondary fine-grained mode. The gravel fractions consist mainly of shell fragments and angular flint pebbles. The coarse- and very coarse-grained sand fractions are similarly composed of biotic fragments (shells, teeth) and flint chips. The finer fractions consist of quartz sand, glauconite and fine biotic debris. The light fractions (SG < 2.90) are typically composed of angular to subrounded quartz, rounded and broken glauconite grains (probably detrital) and biotic fragments. Minerals identified in the heavy fractions are garnet, tourmaline, zircon, rutile, muscovite, biotite, collophane, greyish green kyanite (X 8118), brown-yellow apatite (X 8120), dark and pale green amphiboles (X 8124, 8125), yellow staurolite (X 8126), magnetite and hematite (X 8129). The hematite appears to have replaced magnetite by oxidation. GES

Pebble beds above the base of the Crag have not been positively identified in existing borehole logs, although they are known to occur in the Stowmarket area (R Markham, personal communication).

The Crag base rises north-westwards from 13 m above OD in the extreme south-east to over 50 m above OD in the Rushbrooke [89 62] and Kingshall Street [91 62] areas. The thickness ranges from 0 m at the feather edge to a maximum of 21.3 m at Bradfield St George [9096 5886] (see Bristow, 1983, fig. 3).

The only fauna from the district is that recorded from the Woolpit Borehole. The fossils, identified by Mr D Graham, are mostly stout-shelled molluscs of near-shore or littoral aspect. They include: *Buccinum?*, *Turritella?*, *Nucella lapillus*, *Astarte?*, *Cerastoderma?*, *Chlamys opercularis?*, *Mya arenaria*, *Corbula gibba*, *Spisula sp.* and *Balanus sp.* This fauna has a closer affinity with that from the Red Crag than from the Norwich Crag. Foraminifera include: *Buccella frigida*, *B.* cf. *vicksburgenis*, *Bulimina elongata*, *Cassidulina obtusa*, *C. teretis*, *Cibicides lobatulus*, *Elphidiella hannai*, *Elphidium* cf. *asklundi*, *E. clavatum*, *E. pseudolessoni*, *Pullenia bulloides* and *Trifarina angulosa*. Miss D Gregory, who identified the fauna, notes that the assemblage differs from that of the type section of the Norwich Crag at Bramerton in the presence of *Bulimina elongata* and *Cassidulina obtusa* below 28.11 m, possibly indicating deposition in slightly deeper water. The relative abundance of *E. clavatum* at Woolpit implies that this sequence was deposited under colder conditions than that at Bramerton. *Cibicides lobatulus grossus*, recorded at Bramerton, was not recovered at Woolpit. CRB

DETAILS

Chedburgh – Whepstead area

Wells [7896 5749; 7917 5812; 7896 5749] at Chedburgh airfield proved between 0.9 and 8.9 m of green loam, sand and shale, locally with a flint base, resting on Chalk.

Farther east near Whepstead [833 580], grey sand between 4.3 and 5.2 m thick is recorded in two wells [8158 5806; 8347 5886] between Boulder Clay and Chalk. The evidence for suggesting that this sand is Crag is a borehole [8340 5666] just beyond the southern margin of the district where, beneath Boulder Clay, 6.7 m of hard grey sand lie above 3 m of hard green sand, which in turn rests on Chalk.

Saxham

A small outlier of Crag possibly occurs near Cobb's Hall [7899 6192], Great Saxham. A borehole here proved 0.6 m of 'green loam' beneath Boulder Clay and resting on Chalk.

DETAILS 31

Rushbrooke – Sicklesmere area

A narrow tract of fine-grained sand crops out [around 890 630] north and west of Hare Farm. In the borehole west of the farm [8908 6273] these beds consist of up to 4 m of laminated silts or silty sands with a pebbly sandy base, resting on Chalk; in another borehole south of the farm [8961 6252] they are mainly sands, 14.5 m thick and pebbly in the lower part, with a basal sand containing flint cobbles resting on Chalk. Rust-brown clayey pebbly sand, 2 m thick in a borehole [8877 6062] 600 m south-west of Rushbrooke Hall, is interpreted as Crag.

Near Sicklesmere a small outcrop of fine-grained sand, interpreted as Crag, has been mapped east of the Lark valley. The sand has only a limited subdrift distribution, and is represented by 0.4 m of orange silty fine-grained sand beneath Boulder Clay in a borehole [8799 6059] west of the old railway cutting. A borehole [8805 6061] on the opposite side of the cutting proved chalky Boulder Clay directly on Chalk.

At Cocks Green [around 885 585] a subdrift outlier of Crag has been inferred in the record of a well [8867 5876] at Chapelhill Farm. The following descending sequence was proved beneath Boulder Clay: hard sand, 8.2 m; yellow clay, 3 m; soft sand, 4.9 m; rough gravel, 2.1 m; Chalk.

Rougham area

Several wells around Rougham Green [910 616] prove Crag beneath drift. At the Almshouses [9062 6231] 6.1+ m of 'sand' underlie Boulder Clay. Some 300 m north of the Almshouses, 9.3 m of fine-grained sand, locally silty and micaceous, and pebbly at the base, were proved beneath Boulder Clay [9064 6259]. A similar sequence, 7.3 m thick, was noted in a borehole near Rougham Old Hall [9113 6327]. At Moat Farm [9119 6192], some 1.4 km to the south, 0.9 m of sand, resting on 0.9 m of rough gravel, is present between Boulder Clay and Chalk. Immediately to the south, a well [9119 6185] at Greenway House has a much thicker overall sand and gravel sequence, of which the upper 4.7 m of 'ballast' are regarded as Glacial Sand and Gravel, and the lower 7.3 m of sand as Crag. Only sand, 11.3 m thick, was proved in a borehole [9080 6175] at the Old Rectory. A farther 400 m to the south-west, the Crag consists of 7.3 m of red sand [9048 6154]. The only well in which green sand is recorded is that at the council houses [9162 6156] where, beneath 27.4 m of drift, 6.1 m of green sand rest on Chalk.

The Bradfields

At Bradfield St George, the Crag is represented by 1.2 m of brown sand and clay, overlying 8.5 m of brown sand [9137 6013]. A well [9096 5996] at the Pumping Station records beneath Boulder Clay: 14.3 m of red sand; 4.3 m of light sand; and 2.7 m of large black flints, resting on Chalk.

Towards the old railway line at Bradfield St Clare, the Crag consists of 19.8 m of yellow, grey and red sands [9030 5819]. At Pitcher's Green, the Crag, 15.8 m thick, is described as loamy and red sand, and is overlain by 6.1 m of 'ballast' [9154 5834].

Felsham and Gedding area

Around Felsham [945 570], the Crag has been recorded beneath drift in several wells. West of the village a well [9438 5704] at the council houses proved, beneath Glacial Sand and Gravel: gravel and sand, 7.9 m; green sand and shingle, 4.1 m; grey silt, 1.1 m; resting on Chalk at 29.6 m OD. Some 220 m to the east-north-east, the Crag consists of 4+ m of whitish, laminated, sandy clay and hard stone [9458 5712]. Eastwards, a well [9479 5704] at the council houses proved 10.7 m of yellow sand and 6.1 m of green sand. In an adjacent well [9484 5703] at the Rectory, the Crag is recorded as

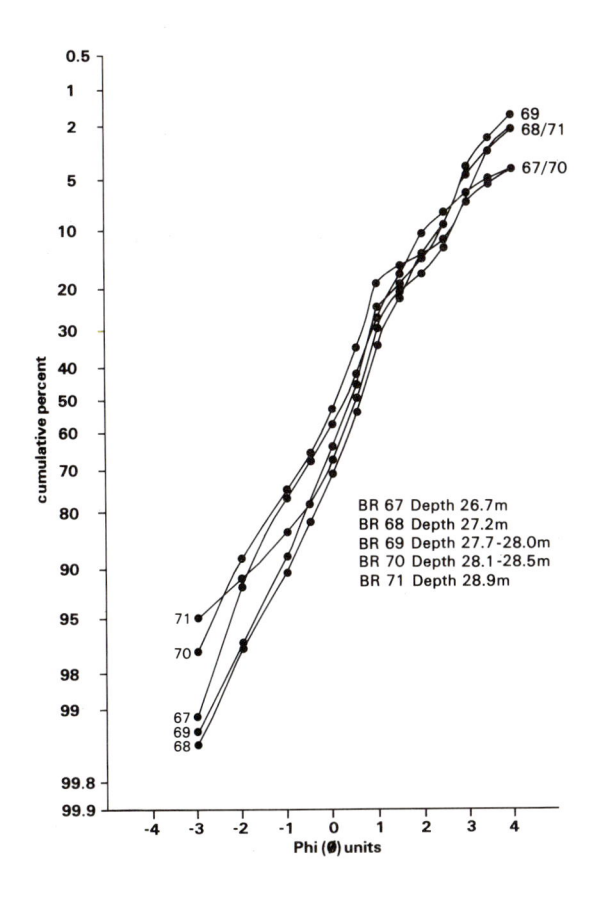

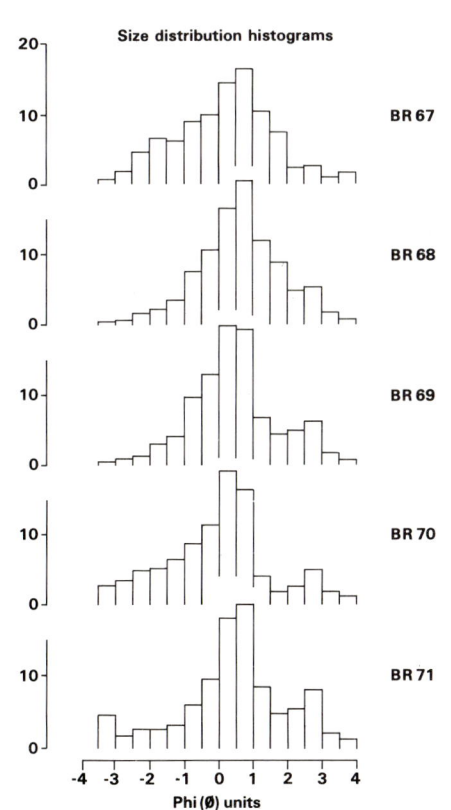

Figure 11 Grading curves and size distribution histograms for samples of Crag sand from the Woolpit Borehole [9820 6238]

8.2 m of brown sand overlying 2.1 m of yellow sand. At Felsham House [9437 5763], the Crag contains a 0.4 m flint bed at the base which is succeeded by 8.8 m of sand, including a 1.8 m bed of green sand in the middle. Green sand is also recorded in the well at Gedding House [9465 5777], some 300 m north-east, where the Crag consists of 4.7 m of red, white, green and brown sand. At Gedding Hall, a well [9528 5861] passed through 16.5 m of brown sand and silt into a basal gravel bed 1.5 m thick. An incomplete thickness (the upper part of the well was not described) of 3.7 m of 'sand' is recorded from a well [9522 5771] 900 m to the south.

Rattlesden area

Some 6.1 m of green sand are recorded in the council house well [9713 5835] at Rattlesden; this rests on Chalk and is overlain by 13.7 m of yellow sand. In the school well [9754 5893] 12.8 m of red sand overlie a 2.1 m bed of sand and 'ballast', which rests on Chalk.

A well at Hill Farm [9596 5723] proved, beneath Boulder Clay, 9.1 m of 'ballast' overlying 7.6 m of sand, 3 m of sand and 'ballast', on Chalk. In the Hollybush Farm well [9648 5731] 540 m east, it is not clear whether any of the 11.3 m of sand and stone between the Boulder Clay and Chalk is Crag. At Friar's Hall [9715 5685], the Crag is represented by 18.6 m of sand. A well [9805 6018] at Clopton Hall proved a 1.8 m basal bed of silt, succeeded by 3 m of sand.

Hessett area

South of Hessett, Crag has been proved in three boreholes. At the council houses [9349 6111] a well proved 9.8 m of greyish green, grey, yellow and white sands beneath 23.8 m of Drift. At the former St Ives Sand and Gravel Co. pit [9380 6100] the beds below Boulder Clay and 'clean' gravel comprise 4.9 m of clay, presumably Crag. Some 70 m south-west, another well [9377 6099] passed through gravel and sand, beneath Boulder Clay, into 1.5 m of brown sand with a 0.3 m bed of flints at the base.

A farther 1 km south-south-west, a borehole [9440 6029] proved, beneath Boulder Clay, 16.7 m of dominantly silty, fine- to medium-grained, commonly green or yellowish green sand with thin beds of green silty clay. The basal bed, 1 m thick and resting on Chalk, consists of grey sandy silt and silty sand with black well-rounded flint cobbles.

Drinkstone area

Glacial Sand and Gravel, beneath Boulder Clay, overlies 6.1 m of sand in a well [9499 6165] in Drinkstone Park.

The Crag appears to be absent, or is not readily identifiable in boreholes in the Drinkstone area [960 620]. However, near Drinkstone Green, Crag is recognisable in several wells. At Whitefield House [9528 6053], beneath Boulder Clay and ballast, 4.3 m of dark brown sand rest on 5.8 m of dark green sand, which rests on Chalk. Some 520 m east, at Hill Farm [9580 6047], there are 8.5 m of sand, beneath 'sand and stone' of presumed glacial origin. However, 120 m north-east at High Barn Hazel [9580 6047], the Crag is locally absent, as 4.6 m of 'ballast' rests on Chalk. In a well [9600 6048] at the council houses, only 170 m south-east, 13.1 m of pale brown sand, with a 0.3 m basal flint bed, rest on Chalk and underlie 'ballast'. Ballast overlies Crag in a well [9596 6006] 430 m south; the Crag consists of 6.1 m of yellow sand, overlying 2.1 m of sand and 'ballast', which in turn rest on Chalk.

A well [9668 5949] at the Chestnuts is one of the few within the district in which shells are recorded in the Crag. The descending sequence beneath gravel is: grey sand, 2.4 m; loam sand, 6.1 m; brown sand, 6.4 m; sand and shells, 1.8 m; small flints, 0.6 m; Chalk. A nearby well [9676 5977], 300 m north-north-east, also proved shelly Crag beneath Boulder Clay, as follows: grey sand, 3.7 m; brown sand, 6.1 m; dark brown sand, 4 m; brown sand and shells, 2.1 m; Chalk.

Thurston – Beyton – Tostock area

Within this area there is an extensive outcrop of fine-grained Crag sands. North of Thurston Station [around 920 653], fine-grained buff and yellow sands have been consistently augered. They were worked to a depth of at least 4 m in a number of pits [e.g. 922 652]. South from Thurston, fine-grained sand is the dominant lithology, but silt was noted at a number of localities [9170 6486; 9262 6423]. A borehole [9338 6472] 1 km east of Thurston House proved the following sequence beneath Boulder Clay and 'ballast': marl, 0.3 m; light green sand, 5.2 m; brown sand and stone, 0.9 m; 'dirty' Chalk. Some 2.7 m of silty sand, sandy silt and silty clay with a gravelly base, resting on Chalk in a borehole [9235 6455] 150 m south-west of Thurston House, is regarded as Crag.

Excellent sections in fine-grained sands were exposed during the construction of the Beyton By-pass. The sands are mainly buff or yellow, well graded, but without obvious stratification. In one locality [9257 6367], coarse-grained ferruginous sand up to 1.2 m thick, very similar to the Red Crag of southern Suffolk, overlies the fine-grained sands. Boreholes along the route of the By-pass showed that the sands were up to 8.3 m thick and rested with a flinty base on Chalk [9236 6364; 9248 6366]. A borehole north of Rougham Place [9214 6383] proved 2.9 m of fine-grained, locally micaceous sands with a gravelly base resting on Chalk.

Several wells near Beyton proved Crag beneath Boulder Clay. The Fruit Farm well [9332 6278] encountered 4.5 m of yellow sand at a depth of 17 m, above 3.6 m of red sand resting on Chalk. The council house well [9304 6267] proved 6.1 m of brown loam between the Boulder Clay and the Chalk. The classification of the school well [9347 6320] is less certain; the driller's log records, beneath gravel, 0.3 m of 'Thanet Sand' resting on 3.96 m of rock-hard fine shingle and clay, which in turn rests on Chalk. Dominantly fine-grained, micaceous sands, locally greenish yellow, were 14.3 m thick in a borehole [9246 6250] 650 m west-south-west Quaker's Farm, Beyton.

A borehole [9481 6346] south-east of Lower Wood, proved 14.4 m of yellow medium-grained sand, pebbly in the lower part, resting on Chalk.

At Tostock, several wells prove subdrift Crag. The council house well [9571 6367] proved in descending sequence, beneath 14.6 m of Boulder Clay: grey sand, 3.7 m; yellow sand, 3.7 m; green sand, 3 m; 'ballast', 11.3 m; Chalk. A borehole [9630 6330] 350 m east of Tostock Place proved, beneath Boulder Clay, 3.4 m of silty sand with a gravelly base resting on Chalk. Some 500 m north-west of Tostock Place [9554 6362], the beds between the Boulder Clay and Chalk consist of 8.5 m of fine-grained silty sand. The lowest bed, 1.5 m thick, is a green pebbly sand with green-coated flints. Some 700 m north of Tostock Place, a borehole [9589 6406] proved 1 m of sandy gravel (?Glacial) beneath Boulder Clay, resting on 7 m of sands, which were pebbly in their lower half; the lowest 2 m contained green 'horizons'. At Tostock House [9536 6330], Crag is represented by 5.18 m of 'dark red sand'.

Boreholes for the by-pass [e.g. 9528 6289], some 200 m south-west of Ticehurst House, encountered 1.45 m of dense grey sand beneath Glacial Sand and Gravel, resting on 6.75 m of dense brown sand and gravel, which in turn rests on Chalk.

Woolpit area

In a well [9726 6304] north of Woolpit, the beds between Boulder Clay and Chalk comprise an upper unit of 5.9 m of coarse-grained [Glacial] sand and gravel, above 6 m of green sand (pebbly at the top, shelly at the base). A borehole [9694 6333] north-west of the village encountered 1.5 m of grey silty sand above Chalk; this was separated from Boulder Clay by 2.9 m of grey silty gravel and sand. The lower sand is interpreted as Crag, and the upper sand and gravel unit is tentatively regarded as Glacial Sand and Gravel.

A well [9745 6237] in Woolpit proved: coarse brown sand, 5.5 m; green sand, 2.4 m; pea shingle and green sand, 0.9 m; shell and shingle, 0.3 m; Chalk. A well [9718 6260], close to the subdrift feather edge of the Crag north-west of the village, recorded 3.7 m of grey sand between Boulder Clay and Chalk. It is presumed that Crag is represented in the 5.2 m of sand and ballast in a well [9742 6257] 250 m east. Some 4.3 m of green sand, overlying 1.6 m of flint, which in turn rests on Chalk, were proved beneath Boulder Clay in a well [9820 6247] at the former brickworks. The Woolpit Borehole [9820 6238], 200 m south-south-west of the above borehole, proved 3.7 m of grey (upper part) and yellow (lower part) shelly sands beneath 'brickearth' and Boulder Clay, resting with a basal glauconitic pebble bed on Chalk. A sparse Crag macrofauna of near-shore or littoral aspect, together with foraminifera, has been listed above (p.30).

At Woolpit Green [around 980 615] the Crag has been proved in several wells. At the former searchlight station [9786 6138] beds beneath Boulder Clay consist in downward sequence of: hard sand, 1.8 m; green running sand, 6.1 m; gravel and flints, 1.5 m; Chalk. Some 200 m north-north-west, the Crag was described as 6.1 m of stone and sand, overlying 5.8 m of 'shale' and greensand [9779 6157]. In a well [9818 6183] at Chestnut Holdings, 1.2 m of 'sand and shell' overlie Chalk; above, and continuing to the surface, are 30.5 m of sands and gravel which may include some Crag in their lower part.

Hunston – Norton – Elmswell New Hall area

Within this area Crag does not crop out, but is thought to have been proved in numerous boreholes. In many of these, the beds between Boulder Clay and Chalk can be divided into an upper gravel, here regarded as Glacial Sand and Gravel and/or Kesgrave Sands and Gravels, and a lower unit of sand. The lower sand is sometimes described as greenish and, just beyond the eastern margin of the district, shells have been recorded within it; in some logs a basal pebble bed is recorded. Accordingly, these locally green and shelly sands are regarded as Crag. They are not everywhere present beneath Boulder Clay, for in some wells [e.g. 9826 6671] Boulder Clay rests directly on Chalk; there is insufficient control to delimit their occurrence.

A well [9800 6699] at Hunston Lodge proved 3.3 m of sand beneath sand and 'ballast'. Some 670 m south-west, a well at Hill Farm [9759 6647] encountered 6.1 m of fine-grained yellowish green sand beneath 'ballast'. The 5.2 m of 'black' sand at High Hall [9807 6650] is here regarded as Crag. Some 270 m north-east, Crag is absent beneath Boulder Clay [9826 6671].

The Crag probably forms part of the 14.6 m of sand and gravel recorded at Crawley Hall [9656 6479]. A borehole [9676 6489] 220 m north-east of the Hall proved 3.4 m of sand, sandy gravel and pebbly sand, locally greenish yellow, between ?Glacial Sand and Gravel and Chalk.

About 1 km south-east of Elmswell New Hall, 1.7 m of sand and gravel, with greenish white flints and brownish green chalk, rest on Chalk and are overlain by Boulder Clay [9781 6363].

North-west of Elmswell Hall, a borehole [9824 6436] proved 0.6 m of sandy gravel beneath Boulder Clay, and then 12.8 m of yellow, grey and green sand. The lowest part of the sequence consists of 0.7+ m of greenish grey sand with subrounded and well-rounded pebbles of flint, quartz and quartzite.

Stowlangtoft – Hunston area

An outcrop of mainly fine-grained sand is present north of the valley which runs through Hunston and Stowlangtoft. A section [9480 6895] in the Stowlangtoft chalk pit showed the following section in February 1979:

	Thickness m	Depth m
CRAG		
Thinly bedded sequence of fine-grained, greyish brown, micaceous sands with thin (2–3 mm) reddish brown clay laminae; locally the clay is fragmented and appears as clasts within the sands. The sands form the dominant part of the sequence. At one point, about 3 m up the face, there is a 5 cm seam of coarse-grained greyish green sand and clay (see below)	4.0	4.0
Flint pebble bed in which the flints are mostly unworn, a few are slightly rounded and one or two well rounded. Some of the flints are green coated	0.1	4.1
UPPER CHALK		
Chalk, firm, white, with flints	10.0	14.1

Samples from the green sand and clay layer, and also from the clays lower down, were examined for dinoflagellates but proved to be barren. The base of the Crag is in general planar, but locally it is very irregular and piped down for 2 to 3 m into Chalk. CRB

An X-ray powder photograph of the green grains in the section shows that the mineral composition is that of illite with less than 10 per cent smectite interlayers. Most grains have been rounded and polished, and some have been subsequently fractured. The bulk of the sample consists of poorly sorted quartz sand with grains ranging from 0.1–2.0 mm across. The degree of rounding of grains is variable, ranging from polished and well rounded, to angular or very angular. RJM

East of the chalk pit, generally only fine-grained sand was augered. North of Twelve Acre Plantation, 1 km north-east of the chalk pit, some 7.8+ m of sandy silt and fine-grained sand underlie Boulder Clay [9545 6972]. Some 350 m south-east of Kiln Farm, surface indications of quartz-rich gravel suggest that the Crag is locally overlain by Kesgrave Sands and Gravels [around 962 692]. Some 900 m north-east of the above locality, a borehole [9701 6984] proved 6.8 m of fine-grained sand with scattered flint and vein-quartz pebbles beneath Boulder Clay and above Chalk.

At Langham, in another borehole [9811 6967], Crag silt and pebbly sand, some 2.6 m thick, underlie Glacial Sand and Gravel.

Kiln Wood – Wyken Wood – Hillwatering Farm – Potash Farm area

Near Kiln Wood, Stanton [around 960 720], there is an extensive area of fine- to medium-grained micaceous sands locally overlain by quartz-rich gravels or chalky Boulder Clay. These sands have a basal bed of glauconite-coated flints and rest on Chalk. Generally only buff or yellow, fine- to medium-grained sands have been augered, but coarse-grained sands and silty clayey sands were encountered locally. At two points [9600 7192; 9630 7205] bluish grey sandy clay was found within the sequence.

One of the best sections in the Crag was provided by a trial pit in Kiln Meadow [9595 7199]:

	Thickness m	Depth m
Topsoil	0.3	0.3
CRAG		
Sand, fine-grained, pebbly	0.4	0.7
Clay, mottled orange and grey	0.1	0.8
Sand, pebbly, coarse-grained, clayey	0.1	0.9
Sand, fine- to medium-grained, greyish orange, with local clay layers	1.0	1.9
Clay, dark grey, silty and micaceous passing down into	0.2	2.1
Sand, pebbly, clayey, locally green	0.1	2.2
Clay, grey	0.3	2.5
Sand, fine-grained, buff	0.1	2.6
Gravel, dark brown, with polished tabular flints, broken polished flints, glauconite-coated flints, small well-rounded black flints, boxstones, and ?phosphatic nodules, set in an iron-cemented micaceous silt	0.1	2.7
UPPER CHALK		
Chalk, firm, whitish cream	0.1	2.8

The dark grey clay at 2.1 m was barren.

Green-coated flints were found at two points [9620 7219; 9616 7225] at the northern end of this same field, but were absent in a nearby trial pit [9615 7229] where the following succession, notable for being essentially argillaceous, was seen.

	Thickness m	Depth m
MADE GROUND	0.7	0.7
?KESGRAVE SANDS AND GRAVELS		
Sand, fine- to medium-grained	0.6	1.3
Sand, clean, medium- to coarse-grained, with diffuse quartz, quartzite and flint gravel layers. At base a matrix-free gravel	1.3	2.6
CRAG		
Clay, brownish grey, micaceous, with scattered sand grains and quartz and flint pebbles	0.1	2.7
Clay, chocolate-brown, micaceous, sandy, with scattered pebbles, becoming darker brown downwards	0.2	2.9
Chalk, redeposited, creamy	0.1	3.0
Chalk, chocolate-brown, micaceous, sandy and gravelly	0.1	3.1
UPPER CHALK		
Chalk, soft, white	0.1	3.2

The Chalk surface in the fields [around 958 713] west of Wyken Wood has a scattering of conspicuous glauconite-coated flints. Although Crag is absent hereabouts, these flints are thought to represent remnants from its basal bed. CRB

XRD analysis of the green coating from one of these flints shows that it consists of randomly interstratified illite/smectite mixed-layer mineral containing approximately 25 per cent expansible layers. This type of green clay is regarded as mineral glauconite *sensu lato* by McRae (1972), and corresponds to 'pigmentary glauconite' in Triplehorn's (1966) classification. Glauconite X-ray diffraction patterns showed contamination by quartz and minor amounts of calcite and kaolinite. Beneath the glauconite coating there is a slightly porous white or yellowish material composed of quartz with traces of calcite. It probably represents the remains of partially silicified chalk cortex, similar to that described by Jeans (1978, p.117) and no doubt facilitated the formation of glauconite. RJM

Similar green-coated flints have been incorporated into the nearby Kesgrave Sands and Gravels and can be seen in a pit [9535 7105] in Burntfirs Plantation (see Plate 1).

South and east of Wyken Wood, fine-grained sands have been augered extensively. A borehole [9665 7069], sited close to the feather-edge of the outcrop, proved 4 m of fine-grained yellowish green sand above Chalk. Fine-grained greenish grey sand was also augered at one point [9544 7029] 350 m east of Woodstreet Farm. Towards the east of the outcrop, grey silt is associated with fine-grained sand [9754 7083].

Fine-grained sand extends eastwards from just south-west of Potash Farm [around 981 712], to just west of Walsham-le-Willows in the adjacent Eye (190) district. A well [9842 7165] at Potash Farm proved 5.2 m of sand between Boulder Clay and Chalk. CRB

CHAPTER 5

Quaternary Drift: Pre-Anglian and Anglian

The Quaternary in Britain was a time of marked climatic variation, with alternating cold and warm phases. During some of the cold phases permanent ice-sheets developed. In these glacial episodes, ice moved southwards over the low-lying areas of eastern England and what is now the North Sea, picking up huge quantities of bedrock which were subsequently dumped, largely unsorted, at the margins and base of the ice-sheet. Water under hydrostatic pressure beneath the ice-sheets carved deep, steep-sided channels many tens of metres below the original ground surface; silts were deposited subglacially in these channels. Meltwater, issuing from the margin of the ice-sheets, deposited sheets of sand and gravel. Concurrently, sheets of solifluction deposits flowed down and mantled valley sides and bottoms beyond the ice-front. The lower temperatures led to the development of ice-wedges and cryoturbation structures. During the intervening interglacial stages, faunas and floras show that temperatures were as warm or warmer than at present.

An examination of the fossil pollen and spores allows the vegetational and climatic sequence within any one interglacial to be established with confidence. What is less certain is the exact number of cold and warm stages, and their duration and importance. Conventionally the British Pleistocene sequence is assigned to 13 stages (Mitchell and others, 1973). Evans (1971), however, has recognised globally a total of 48 warm and cold episodes for the whole of the Pleistocene, of which 14 are 'glacial'. The problem of identifying individual glacial and interglacial stages was discussed by Sutcliffe (1975), who remarked 'that counting up or down from supposedly identifiable warm or cold stages may lead to false correlation of deposits which are not contemporary'. This difficulty relates both to British regional correlations and to correlation between British and Continental sequences. This was expressed by Gallois (1978), who stated that 'the establishment of a standard sequence by adding together type sections which are geographically widely separated defies all the rules of stratigraphical nomenclature'. It is accentuated by the difficulty in recognising which of the many breaks in all the sedimentary sequences are insignificant and which mark breaks between stages.

The deposits of this district exemplify many of these unresolved problems of correlation and nomenclature. Nevertheless, it is convenient to have a working set of stage names, however unsatisfactory it may be, and the nomenclature here adopted for the district is given in Table 4. The post-Anglian deposits are described in Chapter 6.

HISTORY OF RESEARCH AND NOMENCLATURE

Past research into the Pleistocene deposits of East Anglia has been summarised by Bristow (1985), but is confused by the gradual and continuing evolution of the nomenclature. The name Kesgrave Sands and Gravels has been given to quartz-rich gravels that lie beneath the boulder clay and which are believed to have been largely deposited by a pre-Anglian proto-Thames (Rose, Allen and Hey, 1976). More recently, Hey (1980) has divided these into a high-level Westland Green Member, including all the localities within the Bury St Edmunds district, and a later, low-level, unnamed member occurring farther south. The Kesgrave Sands and Gravels are commonly capped by a reddened, clay-rich layer which is thought by the above authors to represent a palaeosol developed during a humid warm temperature period, presumed to be the Cromerian interglacial; within the district this horizon has been seen only at Badwell Ash [955 692], a short distance east of the district. Other sands and gravels occur beneath the Anglian boulder clay. In the north-west some have a very high content of brown quartzite ('Bunters') and have been named the Ingham Sand and Gravel: their relationship to the palaeosol is, however,

Table 4 Classification of the Quaternary deposits (Drift) in the Bury St Edmunds district

	Stage	Temperature	Deposits
HOLOCENE	Flandrian	Warm	Alluvium and Peat
	Devensian	Cold	Cover Sand River Terrace Deposits Head and Head Gravel Glacial Silt (part)
	Ipswichian	Warm	
	?Wolstonian	?Cold	
	Hoxnian	Warm	Lacustrine Deposits: silt and clay at Sicklesmere; tufa at Icklingham
PLEISTOCENE	Anglian	Cold	Woolpit Beds Glacial Silt (part) Upper Glacial Sand and Gravel (including Haughley Park Sands and Gravels) Boulder Clay Lower Glacial Sand and Gravel (including Barham Sands and Gravels)
	Pre-Anglian	Cold	Kesgrave Sands and Gravels; Ingham Sand and Gravel

uncertain. Overlying both the Ingham Sand and Gravel and the Kesgrave Sands and Gravels there is a separate suite of poorly sorted sands and gravels, with a high chalk content and much less quartzite and vein-quartz. This suite is termed the Barham Sands and Gravels (Rose and others, 1976). It overlies the ?Cromerian palaeosol and is believed to represent the advance outwash from the Anglian ice sheet.

The Anglian boulder clay was called the Chalky Boulder Clay by Harmer (1902). It was subdivided by Baden-Powell (1948) into a Lowestoft Till (Lower Chalky Boulder Clay) and a Gipping Till (Upper Chalky Boulder Clay), which he believed to be products of two glaciations separated by the Hoxnian Interglacial. This interpretation was supported by West and Donner (1956), who thought that both tills were present within the district. More recently, Straw (1979) has maintained that there are three tills within this general area: Breckland Tills of mixed lithology in the north-west; Marly Drift in the north-east (both of Wolstonian age, that is, the Gipping Till of Baden-Powell); and an older Anglian Till (?Lowestoft Till) to the south. He drew the southern limit of his Wolstonian ice approximately west–east through Bury St Edmunds, and then north-eastwards towards Diss.

The traditional stratigraphical sequence outline above was first challenged by Bristow and Cox (1973a), who claimed that all the Chalky Boulder Clay south of Norwich formed a single pre-Hoxnian sheet (the Lowestoft Till), and who concluded that the Gipping Till was a lithological variant of the Lowestoft Till. This view was supported by Perrin and others (1973), who demonstrated that the Chalky Boulder Clay of both East Anglia and the East Midlands are remarkably uniform mineralogically and mechanically, and hence that they are probably all broadly synchronous. Sumbler (1983) has taken the argument further, arguing that the type-Wolstonian sequence in Warwickshire and the type-Anglian sequence of East Anglia were laid down during the same pre-Hoxnian stage, though this is not generally accepted.

The Woolpit Beds overlie Boulder Clay at Woolpit [975 625]; they are probably late Anglian in age. Gravels overlying the same Boulder Clay at Woolpit and Tostock have been named the Haughley Park Sands and Gravels by Rose and others (1978). Straw (1979) regarded them as outwash gravels from the Wolstonian ice, but the absence of any proof of the existence of this ice-sheet makes an Anglian age for them seem more likely.

KESGRAVE SANDS AND GRAVELS

The Kesgrave Sands and Gravels extend north-eastwards across East Anglia from mid- and north Essex through Suffolk into Norfolk (Rose and others, 1976; Rose and Allen, 1977; Funnell and others, 1979). They have, however, been identified with certainty only in the north-eastern part of the present district around Stanton [965 735] (Plate 1), though small patches of quartz-rich gravels above the Crag near Stowlangtoft may belong to this division.

Rose, and others (1976, fig. 1) have claimed that the Kesgrave Sands and Gravels occur at two localities (Denham [745 635] and Tostock [956 628]) within the district, and at another just to the east (Badwell Ash [995 692]). In 1977 the Denham pit was largely overgrown; the only gravels visible were poorly sorted and did not contain a particularly high quartzite content; they resembled the Barham Sands and Gravels more than the Kesgrave Sands and Gravels. At Tostock, the above authors recorded both suites, but sections examined during 1977 and 1978 were in about 3 m of coarse, poorly sorted, flint gravel, with only very little white vein-quartz and quartzite. These beds also resemble the Barham Sands and Gravels; reputedly the gravel rests on Crag. Only at Badwell Ash can gravels beneath Boulder Clay be convincingly shown to belong to the quartz-rich Kesgrave Sands and Gravels. They are capped by a clay-rich rubified surface, overlain by poorly sorted, chalk-rich Barham Sands and Gravels, locally containing chalky flow-till. Kesgrave Sands and Gravels have been proved in some boreholes between Hunston and Woolpit (Clarke, 1983), where they overlie Crag or Chalk. In others, Kesgrave Sands and Gravels are absent. The base of the deposits ranges in altitude from 39.2 to 45 m above OD; the thickness ranges from 1.4 to 8.4 m, with a mean of 3.5 m (Clarke, 1983).

At the Badwell Ash pit the Kesgrave Sands and Gravels consist of well-bedded, medium- to coarse-grained, pebbly sand. They have a high proportion of well-rounded quartz

Plate 1 Kesgrave Sands and Gravels and Head, near Stanton. (A13045)

and quartzite pebbles, and generally a clay-free matrix. One unfossiliferous bed of grey clay, 0.3 m thick, was noted in the floor of the pit within ferruginous medium-grained sand. Near Stanton, the sequence is much more clayey, and the dominant lithology is mottled orange and grey sandy clay or clayey sand with scattered well-rounded white quartz, quartzite and flint pebbles. East of the district, around Wattisfield, Botesdale and Burgate, there are beds of clay up to 5 m thick and of sufficient extent and thickness to have been worked for brick-making (Bristow, 1980; 1986).

Incomplete thicknesses of 3.6+ m were proved in trenches between Stanton and Bardwell; up to 6 m of sand and gravel, possibly in pockets, have been proved in wells. The proven thicknesses just outside the Bury St Edmunds district are 5 m at Badwell Ash, 10 m at Wattisfield to the north-east and 12.2 m at Botesdale to the east-north-east (Bristow, 1980; 1986).

Outside the district, Hey (1967) recognised quartz-rich, pebbly gravels overlying the Westleton Beds at Holton in East Suffolk. West and Norton (1974) concluded, on the basis of pollen, that the Westleton Beds from the Wangford pit, which lies close to Holton, are of Pastonian age, and implied that the overlying quartz-rich gravels are of post-Pastonian age. Rose and others (1976) followed Turner (1973) in believing that these quartz-rich post-Pastonian gravels are of Beestonian age and correlated them with the Kesgrave Sands and Gravels. However, an Anglian age cannot be excluded.

The generally accepted interpretation that the Kesgrave Sands and Gravels are of Beestonian age, and separated from the Anglian Barham Sands and Gravels by a Cromerian rubified *sol lessivé*, has been questioned by Lake and others (1977), Lake (1977), Bristow (1977) and Read (1977). These authors disputed the conclusion that the *sol lessivé* formed in a warm-temperate climatic regime, and Lake (1977) noted that the preservation of the rubified horizon over such a wide area suggests that there was no significant time-break at this level. Bristow (1977) has put forward evidence from the Chelmsford district which suggests that the Kesgrave Sands and Gravels overlie the Maldon Till, which is widely accepted, though on scant evidence, to be an early phase of the Anglian glaciation. Until fossil evidence or radiometric age determinations are available, the assignment of the Kesgrave Sands and Gravels to the Beestonian, and the rubified horizon to the Cromerian, is speculative. CRB

Details

Thurston, Tostock and Woolpit

Over much, if not all of this area the Kesgrave Sands and Gravels are probably absent. They were recorded in the Tostock pit [957 628] by Rose and others (1976, fig. 1), but no section was visible in Kesgrave Sands and Gravels in 1977 and 1978 when exposures showed 3 m of poorly sorted, cobbly, flint gravels with interbeds of medium-grained sands (Barham Sands and Gravels). According to the pit operator, these gravels are underlain by fine-grained sand, here interpreted as Crag.

South-west of Thurston, temporary sections for the Beyton Bypass revealed chalky Boulder Clay resting on fine-grained sands of the Crag. Similarly at Woolpit, at least locally, Boulder Clay rests directly on Crag [9820 6238].

Stowlangtoft

At the top of the Stowlangtoft chalk pit [9481 6896] up to 1 m of pebbly sand, containing many quartz and quartzite pebbles, overlies Crag. The fields east of the pit have a surface covering of gravel, but auger holes generally entered fine-grained Crag sands beneath the soil. At only one place [9620 6913] were small (1–2 cm) white quartzite pebbles very common on the surface. Therefore, although there are patches of Kesgrave Sands and Gravels on top of the Crag, they are too small to map.

Stanton

On the south side of Wyken Wood, white quartzite pebbles are common on the surface of the fields [9645 7092], but elsewhere in this vicinity all that is generally found is fine- and locally coarse-grained Crag sand. This small spread has not been mapped separately.

A small pit [9535 7105] at Burntfirs Plantation, 1 km west of Wyken Wood, exposes (Plate 1) in descending sequence: fine-grained sand with scattered flints (Head), 1 m; bedded, well-sorted, well-rounded to subrounded with pebbles of white vein-quartz and quartzite (forming up to 50 per cent of the total pebbles), and subrounded flints, including glauconite-coated ones derived from the Crag, set in a coarse-grained sandy matrix, 4 m; Chalk, exposed in the floor of the pit. White quartz and quartzite pebbles are common on the surface of the fields to the south [953 710], north-west [951 714] and north [9525 7147], where they overlie gravel. Some 450 m north-east of the pit, white vein quartz is common on the Chalk surface [9560 7145].

North of Wyken Hall, a ditch [9643 7175] showed up to 1.5 m of quartz-rich gravel overlying Chalk. White quartz pebbles are again common on the surface of the fields [963 717] west of Wyken Hall.

On the south-west side of Kiln Wood a small spread of Kesgrave Sands and Gravels rests partly on Chalk and partly on Crag [around 956 720]. North of Kiln Wood, the Kesgrave Sands and Gravels have their most extensive outcrop. White quartz and quartzite pebbles are common on the surface of the fields in two areas [960 731; 960 727] on either side of Bury Lane. From here northwards the Kesgrave Sands and Gravels become much more clayey. A number of trial pits close to the north-east corner of the now removed Fir Wood were excavated in these clayey beds. One of these [9552 7333], which can be taken as typical of the Kesgrave Sands and Gravels in this vicinity, showed:

	Depth m
Top soil	0.3
a Boulder Clay, chalky	1.1
b Clay, sandy, mottled orange and grey, with lenses of medium- to coarse-grained sand in mottled orange/grey clay	1.5
c Clay, pebbly, sandy; pebbles up to 8 cm diam. of well-rounded quartzite and subrounded flints	1.6
d Clay, mottled orange and grey, sandy; sandier than bed b	2.5
e Pebbly sandy clay	2.6
f Sand, orange-brown, clayey, fine-grained	2.9
g Sand, grey and orange mottled, clayey	3.2
h Clay, mottled orange and grey, sandy, as bed d	3.6

A similar sequence, more than 3.3 m thick, was revealed in another trial pit [9554 7343]. A count of 50 pebbles showed that they consisted of equal proportions of quartz, quartzite and flint. Chalk was encountered at a depth of 2.8 m immediately north of Glassfield Road.

The base of the sand and gravel, and also the base of the chalky Boulder Clay, is very irregular in this vicinity. A well [959 732] at the Rose and Crown proved 6.1 m of sand and gravel, despite being situated only 50 m away from a Chalk inlier. Several other small inliers of Chalk have been mapped, and there are numerous small outliers of Boulder Clay capping the sand and gravel, all of which indicate an irregular top and bottom to the deposit. Locally, the deposit must be sufficiently thick and clay-free to have been exploited for sand and gravel, as evidenced by several old pits [9530 7293; 9550 7327; 958 730].

White quartz pebbles are common on the surface of the fields south-east [9705 7280; 9700 7305] and east [974 735] of Stanton, which is the most north-easterly point within the Bury district at which the Kesgrave Sands and Gravels have been identified with certainty.
CRB

INGHAM SAND AND GRAVEL

Sand and gravel containing up to 54 per cent of rounded, reddish brown, 'Bunter' quartzite pebbles are intermittently exposed in the floor of a sand and gravel pit [853 716] at Ingham. Mr T E Lawson (internal BGS report, 1982) proposed that the deposit should be called the Ingham Sand and Gravel (Table 4), and this term has since been used by Clarke and Auton (1982) and Clarke (1983). There is only a small outcrop near Ingham, but more extensive spreads occur on either side of a shallow valley at Honington [885 736; 890 744] and along The Black Bourn north of Bardwell [around 940 745]. Similar deposits are recorded in boreholes to the south, south-east, east and north-east by Clarke and Auton (1982).

At Ingham, these Bunter-rich sands and gravels rest in irregular hollows on Chalk (Plate 2). They can be divided into a lower unit with disturbed bedding and an upper unit with undisturbed bedding: it is thus possible that they represent more than one deposit. These gravels are up to 2 m thick and are overlain by (Anglian) Glacial Sand and Gravel.

Pebble counts by Clarke and Auton (1982) show quartzite and sandstone percentages varying from 18 at Timworth [8672 6916] to 60 north-east of the present district. Other major constituents are vein-quartz, which varies from 5 to 47 per cent, and flint and chert which total between 16 and 56 per cent. The mean percentages of flint and chert, vein-quartz, and quartzite and sandstone in forty-seven samples were 42, 14 and 40 respectively, with 4 per cent of other pebbles.
CRB, TEL

Details

At the type locality [853 716], the Ingham Sand and Gravel consists of up to 3 m of well-rounded, reddened 'Bunter' quartzite gravel resting on a very irregular Chalk surface. Locally some of the 'Bunter'-rich gravels seem to pass laterally into a mélange of chalk.

East of Livermere Heath [around 887 738] and on the opposite side of a shallow valley at Black Hill [890 745], there are two spreads of sand and gravel on the surface, in which there are abundant rounded, reddened quartzites.

The most widespread occurrence of Ingham Sand and Gravel is between Sapiston [918 751] and Bardwell [930 746]. These gravels were formerly extensively worked in a pit [923 742] 1 km south-south-east of Sapiston where they appear to be at least 3 m thick. The abundant reddened quartzites are here associated with rounded flints. On the opposite side of the river, up to 2.5 m of poorly sorted 'Bunter'-rich sand and gravel were noted in an old pit [9338 7427].

Near Pakenham, the deposit was proved in a single borehole [9368 6956] where 2.6 m of sand and gravel were recorded (Clarke, 1983).
CRB, TEL

DRIFT-FILLED CHANNELS

Deep channels filled with Glacial Silt, Boulder Clay and sand and gravel (including Glacial Sand and Gravel) underlie the River Lark, The Black Bourn and their tributaries. The River Kennett, however, does not appear to be underlain by a drift-filled channel; indeed, at Kentford its valley is crossed at right angles by a channel that extends down to 5 m below OD [7053 6800]. Other channels also, such as those near Kennett [700 683], at Troston [910 715] and in the north-east of the district (see Figure 12), are not followed by the modern drainage.

Woodland (1970) referred to the drift-filled channels of East Anglia as 'tunnel valleys' and believed that they were cut along pre-existing valleys by pressurised water flowing beneath the 'Chalky Boulder Clay ice', and were largely filled by melt-water debris from that ice. In particular, he

Plate 2 Ingham Sand and Gravel overlain by chalky Boulder Clay, Ingham. (A13980)

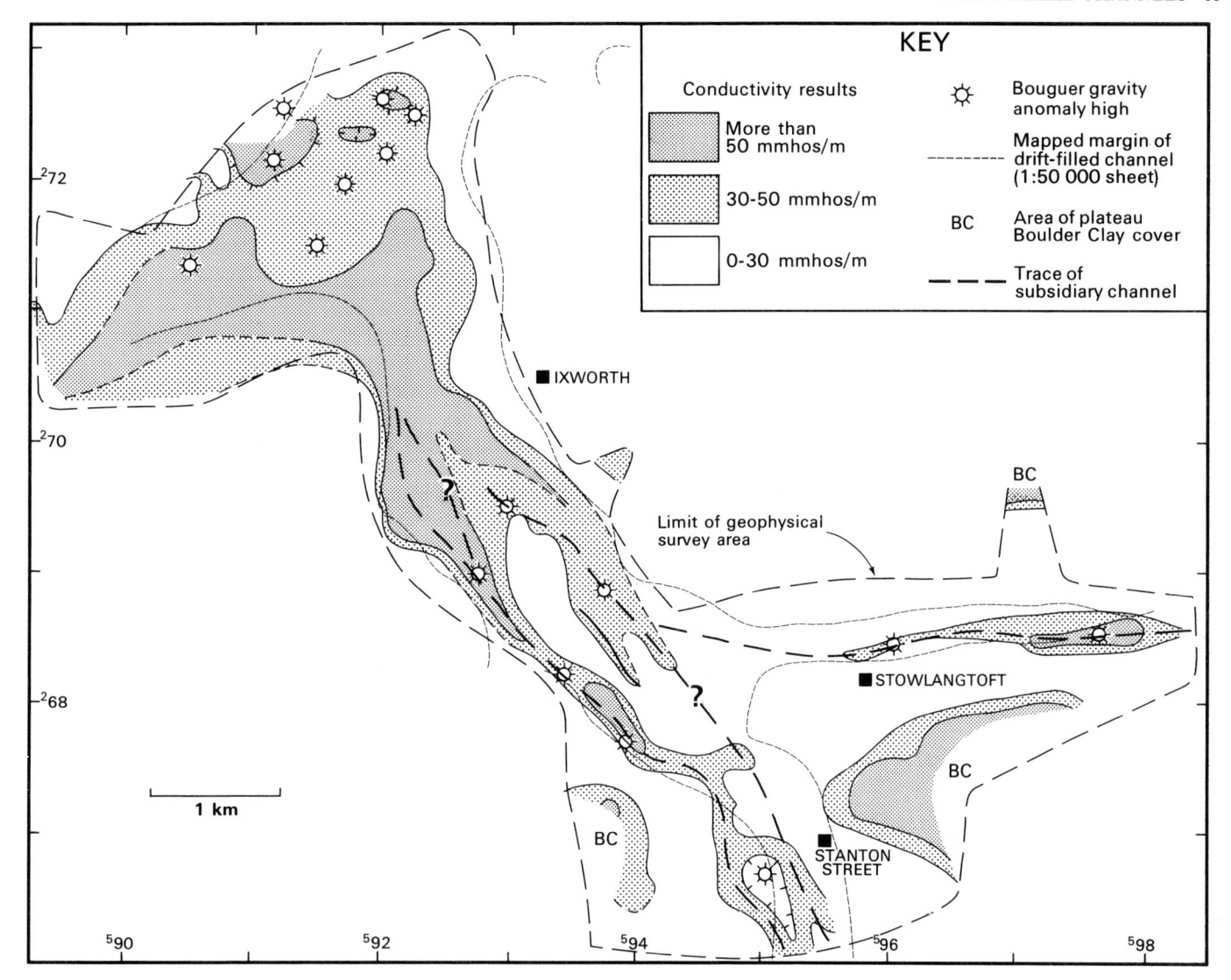

Figure 12 Conductivity map of part of the drift-filled system in the Ixworth-Woolpit area based on ground conductivity meter measurements with a 40 m coil separation (EM34); conductivity and Bouguer anomaly highs indicate thick clay (after Cornwell, 1985)

described a buried channel underlying The Black Bourn valley near Ixworth and noted its great depth (82 m) (35 m below OD) at Norton [9573 6556]. Greater depths are known elsewhere: at Grimstone End [9372 6948] the base of the drift is at 43 m below OD; a borehole [9283 6884] at Old Hall proved 84.4 m of drift with a base at 42 m below OD; at Troston [9091 7127], 102.7 m of Boulder Clay, the thickest known drift in the district, extends down to 51.5 m below OD; at Honington [9129 7456], some 87.9 m of drift has its base at 63 m below OD.

A buried west-south-west-trending channel joins that underlying The Black Bourn north of Bardwell. This channel, which originates in the adjacent Diss (175) district, has a maximum depth of 11 m below OD [9788 7597] within the present district. It may cross that of The Black Bourn and continue via Troston and the valley leading westwards from Great Livermere to the River Lark. In the Lark valley, the maximum depth to which the channel has been proved is 41 m below OD at Lackford [7928 7101], but 96.6 m of 'clay' extending to a depth of 34 m below OD was proved in the upper reaches at Hawstead [8600 5880]. Another drift-filled channel underlies the stream which flows through Stowlangtoft and is tributary to that beneath The Black Bourn. West of the latter, between Pakenham [920 670] and Grimstone End [935 690], there are several subsidiary drift-filled channels trending parallel to The Black Bourn.

Despite the northward increasing maximum depth of The Black Bourn channel, there may not be a regular fall in this direction. Many workers (Woodland, 1970; Clarke and Cornwell, 1983; Bristow, 1985) have thought that the floors of drift-filled channels are irregular, with several lows apparently separated by highs, and have explained the irregularity as being due to erosion by pressurised water. In some cases, however, the irregularity may be illusory, for the location of boreholes in the steep-sided, locally sinuous, channels may be too random to reveal the true gradient of the floor; more closely spaced boreholes or geophysical traverses are necessary to determine this. Clarke and Cornwell (1983), using different methods, have attempted to determine the cross-section and longitudinal profile of a section of the Black Bourn channel between Woolpit and Ixworth. The computer-generated model of Clarke has gently sloping valley sides and fails to recognise the minor channels between Pakenham and Grimstone End. However, the model is based on inadequate data points along the critical channel margins, and where data are closely spaced, as at Grimstone End [94 69], the valley side is manifestly steep-sided. CRB

The fill of the drift-filled channels has also been investigated by geophysical techniques (Clarke and Cornwell, 1983; Barker and Harker, 1984; Cornwell and Carruthers, 1986). The clay fill has a higher density and electrical conductivity than both Chalk bedrock and sand and gravel fill. Using detailed gravity surveys, the small consequential Bouguer gravity anomaly highs (usually less than 1 mgal in amplitude) can be located and interpreted to provide cross-sections of the clay fill. These demonstrate that the fill in the Ixworth area commonly has an assymetric form, with one side of the valley having slopes of 50° or more. The courses of the clay fill, as traced by conductivity mapping equipment, are complex, with the clay variously comprising between all and none of the fill, and in places filling more than one subsidiary channel within the main channel (Figure 12). The sand and gravel which form the rest of the fill is commonly difficult to distinguish by geophysical techniques from Chalk bedrock, particularly where the latter is weathered, because of an overlap in their physical properties. In the Ixworth area, however, there is some evidence that the tendency for the sand content to increase down-channel (Woodland, 1970) can be reversed at the intersection of two channels. JDC

The fill of the channels varies from one valley system to another. In The Black Bourn, it is mostly an alternating sequence of boulder clay and sand and gravel, with the former being generally dominant in the upper part of the sequence. Along the stream which flows through Stowlangtoft, Boulder Clay is dominant, but at two boreholes [9491 6847; 9801 6868] extremely soft reconstituted Chalk, or chalk-fragmental clay, was encountered. In the first borehole the reconstituted Chalk is 26 m thick. In the channel which joins The Black Bourn at Bardwell, Boulder Clay forms the main fill, as it also does at Troston, where 102.7 m of Boulder Clay occur. The channel of the River Lark below Bury St Edmunds and that of its north bank tributary, which enters near West Stow, is mostly filled with Glacial Silt; but, locally, chalky Boulder Clay or sand and gravel occur. The Kentford channel is filled with Boulder Clay in the south-east [73 66], and with Glacial Silt overlain by Boulder Clay farther west [700 683].

The age of the channels is not proven. Where chalky Boulder Clay occupies the channels it commonly appears to be in continuity with the plateau Boulder Clay, which is generally regarded as Anglian in age. The channels must, therefore, have been cut during Anglian times or earlier. Elsewhere, where Glacial Silt is the dominant fill, there is evidence (see p.55) that the top of the silt sequence is Devensian in age, but in other localities Boulder Clay of presumed Anglian age overlies silt. This problem is discussed more fully on p.55. It is possible that there were two or more periods of cutting in different areas, so that the fill in different channels is of different ages; it may even be composite in any one channel. For example, the fill of the Troston-Bardwell–North Common channel (with no surface expression) may be wholly Anglian in age, whereas the silt-filled topographic low of the present Lark valley may have been partly filled by Devensian fluvial deposits, for there is no reason why the tunnel-valleys should have been completely filled during the Anglian melt, and post-Anglian deposition could have continued episodically in the resultant depressions until the present day. CRB

Details

Valley of The Black Bourn and tributaries, Woolpit – Norton – Bull Bridge

The farthest point upstream where a drift-filled channel has been proved is at Woolpit. A borehole [9675 6330] in the stream bed showed that the base of the Boulder Clay is below 25.8 m above OD, whilst in another borehole [9694 6333] on the valley side the base lies at 35.6 m above OD. Similarly, north of Woolpit, in a tributary valley of The Black Bourn, a number of boreholes [e.g. 9744 6350] have proved more than 19 m of Boulder Clay, the base here lying below 26.8 m above OD. Below the confluence with The Black Bourn, Boulder Clay rests on sand and gravel at a depth of 8.2 m in a borehole at the road crossing [9672 6388]. Farther downstream, Boulder Clay, beneath 7.4 m of peaty alluvium, is 7.6+ m thick and its base is below 17.2 m above OD.

At Street Farm, Norton, on the eastern flank of the present-day valley [9573 6556], the drift consists essentially of 35 m of Boulder Clay above 46.9 m of alternating thick beds of sand and gravel and thin beds of 'pug' (boulder clay). The base of the channel lies 35.34 m below OD. A similar sequence was proved in a borehole at Little Haugh Hall [9530 6680]. There, beneath 3.6 m of alluvium, peat and alluvial gravel, occurs in descending sequence: boulder clay, 25.9 m; sand and gravel, 4.1 m; boulder clay, 14.7 m; sand and gravel, 17.5+ m. The base of the drift lies below 34 m below OD.

A borehole [9391 6773], south-east of Bull Bridge, sited within 50 m of the eastern margin of the channel, proved a variable sequence or organic clayey sand, sandy clay and silty clay to a depth of 6 m. Below this occurred 1.6 m of boulder clay and 0.1 m of peat, above 10.8+ m of boulder clay. Another borehole [9474 6787] just south of Bull Bridge proved 2.4 m of River Terrace Deposits above 6 m of chalky Boulder Clay which in turn rests on 13.6+ m of sand, the base of the drift lying below 12.6 m above OD.

Bridge Farm – Stowlangtoft – Hunston

Just north of Bull Bridge, The Black Bourn is joined by an unnamed westward-flowing tributary, the present course of which overlies a drift-filled channel. A borehole [9491 6847] close to the confluence proved in descending sequence: clayey sand and gravel (Head), 2.3 m; chalky and flint gravel (?River Terrace Deposits), 4.7 m; grey silty chalky clay, 12 m; soft, putty chalk, 3 m; loose rubbly chalk with flints in a chalk paste, 23 m; firmer, less rubbly chalk, becoming firmer with depth, 7+ m. The 26 m of soft rubbly chalk is regarded as redeposited chalk. A similar deposit has been noted upstream at Stowlangtoft (see below) and in the Lark valley (see p.40).

Upstream from Bridge Farm, a narrow strip of Boulder Clay crops out on either side of the valley bottom, with Chalk cropping out higher up the slopes. A borehole [9547 6858] on the flood plain, north-west of Stowlangtoft Church, encountered chalky Boulder Clay at 11 m and failed to penetrate it at a depth of 15.3 m (17.3 m above OD). Another borehole [9642 6865], south-east of Stowlangtoft Hall, passed through 3 m of River Terrace Deposits into 20.2 m of brown silty chalky clay, and then into 4.2+ m of grey laminated silt which was not penetrated (11.3 m OD).

A borehole [9772 6866] at Dairy Hall, Hunston, proved in descending sequence: medium-grained, orange sand, 0.9 m; very stiff, bluish grey, chalky clay, 4.8 m; soft, silty, chalky clay, 19.2+ m (base below 13 m above OD). Some 270 m farther upstream [9801 6868], the channel fill differs: there is an upper unit of very stiff bluish grey clay, 9 m thick, above 9.5 m of soft, waterlogged, chalk-fragmental clay, resting on 1+ m of stiff, greyish brown, flinty and chalky clay. The base of the channel here lies below 17.5 m above OD, yet close by, in a third borehole [9796 6873], the base of the drift was only 6.6 m from the surface at 30.4 m above OD. As at Bridge Farm (see above), the Chalk is soft and putty-like, and may have been redeposited. A fourth borehole [9744 6851], west-south-west of Dairy Farm, failed to penetrate dark grey silty chalky clay at a depth of 19.1 (21.4 m above OD).

Bridge Farm – Grimstone End

In the bottom of the east side of The Black Bourn valley, below Bridge Farm, there is a strip of Boulder Clay about 100 m wide, which passes under River Terrace Deposits east of Baileypool Bridge. At the bridge, a well [9398 6899] sited on the Alluvium proved: topsoil and alluvium, 1.2 m; 'ballast', 6.1 m; Chalk. West of The Black Bourn, the Boulder Clay outcrop is about 500 m wide, although partially obscured by River Terrace Deposits. A borehole [9377 6873] within this tract proved 18.7+ m of Boulder Clay with minor amounts of silt and of clayey and sandy gravel, the base of the drift being below 16.1 m above OD.

At Grimstone End, a well [9372 6948] proved 35.4 m of Boulder Clay (with some overlying River Terrace Deposits), above 40.5 m of sand and gravel which rests on Chalk at 44.8 m below OD. The margin of the channel passes between this borehole and another [9368 6965] 90 m north-west, where River Terrace Deposits, 8.1 m thick, rest directly on Chalk at 22.3 m above OD.

Boulder Clay appears to be absent under Mickle Mere. Two boreholes [9377 6966; 9364 6999] proved 5.6 and 2.9 m respectively of alluvial clay and gravel resting on Chalk. A third [9341 6977], just south of Mickle Mere, sited over the channel, proved stiff, grey, chalky clay under River Terrace Deposits. South of this borehole, the Boulder Clay fill of the channel is over 1 km wide. The southern boundary is well defined and appears to be steep-sided, for a borehole [9235 6924] within 30 m of the Chalk outcrop proved chalky Boulder Clay to a depth of 26 m (9 m above OD). Another [9283 6884] at Old Hall proved dominantly chalky clay, with some gravel beds, to a depth of 84.4 m, resting on 3.9 m of sand and gravel which overlie Chalk at 42.1 m below OD.

Grimstone End – Pakenham – Barton

Maulkin's Hall [9368 6807] overlies a drift-filled channel that lies parallel to that of The Black Bourn, and is probably the southern continuation of the channel at Old Hall. A well at Maulkin's Hall proved 59.7 m of 'blue clay' resting on Chalk at 15 m below OD.

Pakenham Fen is constricted between Old Hall and Maulkin's Hall by a low ridge of Boulder Clay. A borehole [9330 6826] close to the Boulder Clay/Alluvium contact proved 25 m of chalky Boulder Clay (6.8 m above OD), above 2 m of soft chalky silts, which rest on very soft Chalk. Some 60 m south-west, a second borehole [9326 6824] proved Boulder Clay to 17.9 m (13.8 m above OD), above 0.4 m of soft putty Chalk and 0.3+ m of firmer Chalk. The drift fill, if any, under Pakenham Fen is not proved, but Chalk extends down to the Alluvium to the east, while Chalk was encountered in several ditches to the west. The Chalk in one of these [9282 6812] was very soft and puggy.

North of Pakenham, a channel filled by Boulder Clay extends down to the fen and appears to cross it. The margins of the channel seem to be steep.

Bull Road, north of Newe House [9335 6747], is cut into Chalk on the north side and into Boulder Clay on the south. The westwards continuation of this channel probably passes beneath Upper Town and Manor Farm, but west of the latter it is obscured.

South of Upper Town a tongue of Boulder Clay is preserved in a channel that extends at least as far as the lake [923 668] west of Nether Hall. South of the lake, an east–west channel can be traced from the stream [926 665] at Sheep Lane, beneath Thurston Grange Hotel [914 665], to a point [c.900 663] south-east of Great Barton. Much of this channel is filled with Boulder Clay, but steep-sided channels filled with Glacial Sand and Gravel occur locally [9160 6655].

No channel could be recognised with certainty in the main branch of the stream which passes through Thurston and Beyton. However, at two points [928 646; 9290 6415], Chalky Boulder Clay was mapped low in the valley. At a third point [9321 6365], a well proved 9.1 m of brown clay and stone, above 27.3 m of blue clay, which rested on Chalk at 13.1 m above OD. Closely spaced boreholes for the By-pass immediately north proved only thin sand and gravel above Chalk.

Grimstone End – Bardwell – Honington

A drift-filled channel lies west of The Black Bourn as far as Bangrove Wood [around 928 720]. Its western margin is clear between Old Hall [928 688] and Brewster's Farm [920 703], but the eastern margin is hidden beneath River Terrace Deposits and Alluvium.

Part of the Boulder Clay spread that extends along the valley from just north-east of Woodstreet Farm [960 707] to Bangrove Wood occupies a channel. Depths of 19 and 19.5 m have been established [9542 7076; 9605 7075] along its eastern section.

A borehole [9227 7202] west of Bangrove Wood proved drift to 35 m (9 m below OD). In the Troston Borehole [9080 7120], some 1.5 km south-west, 102.7 m of Boulder Clay, with a base at 51.5 m below OD, were proved. The probable north-eastward continuation of this channel may account for a prominent north-east swing of the river to Bardwell, and its subsequent west-south-west swing back to Ixworth Thorpe, although Boulder Clay has been proved only to 4 m above OD [9399 7368]. Farther east-north-east a channel follows a tributary as far as Stanton Chare [955 746], and then extends to North Common where 49.5 m of Boulder Clay, with its base at 11 m below OD, has been proved [9788 7597]. At Honington [9129 7456], the channel has been proved to its greatest depth (63 m below OD). River Terrace Deposits overlie 26.5 m of Boulder Clay, which in turn overlie 52 m of Glacial Sand and Gravel. The margin of the channel lies between this borehole and another 400 m north-east [9151 7486], where the chalky till rests on Chalk at 6 m above OD.

Lark valley and tributary channels

The farthest point upstream in the Lark valley at which a channel has been proved is at Hawstead Green, where 'clay' extends to 96.6 m (34.1 m below OD) and rests on Chalk [8600 5880].

At Hawstead Hall, just north of the River Lark, a borehole [8630 5983] proved 57.3 m of 'clay with chalk and stones' resting on Chalk at 2.1 m OD. Farther downstream a borehole [8749 5995] proved: peat, 0.3 m; soft, shelly, grey clay, 5.7 m; yellow, chalky and flinty clay, 0.5 m; very soft granular chalk, 38.5 m; firmer white chalk, 4.4 m; the soft chalk, whose base lies at 3 m below OD, is regarded as redeposited chalk. Similar material has also been found at Stowlangtoft (p.00) and north of Pakenham Fen (p.00).

At Sicklesmere, the Lark is joined by a north-west-flowing tributary. A borehole [8920 5910] east of Copy Farm proved a dominantly clayey unit to 12.6 m, above a dominantly sand and gravel unit to 52.1 m. The lowest bed, 2.7 m thick was Boulder Clay and rested on Chalk at 3 m above OD. From Sicklesmere to Nowton Lodge Farm [870 612], the channel is not proved, but it probably underlies Sicklesmere [875 615]. At Nowton Lodge Farm, on the plateau, a well [8697 6115] proved 38.1 m of Boulder Clay above 42 m of green sand and ballast, resting on Chalk at 29.9 m below OD. A nearby well [8660 6102] proved a similar succession, but with reduced thicknesses of Boulder Clay and of sand and gravel (25.9 and 7.6 m respectively), the base of the drift lying at 21.3 m above OD. A third well [8633 6126], west-north-west of Nowton Lodge Farm, proved 42.7 m of Boulder Clay above 22 m of sand and gravel, resting on Chalk at OD. The thick drift in these boreholes is interpreted as filling tributary channels to the main Lark channel, though the latter may hereabout not be coincident with the present river. A borehole at Nowton Court [8648 6149] provides a fix on one side of the channel, as it encountered Chalk at 18 m (42.5 m above OD).

There is insufficient borehole control to establish the exact course of the channel through Bury, though a well [8565 6467] proved 11 m of sand and gravel and grey silt above 6.5 m of soft dirty chalk, which in turn rested on 1 m of rubbly chalk, before entering firm Chalk with flints at c.12.9 m above OD. Another well [8553 6514] proved a dominantly sandy sequence, 38.4 m thick, resting on 6.4 m of grey sandy clay with a basal flint bed, which in turn rested on Chalk at 13.1 m below OD.

At Fornham St Martin, a channel runs at right-angles to the Lark valley. Its steep-sided southern margin can be traced in fields north-west of the Church. A borehole [8504 6747], north-west of the Church, proved in descending sequence: sand (River Terrace Deposits), 5.6 m; shelly silt, 6.9 m; gravel, 1.2 m; chalky Boulder Clay, 11.2+ m: the base of the drift lies below 12.2 m above OD.

At the old barracks in Bury St Edmunds, Boulder Clay occupies a circular depression in Chalk, unconnected with the Lark valley. A well [8424 6458] recorded 18.3 m of Boulder Clay before reaching Chalk. However, a temporary section [8424 6450] revealed that the 'boulder clay', at least in its upper part, is a sandy silt.

Just north of Bury St Edmunds, a well [8490 6662] on the alluvium penetrated 35.5 m of drift before entering Chalk. An adjacent well [8491 6668] proved only 6.4 m of drift on bedrock. This gives a minimum slope for the channel side of about 30°. The channel continues north-westwards along the Lark, but its depth and profile are unknown. Two boreholes [8247 6944; 8326 6851] proved dominantly silt to depths of more than 16.8 and 12.5 m respectively, beneath alluvial deposits. Just north of Hengrave, this channel is joined from the east by another, underlying an unnamed stream. The Ingham Borehole [8478 6967], sited on the tributary channel, proved 36.5 m of silty, chalky, grey clay on Chalk. The westward continuation of this channel is proved by a borehole [8387 6965] south of Culford, which penetrated 44.5 m of drift before entering Chalk.

At Lackford [7928 7101], 48.6 m of soft water-saturated silt, underlain by 6.4 m of gravel and redeposited chalk, has its base at 41 m below OD. North-east of Tuddenham, the channel is much wider. Grey silt was seen in trial pits on Tuddenham Heath [7402 7298; 7397 7234; 7411 7205]. A borehole [7430 7301] on the Heath proved 2.9 m of sand and gravel on 6.7 m of clay with sand, on 0.6+ m of gravel. Several boreholes close to the point where the cut-off channel diverges from the Lark show more than 10 m of sand, gravel and clayey silt.

There is no evidence for a channel beneath the Lark south of Mildenhall, but it continues east of the town where a borehole [7286 7457] just west of the 'cut-off channel' proved 10.4 m of sand and gravel on 8.8+ m of grey silt. East of Mildenhall, 9.5 m of sand and gravel overlie 13.4 m of clay, which rest on Chalk at a depth of 13.8 m below OD [7218 7498]. On the opposite side of the cut-off valley, 44.2 m of sand, 'pea shingle', white clay and marl rest on Chalk.

Some 800 m north-north-west, two boreholes [7290 7580; 7296 7593] showed 9.9 and 7 m of sand and gravel respectively, above Chalk, whilst a third [7229 7542] proved: brown sand with pebbles, 2.9 m; grey clay, 9 m; chalk gravel with flints and clay, 10 m; chalk and silt, 10.8 m; on Chalk, to 11.8+ m. CRB

East of Gazeley to Kennett

A tongue of Boulder Clay descends from the plateau east of Gazeley and fills a channel in the Chalk. A borehole [7316 6576] about 1 km east of Needham Hall proved:

	Depth m
Sand, chalky	0.9
Clay, chalky	1.0
Silt, brown, with chalk pellets, possibly laminated	9.8
Silt, yellow-brown, with common chalk pellets and some Jurassic shell fragments	12.2
Chalk, white, soft, with harder chalk pellets; ?redeposited	13.7

Two other boreholes in the same channel just north of the A45 road proved 17.7 and 25 m of drift respectively. One of these [7264 6667] encountered:

	Depth m
Sand and gravel	3.0
Clay, buff, chalky, on brown silt	6.1
Sand, with scattered flints	7.9
Clay, silty, chalky, with scattered flints	9.1
Silt, less chalky, softer, somewhat sandy at 12.2 m	15.2
Clay, very silty, sandy, with flint and chalk	16.3
Silt, clayey, buff-yellow, with fine-grained sand	17.7
Chalk, whitish cream, soft; with subangular flints; probably redeposited	18.9

The other [7239 6676] proved, beneath made ground, 2.2 m of chalky silt on Chalk.

Grey silts in the base of gravel workings [7180 6750] about 1 km north-west indicate the probable north-west extension of the channel. Still farther north-west, a borehole [7085 6809] proved 14.2 m of drift on Chalk. Another [7025 6820] proved 31.4 m of clay, silt and sand above Chalk at 5 m below OD. To the west of this, grey silt was seen in an old pit near Kennett Church, though other boreholes about 100 m north of the above borehole proved only thin drift. Another borehole [7000 6746] in a disused gravel pit proved: silt, pale buff with shells, 6.1 m; clay, sandy, silty, slightly chalky, with some flints, 0.6 m; sand, coarse-grained, with flints, dark brown, with chalk pellets, 13.7 m; chalk, soft, putty, 1.0+ m.

South of Herringswell Manor Farm

South of Herringswell Manor Farm, there is a narrow east–west drift-filled channel. A borehole [7130 7051] close to the edge of the channel proved 1.5 m of sand on 9.5 m of grey silty clay with few flints. Several trial pits [around 720 710] sited within the channel proved very sandy and silty clay with minor sand beds and abundant Jurassic fossil fragments and septaria.   BSPM

LOWER GLACIAL SAND AND GRAVEL

Sands and gravels associated with the Boulder Clay occur both above and below it. It is not always possible to assign particular spreads to either category, and these have been left unclassified on the geological map.

The Lower Glacial Sand and Gravel (Table 4, Plates 3 and 4) has an irregular distribution. Some occurs in the buried channels, and other deposits form fragmented outcrops from west of Barrow [75 63], through Hengrave [81 69] and Fornham St Genevieve [840 685], to Bury St Edmunds [86 63]. Some occurrences, for example near Conyer's Green [888 685] and Stanton [979 740], have the appearance of outliers of Upper Sand and Gravel but have been proved by drilling to underlie the Boulder Clay. The Lower Glacial Sand and Gravel includes the Barham Sands and Gravels (Rose and others, 1976); the latter are apparently discontinuous, though the logs of older boreholes are not sufficiently detailed to enable them to be distinguished from Ingham Sand and Gravel, Kesgrave Sands and Gravels, or Crag; some of which may have been locally included with Glacial Sand and Gravel.

There is no regular form to the base of the deposits. Where gravel is present beneath Boulder Clay, the base varies from c.70 m above OD near Barrow [765 635] to c.60 m above OD north-east and east of Horringer [84 62] and Bury St Edmunds [885 645], and is between 20 and 40 m above OD in the south-east near Felsham (Bristow, 1981). Considerable thicknesses of Glacial Sand and Gravel occur in some of the drift-filled channels and extend to below OD.

The thickness of the sand and gravel varies markedly and shows no regional trend. In the drift-filled channels, thicknesses in excess of 23 m have been proved [7432 7118] (Clayton, 1983). Outside the channels, an irregular sheet of sand and gravel, varying from 0 to 22 m, has been proved beneath Boulder Clay in the central and eastern part of the district. There is no regular eastward and south-eastward thickening within the area of Sheet TL 96 as was thought by Clarke (1983, p.5).

The composition of the sand and gravel within and outside the drift-filled channels differs slightly. Angular and subangular flint is the commonest component in both deposits and minor amounts of quartz, quartzite, chalk, limestone and igneous material are present. The matrix is dominantly fine- and medium-grained quartz sand, with

Plate 3 Chalky Boulder Clay overlying contorted Glacial Sand and Gravel Fornham Park. (A 12825)

Plate 4 Chalky Boulder Clay overlying Lower Glacial Sand and Gravel, Fornham Park. (A12823)

some chalk and flint locally. The deposits overall are clayey sands and gravels, but the sand and gravel in the channels has either a much smaller percentage (<10 per cent) of 'fines' or a much lower gravel content (Clayton, 1983, fig. 5).
CRB

Details

High Lodge – Ingham – Troston – Bradwell

Excavations at High Lodge, about 500 m north-east of Barton Mills, revealed 6.1 m of Glacial Sand and Gravel beneath about 1.5 m of Boulder Clay. The sand and gravel, which is underlain by Glacial Silt and another Boulder Clay, consists of crudely bedded, angular to subangular flints and quartzites with some fine-grained sandy beds.

Chalk was augered at about 3 m from the original surface in one of several old gravel pits [7417 7442] south of Warren Belt. A section [7456 7421] in one pit showed 0.5 m of chalky laminated silty and fine-grained sands about 3 m below the original ground level. A trial pit here [7400 7433] revealed:

	Depth m
Soil, sandy, flinty	0.2
Sand, gravelly, dirty brown, with abundant angular patinated flints up to 10 cm diameter in a medium-grained sand matrix	0.8
Sand, medium-grained, orange, unbedded, possibly decalcified, with sparse flints and small pods of chalky sand; dark brown at base	1.8
Sand, fine-grained; a seam of chalky, sandy gravel with chalk pebbles up to 3 cm diameter just below top; the sand below is free of gravel except for thin seams throughout	3.0
Silt, chalky with chalk pebbles up to 5 cm in diameter, some sand and scattered flints	seen to 3.3

A second pit [7427 7432] to the east proved 0.6 m of fine- to medium-grained chalky sand, with scattered subangular and angular flints up to 3 cm in diameter and chalk pebbles, underlying 3 m of made and disturbed ground.
BSPM

A small isolated area [7755 7430] of fine gravel lies west of the valley running north-east from Icklingham. In a disused gravel pit [7908 7199] east of Weatherhill Farm, Icklingham, a trial pit proved:

	Depth m
Sand, medium- to coarse-grained, fawn, unbedded	2.0
Gravel, fine, poorly sorted, unbedded	2.5
Sand, medium- to fine-grained, fawn, with patches of iron-staining emphasising the bedding; some stringers of fine gravel, with chalk pellets and a few 'Bunter' quartzites	5.5
Cobble gravel containing large, relatively fresh, nodular flints and flint pebbles, with some quartzites, in a matrix of coarse-grained flinty sand and fine gravel; a few lenses of chalky sand	seen to 7.9

The dip of the bedding increases up the section from about 10° at the base to approximately 25° at the top. The Chalk lies in the floor of the pit only 20 m south of the section and was also augered 100 m to the north; the gravel thus occupies a very narrow channel capped by chalky Boulder Clay. South-west of the pit, the area known as Rampart Field [789 716] consists of a ridge of sand and gravel.
TEL

The dry valley of the King's Forest [around 82 74] is largely floored by Head, but in one area [820 737 to 826 737] a low mound of angular flint gravel divides the valley into two.

A section in a small pit [8351 7160], in Limekiln Plantation near Culford, was recorded by Mr T E Lawson in 1977:

	Depth m
Unrecorded	1.0
Gravel, with angular flints set in a reddish brown sand matrix, involuted into underlying bed; becoming finer downward	1.5
Sand, fine-grained, very silty, micaceous, yellowish fawn, locally greyish fawn; small-scale ripple-drift cross-bedding; some lenses, 1 to 2 m across and up to 0.6 m thick, of rounded gravel in a sand matrix; lower part more chalky, with iron-staining at its top; gravelly base with pebbles up to 70 mm	2.5
Sand, fine-grained, silty, laminated, yellowish fawn, becoming greyer and passing into chalky sand and gravel at depth; clasts are dominantly flint and chalk, but include chert, jasper and red micaceous sandstone; clasts commonly between 2 to 30 mm, but with some up to 80 mm across; asymmetric cross-bedding emphasised by iron-staining at the base of each cross-bed; foresets dip predominantly east, but some dip west	3.0

North-west of Ingham there are a number of partially back-filled pits with rapidly changing faces. The bases of the pits are formed by an irregular and locally very hard surface of Chalk. Resting locally on this surface, and mainly occupying the hollows in it, is the 'Bunter'-rich Ingham Sand and Gravel (p.38), which in turn is succeeded by a chalky, cobbly gravel up to 10 m thick. Boulder Clay, locally split into two by a cobble gravel, caps the pits. The Glacial Sand and Gravel has cobbles and boulders up to 1 m in diameter, consisting mostly of worn nodular and tabular flints; some of the largest boulders are ?Kimmeridgian septarian cementstone nodules with dog-tooth spar in the cracks, together with subangular to subrounded chalk clasts (up to 0.4 m) particularly towards the base, '*Ostrea*' limestone, iron-stained fine-grained sandstone, and light greenish grey, glauconitic, silty sandstone with oyster fragments and clusters of small serpulids and belemnites. A typical section [8518 7161], recorded by Mr T E Lawson in 1978, is:

	Thickness m
BOULDER CLAY, with irregular base	6.0
GLACIAL SAND AND GRAVEL	
Gravel, fine to medium, with scattered larger flints in a silty, coarse-grained, light fawn sand matrix; many rounded chalk clasts and worn subangular flints	0.6
Silt, coarse-grained, light yellowish brown, cross-laminated; becoming a silty fine-grained sand downwards, locally flaser bedded and horizontally bedded, with small chalk and flint pebbles; sharp irregular base	0.3
Gravel, fine, in a medium- to coarse-grained sand matrix; abundant rounded chalk clasts; many subangular flint chips in matrix; some subhorizontal imbrication, otherwise unbedded; sharp planar base	2.6
Gravel, medium to coarse, with the medium grade composed dominantly or rounded chalk clasts, and subangular flints, and the coarse grade of large, slightly worn nodular flints, set in a fawn fine-grained silt matrix; some siltstone clasts and a few scattered 'Bunter' and vein-quartz pebbles	2.5
CHALK	

At Brush Hills, 6 km north-east of Ingham, sand and gravel crops out from beneath Cover Sand. At the south-western end of the outcrop, the deposit contains much rounded quartzite and white patinated flint [8705 7365]. A borehole in this vicinity [8723 7421] proved 10.7 m of sand and gravel.

North-west of Troston, another small patch of sand and gravel [895 730], chert- and quartzite-rich in the east [896 730], has been worked in shallow pits. One [8938 7286] exposed 1.5 m of sand and gravel resting on silts. Nearby boreholes [8989 7356; 8942 7473] proved 9.5 and 10 m respectively of sand and gravel beneath Boulder Clay.

Patches of sand and gravel south and south-west of Great Livermere [875 708; 883 708; 89 71] appear to be quite thin and to overlie silt. There are abundant rounded quartzites and angular white flints on the surface of the western spread; in the east, the gravel is locally very chalky [8922 7114; 8905 7105]. Although the sand and gravel appears to be fairly thin, boreholes north of these patches, at Great Livermere, which commenced in Head, proved thicknesses of up to 29.5 m [8881 7127; 8881 7116]. Farther south, sand and gravel is 13.4 m thick in one well [8809 7031] and absent in another [8963 7038].

CRB, TEL

Barton Mills – Higham – Ousden

The flat-topped ground which extends eastwards from Chalk Hill, near Barton Mills, is capped by sand and gravel, which varies from an angular flint gravel through a predominantly reddened, rounded quartzite gravel, to sand. In the road cutting at Chalk Hill, pale cream to buff sands are poorly exposed in the bottom of the cutting; Boulder Clay occurs higher in the cutting. The sand and gravel overburden in Howe's chalk pit at Chalk Hill ranges from poorly sorted, angular and subangular flint gravel in a silty or clayey matrix, to a predominantly rounded quartzite gravel, and even to a clean sand. Locally the gravel consists almost entirely of chalk pebbles. In places the gravel has been let down into solution pipes in the Chalk. At the eastern end of the pit the sand and gravel is very deformed and probably cryoturbated.

Angular to subangular flint gravel with varying quantities of rounded reddened quartzite pebbles caps a ridge south-east of Tuddenham. In the north face of a disused chalk pit [747 703] south-east of the village, up to 2 m of large flint cobbles in a chalky sandy matrix occur at the top of the section.

BSPM

At the western end of a nearby pit [7506 7038] the section was:

	Thickness m
MADE GROUND	0.8
GLACIAL SAND AND GRAVEL	
Gravel, medium to coarse, fawn, locally stained reddish brown, angular to subrounded, in a medium- to coarse-grained sand matrix, locally clayey; the gravel contains chalk pebbles and silt-grade chalk; irregular base	2.3
Sand, medium-grained, fawn, horizontally bedded	0.5
Sand, medium-grained, locally clayey, pale fawn, locally slightly reddened; clay bands up to 4 mm thick; sparsely scattered flints and small chalk pebbles; at 1.1 m from the top, a rippled horizon is capped by 2 to 4 mm of reddish sandy clay; clay pellets at 0.4 m above base, with thin (c.30 mm) coarsening-upward cycles below; iron staining in	

basal 0.3 m; thin ironpan at base	1.9
Sand, fine-grained, and interlaminated silt, grey and purplish grey, micaceous; thin ironpan at base	0.3
Sand, fine- to medium-grained, fawn; lenses of purplish coarse silt and fine-grained sand, randomly iron stained, horizontally bedded	1.4
Sand, fine-grained, with chalk blocks and pellets	1.0

Gravel underlying till-like material in a trench [7515 7028] in the pit (see p.50) consists of up to 1.5 m of unbedded, poorly sorted, angular flint gravel in a medium- to coarse-grained, locally clayey, sand matrix. It is underlain by fine- to medium-grained, bedded sand with thin (c.0.1 m) beds of silty clayey sand, at the base of which is a red and grey mottled silty clay with scattered flints, overlying unsorted flint gravel with red clay stringers throughout.

TEL

Small outcrops of Glacial Sand and Gravel emerge from beneath Boulder Clay along the valley sides of the River Kennett near Dalham and Ousden. Most have been worked for sand and gravel [7150 5979; 7050 6165; 7315 6118]. In one pit [7338 6167], 5 m of sand and gravel are overlain by thin Boulder Clay. The gravel is bedded, chalky and poorly sorted, and ranges from large, slightly worn flint cobbles, to fine, angular flint gravel in a matrix of medium- to coarse-grained sand.

A poorly exposed section near Denham [750 630] showed 2.5 m of extremely poorly sorted flint gravel and chalky sands. The gravel, locally decalcified, contains cobble-sized, slightly worn, nodular flints; Boulder Clay occurs at the top of the section. At Heath Farm [755 667], near Higham, a sandy flint gravel, locally containing abundant purple-red quartzites, caps the hill.

A gravel pit [789 692] south-east of Hall Heath exposed an extremely variable sequence of Glacial Sand and Gravel 'draped' over an irregular Chalk surface, with the bedding in the sand and gravel paralleling this surface. Several 'lows' in the gravel were filled with laminated silts and silty clays showing that the dips in the gravels are original and not due to solution of the Chalk. Some gravel contains about 50 per cent rounded, red and white quartzites; the rest consists of angular and subangular flints. About 125 m to the east, a trial pit [8017 6889] proved 0.7 m of fine-grained sand with coarse silt lenses under 3 m of made ground and Boulder Clay. Still farther east, another trial pit [8198 6838] proved:

	Depth m
Soil, Cover Sand and Boulder Clay	1.15
Sand, fine-grained, orange-buff, no bedding, with scattered angular flints	1.90
Gravel, with round and angular flints generally less than 5 cm in diameter	2.15
Sand, flinty, orange	3.30

Small pits [8100 6953; 8160 6805; 8155 6898] south of Flempton provide sections of some 5 m ranging from unbedded coarse flint gravel with clasts up to 0.6 m across, to bedded orange sand resting on Chalk. Funnell (1955) recorded about 1 m of micaceous grey loam below 6 m of 'alternating sand or loam, and gravel' from a section [810 683] in the now landscaped western part of one pit.

Thin patches [815 653; 825 652] of gravelly sand occur adjacent to the A45 north of Westley. Up to 2.4 m of pebbly sand and gravel have been proved [8102 6551], but its relationship to the chalky Boulder Clay is obscure. A little to the south, however, sand and gravel crops out from beneath the Boulder Clay on the hillsides north, east, and south-east of Little Horringer Hall [818 639], although a well at the Hall entered Chalk directly beneath Boulder Clay.

West and south-west of Horringer Court, there are several overgrown gravel pits [8360 6285; 8355 6270; 8350 6275] which bottomed in Chalk. A well [8363 6318] north-west of Horringer Court proved 12.2 m of sand and gravel on Chalk.

East of the Lark, gravel has been worked extensively at Fornham Park, Fornham St Genevieve. An old face [8405 6867] was cut through 5 m of boulder clay and intercalated gravel into 2.6 m of Glacial Sand and Gravel. The latter is bedded, with angular, subangular, and subrounded flints and rather less common round red quartzites, set in a sandy matrix. Another section [8438 6844] showed 2 m of gravel, consisting mainly of medium pebbles containing about 50 per cent red quartzites and 50 per cent flints, in a medium- to coarse-grained sand matrix; orange sand underlies the gravel. A third section [8440 6836] exposes about 4 m of Boulder Clay overlying 4.5 m of medium- to fine-grained sand with some gravel bands. Silt and clay beds up to 5 cm thick occur in the lowest 1.5 m. Slump structures in the sand are truncated by Boulder Clay.

BSPM

Timworth – Fornham St Martin – Great Barton

Over much of this area Boulder Clay rests directly on Chalk, though sand and gravel, up to 15 m thick, occur at depth south-west of Timworth and are presumably in continuity with those exposed in the pits at Fornham Park, though the relationship of many of the deposits to the Boulder Clay is uncertain. However, a borehole [8823 6931] near Cage Grove proved 8.9+ m of dominantly sand with a 0.5 m bed of boulder clay in it middle, and another [8869 6865] proved 6.7 m dominantly of sand which rests on chalky Boulder Clay and is overlain by a further thin boulder clay.

Boreholes farther south generally prove chalky Boulder Clay on Chalk, though near Great Barton [8886 6795; 8959 6622; 8968 6662] up to 7 m of Glacial Sand and Gravel have been proved.

Glacial Sand and Gravel emerges from beneath Boulder Clay south-west of Moreton Hall. Closely spaced boreholes between here and the old airfield have allowed the northern limit of the sand and gravel beneath Boulder Clay to be followed as far as Eldohouse Farm [88 64]; south of this line up to 4.8 m of somewhat clayey sand and gravel are present.

Nowton to Bradfield Combust

Except for 6.09 m of 'sand and gravel' in a well [8789 5793] south-west of Cocks Green (which may include some Crag), there is no Lower Glacial Sand and Gravel preserved between Chedburgh and Bradfield Combust. To the north, at Low Green, thicknesses of 22 m, 7.6 m and 42 m [8635 6125; 8660 6102; 8677 6115] of Glacial Sand and Gravel have been proved, but at the first and last localities these are possibly associated with the buried valley of the Lark. Farther to the north-north-west, 6.4 m of sandy and chalky gravel lie beneath Head and (?interglacial) silt [8618 6193]. Glacial Sand and Gravel crops out north and south of this last locality. An old pit [860 617] west-north-west of Nowton Court, now backfilled, formerly exposed a very coarse, reddish brown gravel consisting mostly of flints, above a buff, white or yellow sand interbedded with gravel and layers of laminated clay; the sand was not bottomed at a depth of 7.2 m (Bennett and Blake, 1886, p.9). The old Southgate brickyard [8615 6275] is about 5 m deep, and poor sections of coarse, nodular, poorly sorted, flint gravels are all that are now visible. Bennett and Blake (1886, fig. 1) show that the Glacial Sand and Gravel occurs within Boulder Clay. A well [8620 6271] at the brickyard proved 6.1 m of gravel and sand resting on Chalk.

A well [8553 6212] at Home Farm just south-west of an overgrown gravel pit, proved: boulder clay, 11.89 m; loamy ballast, 5.97 m; brown sand, 1.52 m; 'brown clay', 7.93 m; on Chalk. To the north, a well [8543 6289] proved: loam and gravel with large flints at the base, 2.74 m; white clay, 0.92 m; loam, 0.91 m; on Chalk. Boreholes at the Hospital [850 627], west of Hardwick

Heath, proved between 3 and 8 m of sand and gravel, overlain by Boulder Clay at the southern end of the site. In many of the boreholes 0.6 to 4.9 m of brown sandy silty clay with flint and chalk pebbles lie beneath the sand and gravel.

Thurston to Gedding

There are scarcely any exposures of the deposit in this tract. A few small patches of flinty sand and gravel, too small to map, crop out north of Green Farm [around 891 623]. Another patch has been worked in a small pit [8923 6213] and consists of well-rounded quartz, quartzite and 'Bunter' pebbles with only a minor proportion of flints; it may be Kesgrave Sands and Gravels.

In the extreme south-east, the Lower Glacial Sand and Gravel is generally absent, but up to 9 m have been recorded from scattered boreholes. Eastwards from Hessett, Glacial Sand and Gravel is more continuous at depth. Thicknesses of 5.48 m, 3.35 m and 2.44 m are recorded at Hessett [9349 6111; 9380 6100; 9377 6099 respectively]; 2.44 m were encountered in Drinkstone Park [9495 6167], and at Drinkstone Green 10.51 m, 4.58 m, 4.26 m and 2.14 m have been proved [9528 6053; 9587 6058; 9586 6049; 9600 6043 respectively]. At Clopton Green, 8.53 m of gravel and silt occur between the chalky Boulder Clay and the Crag [9805 6018].

Rose and others (1976, fig. 1) recorded Kesgrave Sands and Gravels, with a rubified palaeosol at the top, in a gravel pit [957 628] at Tostock, overlain by a thin bed of loess, which in turn is covered by the Barham Sands and Gravels. Sections seen during 1977 and 1978 showed no Kesgrave Sands and Gravels; all exposures beneath the Boulder Clay were in coarse poorly sorted gravel with thin interbeds of medium-grained sand.

South and east of Woolpit, Glacial Sand and Gravel is absent. North of Woolpit, a borehole [9726 6304] proved 5.9 m of sandy gravel or gravelly sand, locally clayey, between Boulder Clay and Crag. There are poor exposures [948 655] of fine-grained yellow sand with rounded 'Bunter' quartzites and subangular flints overlying the Chalk east of Great Green.

Glacial Sand and Gravel rises through Boulder Clay at Great Green where a well [9413 6550] started in sand and gravel and proved 3.05 m of it before encountering Chalk. Possibly the same is true of a small spread of sand and gravel [944 658] north-east of the well, although it may belong to the Upper Glacial Sand and Gravel. Clearly the deposits are patchy, for a borehole at Green Farm [9361 6549] proved 2.9 m of sand, sandy clay and sandy gravel between Boulder Clay and Chalk, but these are absent at outcrop only 250 m west. About 1 km north-west of the farm, a very gravelly deposit of limited extent, which was formerly worked for sand and gravel, crops out from beneath the Boulder Clay [926 662]. Small patches of Glacial Sand and Gravel also occur south-east of Pakenham [928 669; 930 671]. The first of these patches is dominantly sandy; the second is very gravelly and was dug in the past. Patches of sand and gravel, surrounded by and presumably rising through Boulder Clay, occur south-east of the church, and up to 4 m of sand rest on Chalk in two boreholes [9240 6808; 9437 6645]. Considerable thicknesses of sand and gravel, with some interbedded boulder clay, are associated with the buried valley of The Black Bourn: at Street Farm, Norton [9573 6556], 46.4 m of 'shingle and ballast' are present beneath Boulder Clay; at Little Haugh Hall [9530 6680], 40.5 m of sand and gravel, mainly gravelly in the upper part, and sandy in the lower part, were recorded; at Bull Bridge [9474 6787], 12.6 m of sand were proved; at Watermill Farm [9372 6948], Pakenham, 40.54 m of sand and gravel appears to have a higher gravel content than the other deposits. In contrast, a borehole at Old Hall Farm [9283 6884], west of Pakenham Fen, proved only 3.93 m of dominantly flint gravel beneath 84.36 m of Boulder Clay.

Stowlangtoft to Elmswell

South-east of Elmswell New Hall, a borehole [9781 6363] encountered 1.7 m of pebbly sand at a depth of 22.8 m, where it rested on Chalk. To the north-east, another borehole [9824 6436] proved 2.7 m of sand and gravel beneath Boulder Clay, and resting on Crag.

Glacial Sand and Gravel crops out in a shallow valley [969 647] north-west of Norton Wood. A nearby borehole [9676 6489] suggests that it rests on Crag. Scattered boreholes east of Norton show the following thicknesses of Glacial Sand and Gravel beneath Boulder Clay: 3.05 m [9702 6612]; 6.71 m [9759 6647]; 1.22 m [9807 6650]; 11.67 m [9800 6699]. As elsewhere these appear to be local patches, for other boreholes [9826 6671; 9587 6680] have entered Chalk directly beneath Boulder Clay.

At Stowlangtoft [96 68], there is a wide spread of sand and gravel, locally very gravelly, beneath Boulder Clay. The more gravelly parts are in the west where they have been exploited in a number of pits. Boreholes [9542 6798; 9617 6823; 9627 6804] have proved only 2 to 3 m of the deposit.

Langham to Stanton

No Glacial Sand and Gravel has been recorded beneath the plateau at Langham. East of Stanton there are three small spreads of sand and gravel [980 728; 9800 7365; 979 740]. The first consists dominantly of fine-grained sand and may overlie Boulder Clay; the second also contains much sand and is locally very chalky; the third is certainly an inlier of Lower Glacial Sand and Gravel, for old gravel pits [9782 7432; 9783 7427] expose Chalk beneath chalky sand, clayey sand and gravel, and sand and gravel.   CRB

BOULDER CLAY (TILL)

Over the whole of the district, the known occurrences of Boulder Clay form part of the widespread expanse of Chalky Boulder Clay (Harmer, 1902) (till) of Anglian age that covers much of East Anglia. It crops out extensively in the south and east of the district where it variously overlies Chalk, Crag, Kesgrave Sands and Gravels, and Lower Glacial Sand and Gravel (Plate 4). In general, the name Lowestoft Till has been applied to it in recent years, although various authors (e.g. West and Donner, 1956; Straw, 1979) claim to have found evidence of a younger, Gipping Till (see p.36, and Bristow and Cox, 1973).

East of the district, Clarke and Auton (1982) identified and plotted the occurrence of a brown sandy till beneath the chalky Boulder Clay. This sandy till, the Starston Till of Lawson (1982), contains erratic pebbles of vein-quartz and quartzite, subordinate amounts of angular flint, igneous and metamorphic rocks, and minor amounts of fine-grained, well-rounded chalk. The Starston Till has not been recognised within the district.

The Boulder Clay of the plateau area in the south has in general an almost planar base which descends gently eastwards and north-eastwards from a high of 90 m above OD in the Ashley [70 62] and Ousden [74 61] areas, to c.40 m in the extreme east [98 57], though it lies at c.30 m near Flempton [80 70] in the centre of the district. Along the eastern margin of the district the base gently undulates at about 40 m above OD, with local highs of around 60 m above OD, e.g. near Stowlangtoft [965 694]. Locally the base is interrupted where the Boulder Clay falls sharply into steep-sided, drift-filled channels. Many of these are followed by present-day rivers such as the Lark and The Black Bourn, but others, including the deepest, which passes east–west south of Troston [910 715], have no topographical expression. Within the plateau area there are several anomalous local 'highs' in the base of the Boulder Clay. For example, south of Horringer, a borehole [8180 6000] in Lady Katherine's Wood proved only 7.9 m of Boulder Clay resting on Chalk at 87.5 m above OD, whereas only 330 m to the south another borehole [8186 5973] proved 45.1 m of Boulder Clay, the base of which lies at 50 m above OD—a height similar to that proved in other nearby boreholes.

Outside the drift-filled channels, the thickest occurrences of Boulder Clay are on the plateau in the south. An area of consistently thick Boulder Clay lies south and east of Chedburgh [80 57] where thicknesses in excess of 50 m have been proved in several boreholes. In general, the Boulder Clay thins from the interfluves towards the valley sides, except where the valleys follow the courses of drift-filled channels. It is difficult to detect any regular variation in the thickness of the till sheet: this reflects not only the original thickness, but also the degree of erosion since its deposition. Certainly there is no regular eastward and southward thickening of the till in the Woolpit area as implied by the computer-generated isopachyte map of Clarke (1983, Map, diagram C).

The Boulder Clay consists of a stiff, bluish grey, chalky and flinty clay that weathers to a yellowish brown clay. In addition to chalk and flint, the erratic pebbles include vein-quartz, 'Bunter' quartzite, Jurassic limestone, mudstone, cementstone and fossils. Locally [e.g. 9801 6868], soft waterlogged chalky clay has been encountered within very stiff, grey, chalky clay. Beds of sand up to 3.6 m thick also occur within the Boulder Clay, particularly in the south-east. Within the drift-filled channels, silt is associated with the Boulder Clay. Locally [868 660; 890 860; 878 685], silt occurs within, or on Boulder Clay outside the channel: at the first of these localities, silt forms a basal unit to the Boulder Clay.

The lithology and mineralogy of the chalky Boulder Clay has been examined by Perrin and others (1973). They found that the Boulder Clay is remarkably uniform from Lincolnshire to Hertfordshire, although there are minor differences in the fine-grained sand and silt fractions between the extreme north and south of this region. The calcium carbonate content increases southwards from 23 to 43 per cent, and this is thought to be due to the incorporation of increasing quantities of Chalk by ice moving generally southward. The heavy mineral suite (2.5 per cent by weight in the 105–63 µm fraction) shows no regional variation; the heavy minerals suggest the North Sea region as a possible source area. The clay mineralogy also shows no significant differences, the assemblages being of mica and kaolinite, with variable smectite and, locally, a little chlorite. This uniformity makes it impossible to determine which of the local clays in the Jurassic and Cretaceous are the dominant source of the clay minerals. Stone-counts show Chalk to be dominant (56 to 84 per cent), with flints and 'others' (mostly Jurassic) in roughly equal proportions: far-travelled 'exotics' form only 0.1 per cent of the total count. The uniformity of all these aspects of the chalky Boulder Clay led Perrin and others (1973) to conclude that it was the product of one glaciation, thus supporting the earlier views of Bristow and Cox (1973).

There is no conclusive date for the deposition of the Boulder Clay. Within the Bury St Edmunds district it is overlain by Hoxnian deposits at Sicklesmere (West, 1981) and Icklingham (Kerney, 1976; Holyoak and others, 1983), but nowhere does it overlie reliably dated deposits. Since the oldest deposits resting on it are Hoxnian, it is assumed to have formed in an immediately preceding cold stage.

Gregory (1922, reproduced in Boswell, 1929) recorded Pleistocene foraminifera from Boulder Clay at Sudbury, and concluded that the Boulder Clay had formed by the melting of ice in sea-water. More probably, however, the foraminifera were scooped up from the bed of the North Sea. The fauna is not diagnostic.

Details

Mildenhall to Fornham

Much of this tract lies beyond the limit of the Boulder Clay plateau, and outcrops are few and small. One such patch is at the old Mildenhall brickyard [7165 7515], where Boulder Clay overlies Chalk and underlies terrace gravels; its relationship to the nearby Glacial Silt ('Brickearth') is not now clear. However, Skertchly (*in* Whitaker and others, 1891) described a section in which Boulder Clay overlay brick-clay containing flint implements and flakes. Wells and boreholes nearby record up to 18.5 m of 'clay' and 'white clay', which could be chalky till, Glacial Silt, or even Chalk beneath the terrace deposits.

At High Lodge (formerly Warren Hill), about 3 km east-north-east of Mildenhall, several pits have been worked for brickearth. These pits [7390 7538], now overgrown, have long been of interest on account of the flint implements found in them. Skertchly (*in* Whitaker and others, 1891) recorded the following section:

	Thickness m
Sand	0.61
Boulder Clay	1.22
Coarse chalky flint gravel	1.83
Mottled red and blue clay with worked flints	1.52
Boulder Clay seen to	0.61

The upper and lower boulder clays coalesce towards one end of the section; the lower one rests on Chalk. *Cervus* and *Elephas* occur within the clays. The sections were re-excavated in 1965 by G de G Sieveking of the British Museum. In general, the excavations confirm the description given by Skertchly. Holmes (1971), who mapped the High Lodge area and examined Sieveking's excavations, considered that there were two boulder clays at High Lodge; a lower Boulder Clay which has been worked in a now overgrown pit [7405 7535] just south of High Lodge, and a second, younger Boulder Clay cropping out [7391 7546] north-west of the older one. Augering into the lower Boulder Clay at the eastern end of the pit proved buff to greyish buff chalky silty clay, similar to the descriptions of the upper Boulder Clay. In the 1965 excavations up to 1.5 m of the upper Boulder Clay were exposed. A section [7310 7413] noted by Mr S C A Holmes in the cut-off channel east of Barton Mills revealed rather silty, stiff, grey stoneless clay. This was correlated by Holmes (1971) with the younger Boulder Clay at High Lodge. The significance of the faunas and artifacts, and their relationship to undoubted Anglian till, is far from clear.   BSPM

A small isolated patch of chalky and sandy Boulder Clay [7825

7414] occurs north-north-east of Icklingham. On aerial photographs, the Boulder Clay can be distinguished from the surrounding Chalk by the different types of patterned ground it produces.

A low-lying terrace-like feature [782 721] south-east of Icklingham is underlain by Boulder Clay. Another small patch of chalky Boulder Clay [7864 7185], south of Weatherhill Farm, was probably worked for clay in Roman times as there are several sites of Roman kilns nearby [786 719]. Some 2 m of brown, fawn and grey mottled, chalky silty clay were exposed at the top of an old sand and gravel pit [7908 7199] east of Weatherhill Farm, and 9.1 m of brickearth were recorded in a well at the site of an adjacent old kiln [7928 7204]. It is probable that the brickearth is underlain by till by till which fills a small channel. TEL

West of Ingham, there is a large outlier of chalky Boulder Clay. Despite a variable cover of locally gravelly sand, Boulder Clay can generally be augered in the deeper ditches and has been dug from a number of pits. West of Ingham Farm, two boreholes [8490 7032; 8493 7044] proved 3 and 5 m respectively of Boulder Clay on the valley side, but this increases to 26.5 m, beneath the Glacial Silt, in the valley bottom [8483 7003]. BSPM, CRB

Boreholes near Ingham, which commenced in Upper Glacial Sand and Gravel, proved thicknesses of 14.8 m, 10.6 m and 14.8 m of Boulder Clay [8579 7081; 8552 7047; 8551 7084]. Closer to the valley, the Boulder Clay is at least 45.7 m thick [8643 7018], and clearly fills a channel. In Ingham gravel pit [8525 7155], two boulder clays, separated by a cobble gravel, have been noted; the lower varies from 0.7 to 1.8 m, and the upper is at least 4 m thick. TEL, CRB

A borehole [8309 6981] at Dixon's Covert, West Stow, proved 4 m of Boulder Clay beneath River Terrace Deposits. Boulder Clay was also seen in the bottom of a disused gravel pit [8330 6840] 300 m north of Ducksluice Farm, and there are extensive sections of Boulder Clay in gravel workings, now backfilled and landscaped, at Fornham Park. In the south face [8440 6823], approximately 3.5 m of buff flinty chalky clay were seen above Glacial Sand and Gravel (Plate 4). The basal 20 cm of the Boulder Clay consists of laminated, slightly chalky, buff clay with scattered flint pebbles, grading downwards to a laminated sandy buff silt without chalk; the number of flint pebbles increases downwards. Locally, up to 10 cm of calcrete are present at the subhorizontal base of the Boulder Clay.

Another pit [8405 6867], farther north, showed:

	Thickness m
Cover Sand, involuted into Boulder Clay	1.0
Boulder Clay	
Clay, buff, silty, flinty, passing gradationally downwards into fine, medium and coarse gravel, with mainly subangular flint pebbles and abundant rounded quartzites	3.5
Clay, silty, laminated, with scattered flints and quartzites; locally silts and clays are channelled into lower silts	0.5
Glacial Sand and Gravel	2.6

Honington to Bury St Edmunds

Boulder Clay crops out widely over the whole of this area, though with a partial cover of fine-grained sand. North of Bury St Edmunds, except towards the buried channel in the north and near Fornham St Martin, it does not appear to exceed 5 m. It reaches a maximum thickness (outside the buried channel) of 27 m at Conyer's Green [8886 6795].

North of Westfield Farm, the basal part of the Boulder Clay [around 868 660] consists of yellow, grey and brown silt and silty clay. Similar silt, but higher in the sequence, occurs at two localities [880 659; 890 660] south-west and south of Great Barton. A borehole [8898 6589] proved 5.8 m of silt at this latter locality, lying beneath 1.6 m of Cover Sand, and resting on 2 m of chalky Boulder Clay. Khaki silt, presumably at the same level, were also augered beneath Cover Sand at a third locality [8870 6564], but its extent beneath the Cover Sand is unknown. Another borehole [8993 6527] proved 0.2 m of brownish cream laminated silt lying beneath (Upper) Glacial Sand and Gravel and resting on 1.1 m of chalky Boulder Clay.

A well at Barton Stud [8761 6628] proved 2.1 m of gravel in the upper part of the Boulder Clay. Similar interdigitations of sand and gravel and Boulder Clay were proved in two boreholes north [8823 6931] and south [8869 6865] of Livermere Thicks (Hawkins, 1981). The Boulder Clay on the plateau at Fox Spinney, near Great Livermere, varies from 7.9 m [8708 6946] to 39.7 m [8963 7038] in thickness. CRB

Farther north and east, chalky Boulder Clay is 40.8 m thick at Heath Farm [9069 7090] and 32.3 m at Troston Hall [9018 7181]. A third borehole [9092 7127] between these two proved 102.7 m of Boulder Clay, with some sand and gravel, resting on Chalk at 57.5 m below OD. This is the thickest known Boulder Clay within the district.

East of Troston, a borehole [9027 7232] penetrated 28.5 m of Boulder Clay above gravel, though the deposit thins towards the valley sides. Near Honington Airfield, a borehole [8942 7473] on the plateau margin proved 13.4 m of Boulder Clay, and the thickness increases towards the valley of The Black Bourn to 29.8 m [9121 7372]. CRB, TEL

West of The Black Bourn at Ixworth [around 930 695], the Boulder Clay, at least in part, occupies a steep-sided channel. The best evidence for the channel is provided by a well [9372 6948] at Grimstone End where, beneath 4 m of terrace gravels, thick beds of clay alternate with thinner beds of sand and gravel to a depth of 35.4 m, below which occur 40 m of sand and gravel resting on Chalk (see p.41). A borehole [9283 6884] in an adjacent drift-filled channel at Old Hall proved the following much thicker sequence: 84.4 m of chalky clay overlying 3.9 m of gravel, which in turn rests on Chalk. The Boulder Clay contains beds of gravel and sand, especially in the lower part (below 53.7 m), but because of poor recovery their exact thicknesses are unknown. This channel is continuous with the one south of Pakenham Fen at Maulkin's Hall (see p.41). CRB

Sapiston to Langham

North, east and south of Stanton, thick Boulder Clay forms a generally monotonous, featureless plateau. West of Stanton, however, the outcrop is broken into small disconnected patches. Over much of this area, this Boulder Clay is a stiff bluish grey clay up to within 1 m of the surface. Locally, there are thin patches, or 'gaults', of Cover Sand resting on, or let into the chalky Boulder Clay. The latter is generally less than 15 m thick, but two wells north of Hepworth prove thicknesses of 30 and 50 m respectively [9788 7597; 9815 7548]. This thickening is associated with a channel which extends from near Bardwell Mill [936 743] through Stanton Chare [956 742] and thence to Thelnetham [TM 020 780].

North-east of Stanton, the base of the Boulder Clay locally undulates, for there are inliers of both Glacial Sand and Gravel and Chalk on the plateau [978 743]. West of the Stanton, the distribution of the Boulder Clay is even more irregular. North of Fir Wood, it forms small pockets, 20 to 400 m across, overlying Glacial Sand and Gravel or Chalk [around 957 734]. It thickens rapidly northwards, and its base falls into the buried valley north-east of Woodstreet Farm. The Boulder Clay in this buried valley is of two types. In a borehole [9605 7074] north-east of the farm, 12 m of brown silty and chalky clay overlies 7.5 m of soft chalky buff clay,

Barton Mills to Cavenham

which in turn overlies Chalk. Another borehole [9542 7076] to the west proved 6 m of very stiff, bluish grey, chalky clay before passing into soft, less chalky, silty clay and stiff bluish grey chalky clay to 19 m depth, on the Chalk (see also p.51).   CRB

Barton Mills to Cavenham

Very little Boulder Clay is preserved in this tract. A road cutting at Chalk Hill [7095 7212] revealed 2 m of chalky, olive-brown, silty clay presumed to be Boulder Clay. Lower in the cutting, buff sands are present, but their junction with the Boulder Clay is not visible. Slightly farther east, a section [7105 7210] showed a poorly laminated sequence of clays, silts and poorly sorted fine-grained sands, with scattered flints, in a depression in sand and gravel.

A strip of Boulder Clay [7120 7060] south of Park Farm occupies an east–west channel cut in Chalk. The Boulder Clay, which is silty near the surface, is mostly hidden by Cover Sand less than 1 m thick, and has been dug in three pits that are now overgrown [7118 7048; 7145 7063; 7210 7070].

A borehole [7130 7051] SSE of Park Farm, proved:

	Depth m
Soil and sand	1.5
Clay, sandy, silty, chalky, flinty, brown	6.1
Clay, becoming grey, chalky, with few flints	9.7
Clay, becoming pale grey	10.7
Clay, less grey, more buff	11.0
Chalk, soft, possibly redeposited	11.5

At the eastern end of the outcrop, a trial pit [7200 7084] revealed:

	Depth m
Soil	0.3
Clay, silty, chalky, with pockets of fine-grained, clayey, reddish buff sand	0.5–1.3
Clay, rather silty, chalky, with several red chalk pebbles and limestone blocks containing bivalves; becoming increasingly chalky downwards	1.6
Gravel, passing down into chalk gravel with silt matrix; includes an extremely hard band of septarian nodules and large nodular flints	2.7
Silt, buff, laminated, with stringers of chalky gravel at 3.4 m; rather sharp but irregular base	3.5
Clay, silty, chalky, seen to	3.6

Similar silts occur in a trial pit [7206 7074] south-east of Manor Farm, in a borehole close by [7198 7088], in a trial pit [7106 7027] excavated through Second River Terrace Deposits south of the farm, and in another [7137 7031] a little to the east.

A north-east–south-west string of small outcrops of Boulder Clay, ranging from about 43 m above OD in the south-west to 30 m above OD in the north-east, occurs between Kentford and Cavenham. At the surface, the Boulder Clay varies from a brown clay to a chalky, very silty, buff clay. Skertchly (*in* Whitaker and others, 1891) described a pit [probably 7388 6892] in which 'Boulder Clay' has now worked up a loam, contorting it, dragging it from its original position, and so influencing it that in places it is difficult to know whether to call the material 'Boulder Clay made up of loam or loam mixed up with Boulder Clay'.   BSPM

Just to the north, a thin (0.4 to 2 m) bed of compact, pale grey-buff/khaki, silty clay containing unsorted, well-rounded chalk clasts, angular flints, and red chalk and cementstone erratics was proved in an old sand and gravel pit [7516 7028] west-north-west of Cavenham Church. This Boulder Clay lies between gravels and is markedly lenticular, thinning both south and west. The base of the till capping the hill at Bunker's Barn [7738 7019] plunges westwards to the valley floor.   TEL

Ashley to Bury St Edmunds

The bulk of this area makes up the western part of the plateau, beneath which the chalky Boulder Clay is between 20 and 40 m thick around Barrow, while in the extreme south at Chedburgh a well [7896 5749] has proved 58.2 m of Boulder Clay. The sheet thins out and becomes silty around its margin [7828 6832] as at Risby Poor's Heath.

In this same general peripheral area, a trial pit [8013 6891] at Brakey Pin proved a Cover Sand involution to 1.4 m, on 2 m of Boulder Clay; there are similar provings nearby [8188 6899; 8198 6838].

The base of the plateau Boulder Clay, though broadly falling north-eastwards from 80 to 90 m at Ashley to 30 to 40 m at Flempton, is modified by channels. Thus between Gazeley and Dalham, a tongue of Boulder Clay fills a channel that extends northwards from the plateau; only the upper part of the channel contains Boulder Clay, the lower part being filled by Glacial Silt. Apart from such anomalies, the base of the Boulder Clay clearly undulates. East of Dalham, it rises to a high of about 100 m above OD, but drops sharply southwards as shown by a well [7420 5958] at Ousden, which proved 36.6 m of Boulder Clay on Chalk at 77 m above OD. A sub-Boulder Clay ridge extends eastwards from Dalham, through Great Saxham [78 62] and Ickworth Park [81 61]; the base drops gently on both sides of the ridge.

To the east, another anomaly is provided by a well [8081 6306] north of Dairy Wood, Little Saxham, which proved 59 m of 'drift' (probably Boulder Clay), though Chalk crops out within about 100 m of the well.

In Bury St Edmunds, two wells at the Barracks are said to have penetrated 1.2 and 18.3 m of Boulder Clay, but an exposure nearby in laminated silt and fine-grained sand suggests that the wells were sunk into Glacial Silt (see p.57). Farther west, Baden Powell and Oakley (1952) have described an intimate relationship between 'brickearth' and Boulder Clay about 1 km west of Westley, and the same may be true at Bury St Edmunds.   BSPM

Hawstead to Bradfield Combust

In this plateau area the Boulder Clay is usually chalky to within 0.5 m of the surface where it is buff or yellowish. Some of the thickest occurrences of Boulder Clay, outside buried channels, have been recorded in the area. At Rede Hall, a well [8059 5772] passed through 56.2 m of Boulder Clay before entering Chalk. Near Hawstead, 57.3 m were recorded in wells [8630 5983; 8599 5661] at the Hall and just beyond the southern margin of the district. Thick Boulder Clay has also been recorded in a well [8789 5793] south of Great Welnetham Church, where 47.2 m were penetrated. An extremely thick occurrence (91 m) at Hawstead House, between the above two wells, is thought to be related to the buried channel of the River Lark.

North of Hawstead Hall, the chalky Boulder Clay thins towards its feather edge. There is no regular northward thinning, for thicknesses of 42.6 m [8633 6126] and 38.1 m [8697 6155] at Low Green, Nowton, are associated with buried valleys. Similar thinning occurs to less than 6 m [8749 5995] on the southern margin of the Lark valley, and to 9 m [8956 5732] at the Hall, Bradfield Combust.

Rushbrooke to Pakenham

Near Rushbrooke, Boulder Clay reaches a maximum thickness of 30.2 m [8912 6112] and thins towards the valleys. Its base is undulating, and there are small inliers of Glacial Sand and Gravel [around 884 606]. Eastwards towards Link Wood [around 897 607], the Boulder Clay is very sandy at the surface and is not chalky.

Near Rougham Green, the Boulder Clay varies in thickness from 11.6 m [9080 6175] to 30.5 m [9006 6140] over a distance of only 170 m. There is commonly a surface cover of up to 1.2 m of fine-grained sand.

A borehole [9121 6133] south-east of the village proved 18.5 m of silty clay, with 1 m of chalky gravel and 3.2 m of thick grey laminated silt in the lower part. Thin beds of silt within a silty clay sequence were also noted between depths of 1 and 9 m in a borehole [9282 6324] west of Beyton. There, chalky Boulder Clay overlies 6.3 m of pebbly clayey sand, which in turn overlies 3 m of sandy clay regarded as a 'lower boulder clay'. Over 20 m of Boulder Clay in another borehole [9352 6296], south of Beyton, was also dominantly silty with only minor amounts of chalk and flint.

Chalky silt was augered in a ditch [9408 6311] south-east of Beyton, and was also noted at the bottom of a cutting [9390 6355] for the Beyton By-pass where it underlay 2 to 3 m of chalky till, with 1 m of clayey sand and fine gravel at the base. A borehole close by [9390 6357] proved 0.8 m of laminated silty clay between depths of 2 and 2.8 m; in this borehole, more than 4.2 m of Boulder Clay occurred below the silty clay.

Farther north-east, near Great Green, the base of the Boulder Clay is again undulating. A small patch of sand and gravel [943 658] to the south-east may rise through Boulder Clay, as a well nearby [9413 6550] started, according to its log, in sand and gravel, resting on Chalk, even though chalky till was augered nearby.

Small patches of gravel [around 933 666], south-east of Pakenham, are also inliers of Lower Glacial Sand and Gravel. The Boulder Clay hereabouts locally fills deep, steep-sided channels. At Maulkin's Hall, a little to the north-west, a well [9368 6807] proved 59.7 m of Boulder Clay above Chalk, though the latter crops out only 100 m to the west and 150 m to the north-east. West of Pakenham Fen, this drift-filled channel continues near Old Hall [928 689] (see p.41).

Close to Grimstone End, the Boulder Clay occupies a channel associated with the present course of The Black Bourn. A borehole [9377 6873] here proved more than 18.7 m of chalky clay, with 0.7 m of gravel towards the top of the deposit.

East of Maulkin's Hall, another borehole [9497 6787] passed through First River Terrace Deposits into 6 m of Boulder Clay, and then into more than 13.6 m of channel-fill sand.

Tostock to Felsham

This area is one of extensive plateau Boulder Clay which is thickest in the south-east at Gedding [9481 5788], where up to 42.7 m have been recorded. Eastwards from Hessett it contains interbedded sands and gravels, the number and thickness of which increase eastwards.

Around Bradfield St Clare and Bradfield St George, the Boulder Clay varies in thickness from about 27 to 38 m. An old brick pit [9130 6005] at Bradfield St George apparently worked a 'brown loam', 1.2 m thick, above Boulder Clay (Blake *in* Whitaker and others, 1881). Chalky silt was noted to a depth of 1.2 m in a ditch [9148 6003] east of the pit, though elsewhere around the pit it appears to be absent. A well close by [9137 6013] proved 38.1 m of Boulder Clay (this includes 1.5 m of grey sand between 22.6 and 24.1 m).

In the south, around Felsham and Gedding, the Boulder Clay varies in thickness from 22 to 42.7 m, whilst just beyond the district, a thickness of 48.8 m has been recorded [9359 5647]. Around Rattlesden, Drinkstone Green and Hessett, the Boulder Clay is somewhat thinner. On the plateau it varies from 21 to 30 m in thickness; the stream near Rattlesden has cut through it.

Thin sands and gravels appear in the upper part of the till-sheet near Hessett. A well [9359 6189], close to Hessett Church, proved 0.6 m of sand in the upper part of the Boulder Clay, and a borehole [9421 6153] to the south-east, which commenced in Upper Glacial Sand and Gravel, proved in descending sequence below this: silty clay, 0.7 m; pebbly sand, 0.7 m; silty clay and silt, 2.8 m; sandy gravel, 6.9 m; silty clay, 1.1 m; chalky gravel, 0.5 m; silty clay, 3.5+ m.

East of Hessett, significant beds of sand and gravel also occur within Boulder Clay; some of these have been classified as Upper Glacial Sand and Gravel, but may be lenses within Boulder Clay. Thus a borehole [9522 6176] just south of The Moat, Drinkstone, proved the following descending sequence: topsoil and sandy clay, 2.2 m; boulder clay, 3 m; gravel, 0.2 m; boulder clay, 1.3 m; clayey gravel, 2.1 m; boulder clay, 9.4 m; clayey gravel, 0.3 m; boulder clay 2.5+ m. A somewhat different sequence was noted in another borehole [9523 6261] a little to the north: silty sand with pebbles, 1.8 m; sandy clayey silt, 3.7 m; silty chalky sand, 3.6 m; boulder clay, 9.6+ m. At Drinkstone Green, a well [9580 6049] encountered 0.9 m of sand and ballast in the upper part of the till.

Near Woolpit, the chalky Boulder Clay varies from 20 to 27 m in thickness. Clayey gravel, 1 m thick, was recorded at a depth of 23.5 m in a borehole [9762 6177] at Woolpit Green. A well [9672 6259] at the gravel pit north-east of the village proved the following sequence: Upper Glacial Sand and Gravel, 3 m; clay, 9.7 m; ballast, 0.6 m; clay, 2.4 m; Lower Glacial Sand and Gravel, 2.4 m.

Around Tostock, the chalky Boulder Clay is some 7 to 14 m thick, beneath 2 to 7 m of Upper Glacial Sand and Gravel. Chalky till in a gravel pit [9566 6270] south of the village is overlain by 3 m of mottled orange and grey, sandy and stony clay, and in turn overlies 3 m of coarse gravel; the basal till is laminated.

Elmswell – New Hall – Norton – Stowlangtoft – Hunston area

Within this area, the plateau Boulder Clay ranges in thickness from 0 to 21 m. At Norton, it is thicker in a drift-filled channel which follows the line of The Black Bourn. A well [9573 6556] south of the village proved 35 m of Boulder Clay, above an alternating sequence, 46.9 m thick, of 'pug' and 'shingle and ballast'. Farther north, a borehole [9530 6680] at Little Haugh Hall, also sited over the channel, proved 3.6 m of Alluvium and Peat above the following: chalky till, 25.6 m; gravel, 8.3 m; chalky till, 14.7 m; sand and gravel, 17.5+ m. East of the village, but outside the channel, another borehole [9632 6553] proved 5.5 m of chalky till above 6.6 m of unlaminated silt with thin pebble beds, which in turn rest on 2 m of chalky till, followed downwards by 4.6+ m of unlaminated silt.

Around Hunston Green [980 665], the chalky Boulder Clay varies in thickness from 11 to 27 m. A drift-filled channel extends beneath the east–west stream which flows through Hunston and Stowlangtoft. At Bridge Farm, close to its confluence with The Black Bourn, Boulder Clay extends down to a depth of 19 m (13 m above OD) and is overlain by 7 m of sand and gravel. Some 700 m farther upstream, another borehole [9547 6858] proved 11 m of Alluvium and sand and gravel, above 4.3+ m of Boulder Clay; 1 km farther upstream, Boulder Clay was 21.4+ m thick, below 3 m of River Terrace Deposits [9642 6865]. All along this section of the valley, Chalk crops out on either side of a narrow tongue of Boulder Clay. At Hunston, however, Chalk does not crop out south of the valley. A borehole [9772 6866] north of Hunston Hall encountered thin sand over 4.8 m of stiff, bluish grey, chalky clay, that overlay 18.3 m+ of soft, silty, water-laden, chalky silts filling the channel. A similar sequence has been noted in the drift-filled channel north of Woodstreet Farm (p.50). Yellow, grey and brown silts, locally exceeding 18.7 m in thickness [around 979 686], north-east of Hunston Hall, may, however, lie within Boulder Clay.   CRB

UPPER GLACIAL SAND AND GRAVEL

Sand and gravel occurring above Boulder Clay form scattered deposits, mostly in the east between Little Welnetham [89 60] and Tostock [96 63], though other patches are present between Fornham St Martin [86 67] and Timworth [87 69]. The deposits in the south-east have been termed the Haughley Park Sands and Gravels (Rose and others, 1978). These authors noted large-scale cross-set infills in sections east of the Bury St Edmunds district, and also recorded a lens of flow-till within the deposits. They regarded the sands and gravels as having been laid down in a braided channel.

The Upper Glacial Sand and Gravel (Table 4) is distinguished in composition from the Lower by its generally higher content of rounded chalk pebbles (up to 53 per cent) (Clarke, 1983, p.75). Grading figures show that, in general, the Upper Sand and Gravel has a higher percentage of 'fines' and sand, and a lower percentage of gravel than the Lower. The maximum known thickness of the deposit is 7.5 m in a borehole [9974 6180] just east of the district (Clarke, 1983).

Rose and others (1978) regard the Haughley Park Sands and Gravels as having formed at the ice-margin during wastage of the Anglian ice-sheet. Straw (1979), however, thought that they are Wolstonian outwash gravels. CRB

Details

Whepstead and Chevington

Two small patches of sandy, chalky sand and gravel overlie Boulder Clay at Whepstead [8380 5825] and east of Chevington [8025 5930]. At the latter locality, small pits were dug into the gravel.

Timworth Green and Fornham St Martin

Though the deposit is quite thin, several substantial areas of Upper Glacial Sand and Gravel occur near the village. In the railway cutting [8565 6790] west of Brick Kiln Plantation, about 2 m of sand and gravel separate a skin of Cover Sand from Boulder Clay. Gravel was formerly extracted from a small pit west of the cutting. At the southern end of the Plantation, the Cover Sand is absent and the surface is very gravelly; a small disused pit [8600 6756] occurs in the deposit. Northwards, the sand and gravel is not very thick and many of the disused pits [859 687; 8591 6858; 8587 6853; 8595 6817; 8635 6833] are floored by Boulder Clay.

East of the valley that runs from Barton Bottom to Timworth Green, the Upper Glacial Sand and Gravel is again present. A pipeline trench [8660 6807] across the southernmost outcrop showed up to 1.2 m of sand and gravel on Boulder Clay, while surface indications a little farther north are of a very gravelly deposit [around 865 687], which is probably thin, for a small inlier of chalky till occurs hereabouts [866 690] and forms the floor of a small pit [8697 6913] nearby. A borehole north of Timworth Long Court, where the soil is very gravelly [8672 6916], passed through only 0.5 m of clayey fine-grained sand before entering Boulder Clay.

A pit [8733 6940] at Timworth Hall similarly showed only 1.5 m of horizontal, finely laminated, fine- to coarse-grained, chalky pebbly sand, overlain by 1.5 m of bedded subangular to rounded flint and chalk gravel. Gravel was, however, extracted from several shallow pits [c.866 665] south of Hall Farm. The gravel consists of angular and subrounded flints with common rounded 'Bunter' quartz and quartzite; well-rounded flints are rare. A borehole [8561 6715] in an outcrop between Hall Farm and Fornham St Martin proved 2.4 m of Cover Sand, above 2.2 m of clayey sand and gravel and clayey pebbly sand, which in turn rest on chalky till. Farther south on this same outcrop, Bennett and Blake (1886, pp.9–10, fig. 2) recorded several sections during the construction of the Bury–Thetford railway line. One of these [c.857 663], now completely filled in, showed 6.7 m of coarse gravel with boulders up to 0.9 m, resting on an irregular piped surface of the Chalk. A little farther north, Bennett recorded about 0.9 m of fine-grained buff sand, overlain by 2.4 m of coarse gravel, resting on thin (0.2 to 0.46 m) chalky till, which in turn rested on Chalk. Some 3.5 m of sand and gravel were encountered [8555 6617] west of the cutting.

Bury St Edmunds to Battlies Green

Bennett and Blake (1886, p.13) recorded a small basin-shaped deposit of coarse gravel and sand, 1.8 m thick, resting on Boulder Clay, in a pit [c.8655 6442] east of the River Lark. They noted that the gravel is largely composed of flints, but loose belemnites and limestone boulders with ammonites also occur. Farther east, a pit [8785 6460] formerly exposed 3 m of coarse flint gravel irregularly intermixed with sand. Bennett and Blake (1886, p.9) thought that this gravel underlies the chalky Boulder Clay, but Boulder Clay rests on Chalk immediately west of the pit and the sand and gravel probably occupies a depression in the surface of the Boulder Clay. East and south-east of the pit, there is an extensive spread of Cover Sand. Locally, however, this is thin or absent, and the underlying sand and gravel can be recognised [c.890 649]. A borehole [8839 6468] towards the western end of the outcrop of the Upper Glacial Sand and Gravel proved 3.7 m of pebbly sand, clayey sandy gravel and clayey gravel, resting in turn on silt, chalky gravel and chalky till.

Farther south, a small pit [8795 6226] at the western end of North Hill Covert exposes 0.5 to 1.5 m of poorly bedded, but roughly graded gravel. The pebbles are mainly rounded quartz and quartzite, but with a few flints which are mostly large and nodular. The relationship of the gravel to the Boulder Clay is not clear near the pit nor to the north-east; to the south-west, however [c.878 620], it appears to rest on the chalky Boulder Clay.

Great Barton to Pakenham area

South-east of Great Barton, there is an area [c.902 666] of very gravelly, probably fairly thin, sand and gravel partially obscured by Cover Sand, overlying chalky Boulder Clay, which floors several small disused, shallow pits [9021 6654; 8997 6655]. About 1 km to the east, south-east of Barton Mere [c.913 665], sand and gravel probably lie within a channel or a hollow in the till. Separated from this spread by a shallow valley, there is a slightly more extensive deposit [c.918 665]. A pit [9160 6655], about 8 m deep, appears to have been entirely in sand and gravel, though chalky Boulder Clay is exposed close by, and is only slightly topographically lower to the north, west and south. The deposit consists mostly of coarse-grained, slightly clayey, chalky sand and gravel. The sand and gravel on the northern part of this outcrop appears to be quite thin.

There are two patches of Upper Glacial Sand and Gravel near Conyer's Green. A borehole [8869 6865] on the western spread passed through 0.8 m of Cover Sand, 0.8 m of light brown, silty, sandy clay, and then into 6.7 m of fine- to medium-grained sand with a gravelly base, resting on Boulder Clay. Similar spreads of an upper sand and gravel have been mapped north of Great Barton. The largest spread [around 906 680] appears to be quite thin, as two small pits [9068 6806; 9080 6811] are floored by chalky Boulder Clay. However, a borehole [9084 6818] at its north-eastern margin proved 1.2 m of top soil and pebbly sand above 3.8 m of clayey chalky gravel, which rested on Chalk. Nevertheless, the high chalk content of the gravel suggests that all the sand and gravel proved in this borehole is the upper gravel.

At Old Hall [929 688] north of Pakenham, there is another spread of the Upper Glacial Sand and Gravel. Sand and gravel was formerly extracted from several pits [9305 6885] on the eastern side of the deposit.

Pakenham to Hunston

Patches of sand and gravel occur in a belt crossing this area. West of The Black Bourn, the southernmost deposit [945 670] seems gravelly, but there is no exposure. North-west [941 674], it appears to be dominantly sand, locally chalky, although gravel was noted towards the south-east. Patches of gravel also occur along Bull Road [939 677; 945 679]. A borehole [9391 6773] proved a total of 1.9 m of silty sand and very clayey pebbly sand above Glacial Silt. There are two overgrown gravel pits [c.9415 6810] at the northern end of the eastern spread. All that could be seen in 1977 were 2 m of unbedded and unsorted gravel. Over the rest of this spread, sand, locally chalky, appears to be the dominant lithology.

Several patches of Upper Glacial Sand and Gravel occur east of The Black Bourn, and along the unnamed steam which flows westwards through Stowlangtoft. The correct correlation of two small patches [956 669; 9565 6670] south of Stanton Street is, however, uncertain. Bennett (1884, p.8) suggested that they were bosses of sand and gravel protruding through Boulder Clay. He described a section in the northernmost of the two patches as a coarse pebbly gravel containing chalk and seams of sand; boulder clay was exposed in the lower part of the pit, though its relation to the gravel was not clear. The bedding in the sand and gravel was anticlinal, and this suggested to Bennett that the sand and gravel rose from beneath the Boulder Clay. In an earlier description of this pit (Whitaker and others, 1881, p.12), Bennett noted 5.5 m of an upper gravel (like that described in the pit to the south—see below), overlying 2.74 m of well-bedded chalky sand and gravel. A section [9553 6686] in 1978 showed 2 m of horizontally bedded chalky and clayey gravel. A pit [9565 6670] in the southernmost spread was also described by Whitaker and others (1881, p.11). Here, beneath an irregular cover of sandy brickearth, Bennett recorded 1.5 m of Boulder Clay, resting on 4.27 m of gravel composed of well-rounded flints averaging 5 to 10 cm diameter, overlying buff sand. No sand and gravel was found in a borehole [9587 6680] close to the east of the pit, where Boulder Clay rests directly on Chalk, but since Boulder Clay surrounds the pit at the surface, Bennett (1884, p.8) may have been correct in postulating that the sand and gravel protrudes through the Boulder Clay. Alternatively, the sand and gravel may occupy a steep-sided depression in the Boulder Clay.

Near Norton, a narrow strip of clayey fine-grained sand and gravel extends for about 1 km along The Black Bourn. There is no exposure, but the thickness exceeds 1.5 m; the relationship to the Boulder Clay is not clear.

North of Stanton Street a much larger spread of sand and gravel [around 952 672] appears to overlie Boulder Clay. Springs issue from the sand and gravel [9503 6731] to the west and south [9536 6702], and give rise to an extensive area of peat. Gravel is dominant at the surface; at the northern end, the gravels are chalky [9519 6754] and have been worked in a shallow pit, while there is a larger sand and gravel pit [9547 6711] to the south.

The stratigraphic position of the larger spread of sand and gravel at Stowlangtoft [957 681] is also uncertain: south-east of the church [961 680] it appears to be overlain by Boulder Clay, but south-west of the church [955 678] very gravelly deposits appear to rest on the chalky till. At one point [9529 6795] chalky till was augered beneath gravel and at another [9049 6814], west of the church, it lies beneath 1.1 m of sand and gravel. It appears that lithologically similar 'upper' and 'lower' sands and gravels are in contact hereabouts; in the absence of good exposure it is impossible to separate the two.

East of Stowlangtoft [967 684] the sand and gravel certainly overlie Boulder Clay. The spread [974 683] north of the Hall at Hunston consists of sandy clayey gravel, for a trial pit [9748 6836] proved 0.4 m of top soil and 2.7 m of very clayey, coarse, unbedded, unsorted sand and gravel, on Boulder Clay. The gravel consists of nodular and subrounded flints, together with well-rounded quartz and quartzite pebbles. North-east of the Hall [980 684], the dominant lithology appears to be a coarse-grained clayey sand; the fields to the north and west are more gravelly.

Ixworth

Two small patches of sand and gravel cap the Boulder Clay fill of a buried channel east of Ixworth. The more western [952 707] is a coarse, angular flint gravel; the other [957 707] appears to be dominantly fine-grained sand.

Stanton

South of Low Wood [980 728], there is a small area of fine-grained clayey sand. North of the wood, a spread of chalky sand and gravel [9810 7365] was formerly exploited.

The Bradfields

Extensive spreads in this area form the western part of a second belt of Upper Glacial Sand and Gravel paralleling that extending north-north-east from Bury St Edmunds. North-west of Little Welnetham, there are three very small patches of sand and gravel [8835 6040; 885 605; 884 668]. The first appears to be an inlier of Lower Glacial Sand and Gravel, but the others, from their high content of chalk pebbles and minor amounts of quartz, quartzite, 'Bunters' and patinated flints, probably belong to the Upper Glacial Sand and Gravel. At Little Welnetham there is a much bigger spread.

East of Welnetham Church, surface indications are of a very gravelly deposit which has been worked in shallow pits [8974 6005]. Near Link Wood [898 604], the deposits are much more clayey and thinner, with only minor gravel: chalky fine-grained sand was augered to at least 1.2 m at two points [9076 6053; 9079 6043].

In the former railway cutting a little farther south, the base of the sand and gravel is irregular, such that in places the floor of the cutting, some 4 to 5 m below the original ground level, is in sand and gravel [8895 5938; 8915 5930], whereas at other points [8905 5833] it is in chalky till.

South of the stream which flows through the Welnethams, clayey sand and gravel crop over a wide area. In a road cutting [8872 5867; 8885 5850] the deposit is about 3 m thick. Southwards, gravel is dominant locally [e.g. 8930 5780; 8965 5784]. At the latter locality, known as 'gravel field', a small pit formerly existed.

Near Bradfield Combust, the deposit appears to be dominantly clayey, and only locally a gravelly, fine-grained sand. Thicknesses up to at least 1.5 m have been proved. A detached outcrop at Monkspark Wood [925 576] is of dominantly fine-grained sands, locally chalky, which overlie Boulder Clay [9316 5797; 9313 5770]. South of Cargate, angular and subangular flints are common on the surface [9298 5777].

Bradfield St George to Woolpit Green

This area forms the eastern part of the belt of discontinuous outliers that extends from Bradfield Combust. North-west of Millfield Wood, there is a small area of dominantly clayey fine-grained sand [925 604]; gravel was noted only locally.

At Hessett, the Upper Glacial Sand and Gravel was extracted

from a large pit. Exposures are poor, and much of the pit, which appears to be floored with Boulder Clay, is flooded. One exposure [9397 6117] showed 2.3 m of clayey gravel above Boulder Clay. A well [9381 6103] at the western end of the outlier proved 6.71 m of sand and gravel, resting on Boulder Clay. Another spread of sand and gravel occurs about 0.5 km to the north. Fine-grained sand is dominant, but gravel is locally present, particularly in an area [9400 6166] where several small pits formerly existed. Farther north, near Beyton, dominantly fine-grained, clayey, and only locally gravelly, sands occur [around 935 630].

The largest spread of Upper Glacial Sand and Gravel within the district is at Tostock [955 636]. The base is locally marked by springs [9509 6392; 9551 6407; 9623 6357]. Gravel appears to be present over most of the outcrop. A well [9535 6329] at Tostock House proved 4.9 m of sand and gravel above Boulder Clay, and another [9571 6366] encountered 7 m of sand and gravel, though a nearby borehole [9554 6362] proved only 2.5 m of silty sand and sandy clay. South-west of Tostock House, the soil is very gravelly, and gravel was formerly extracted from several pits [9510 6314]. West of Bridge Farm, sand and gravel was extensively worked during the dualling of the A45, and boreholes [e.g. 9623 6307] proved thicknesses of up to 4.85 m. The gravel locally exceeds 4 m in thickness a little farther west [9589 6287]. Some 6.1 m of sand and gravel were proved in a borehole [9593 6300] west of Cindron Wood and near an old gravel pit [9600 6298], while the sand and gravel was 3.3 m thick in another borehole [9630 6330] east-north-east of Tostock Place.

The deposit extends south of the stream which flows to the south of Tostock. A borehole [9523 6261] in this extension proved 1.8 m of silty fine-grained sand above Boulder Clay. A little to the east, a somewhat larger, more gravelly spread occurs. Locally, as in a pit [957 627] south of Tostock, it rests on Barham Sands and Gravels. Probably both the Upper and Lower Glacial Sand and Gravel were worked in another abandoned and overgrown pit [9575 6280] to the east, and up to 3.5 m of sand and gravel were proved in trial pits [around 9576 6290]. The deposit is very gravelly east-south-east of the pit, where it was formerly extracted for sand and gravel [around 9590 6265].

East of The Black Bourn, at Woolpit, there are several large disused pits. Sections [969 627] in one of them showed in descending sequence: clayey, fine- to medium-grained sand, 1 to 1.5 m; chalky till with a brown decalcified top, 0 to 1.25 m; on well-bedded, fine- to coarse-grained sand and gravel. The Boulder Clay is probably a layer within the Upper Glacial Sand and Gravel rather than the feather-edge of the main sheet. Similar interdigitations of Boulder Clay and Upper Glacial Sand and Gravel (Haughley Park Sands and Gravels) have been recorded by Rose and others (1978, p.88). Some 4 m of sand and gravel, with no interbedded boulder clay, were seen on the west side of the adjacent pit [9688 6259]. A borehole [9713 6263] east of the pit proved 7 m of sand and gravel above Boulder Clay. A poor section [9683 6263] on the opposite side of the lane exposed 6 m of sand and gravel, reddened and clay-rich towards the top. A little farther south, a borehole [9640 6224] near the windmill, north-east of Drinkstone, proved 11.28 m of sand and gravel above Boulder Clay.

Much of Drinkstone lies on another outcrop of Upper Glacial Sand and Gravel, the base of which is locally marked by springs [959 617; 9556 6147]. A borehole [9664 6170] at the eastern end of the spread proved 4.5 m of chalky sand and gravel above Boulder Clay.

Clayey sand and gravel also occur near Drinkstone Green [962 602] where about 3 m were proved in a borehole [9596 6006]. There are three small occurrences south of the main deposit [960 596; 961 593; 9635 5905]. The first is locally gravelly [9595 5970]; the second appears to be composed dominantly of clayey sand and gravel which, where seen in ditch sections, exceed 1.2 m in thickness; the third spread is composed of coarse-angular flint gravel.

North of Rattlesden, there are further spreads of clayey sand and gravel [971 593; 978 597]. The former is locally very gravelly; the latter is only rarely so. At one point [9755 5950], the surface of the field is very gravelly, the gravel being composed of well-rounded white vein-quartz, quartzite and 'Bunter' pebbles, and subrounded large flint pebbles.

The western part of a spread of Upper Glacial Sand and Gravel, which consists principally of clayey fine-grained sand, extends into the district near Woolpit Green [around 980 617]. Locally, this spread overlies the Woolpit Beds [980 618]. A similar patch near St John's Church, Elmswell [982 636], is mostly coarse-grained sand and gravel; its base is locally marked by springs [9817 6356; 9819 6368; 9838 6383]. CRB

GLACIAL SILT

The deposits mapped as Glacial Silt vary from clay or silty clay to coarse-grained sand, though silt is dominant. Comminuted chalk, with clasts up to 1 cm across, occurs throughout; small scattered angular flints are also present. At depth, the deposits are bluish grey, but they weather to yellowish buff.

Glacial Silt is confined largely to deep channels, the courses of which are followed by the present-day valley of the River Lark and its tributary which flows through Great Livermere. There are widespread outcrops between Tuddenham and Lackford, and smaller ones near Ingham and at Great Livermere. At Kennett [700 683], a silt-filled channel crosses the River Kennett almost at right angles. This channel extends about 4 km south-east of Kennett and continues westwards into the adjacent Cambridge (188) district, where the silt has been classified as Glacial Loam. Beneath The Black Bourn, thin deposits of silt have been recorded at depth in the Norton area, but they do not crop out, nor do they extend far along the channel. Near Hunston [978 685], Glacial Silt crops out within a channel cut in Boulder Clay, and similar occurrences have been noted near Great Barton [8805 6590; 890 660]. Woodland (1970, pp.559–560, fig. 3) regarded the deposition of these laminated silts, silty clays and clays in the tunnel-valleys of East Anglia as resulting from the thinning of the overlying ice-cap, with a consequent reduction in the hydrostatic head of the englacial waters, so that the channels became filled with stagnant or only gently flowing water.

At Kennett and north-east of Bury St Edmunds [868 660], chalky till overlies Glacial Silt, but along the Lark valley and at Hunston [978 685] the reverse is the case. Commonly, however, in the Lark valley, beds of Boulder Clay and Glacial Silt alternate, and it is not always possible to separate them. The Glacial Silt is mostly unlaminated but, locally [for example, 7928 7101], laminated strata are recorded.

In one of the deeper parts of the drift-filled channel of the Lark, a maximum thickness of 48.1 m of Glacial Silt has been proved [7928 7101]; the silt there extends to 33 m below OD. Near Kennett Church, 25.8 m of Glacial Silt has its base at 5 m below OD.

At Hunston, in the Black Bourn valley system, a borehole [9795 6846] was still in Glacial Silt at a depth of 18.7 m. South-west of Hunston, another borehole [9632 6553] proved an alternating sequence of Boulder Clay and silt; Boulder Clay to 7.4 m; Glacial Silt to 12.1 m; Boulder Clay to 14.1 m; Glacial Silt to at least 18.7 m.

At Kennett, Cavenham, Lackford and Norton, molluscs (Table 6), ostracods and beetles have been collected from the upper part of the silts. Whitaker and others (1891) recorded flint implements and flakes in 'loams' beneath Boulder Clay at the old Mildenhall brickyard [718 752]: the 'boulder clay' at this locality may, however, be a solifluction deposit. The molluscs, whilst not age-diagnostic, indicate deposition in a climate colder that at present. Beetles from Lackford (see p.56) also indicate colder temperatures. Dr G R Coope, who identified the beetles, considers that the fauna is a late Devensian one (c.11 000 years BP), but radiometric age determinations of $25\,030 + 1430/-1210$ years BP and $28\,880 + 520/-480$ years BP (Lackford) and $26\,870 + 260$ years BP (Cavenham) on moss and shells at the top of the silts, and $34\,380 + 510/-730$ years BP (Norton) and $26\,010 + 230/-230$ years BP (Tostock) conflict with the coleopteran date. Possibly the Norton and Tostock deposits are not part of the same deposit as those at Lackford and Cavenham, but the similarity of dates is difficult to discount. In any event, the top of the silt is certainly Devensian in age. Where the silts overlie Boulder Clay, as in the Lark valley, the deposit could be Devensian, but some, at least, of the silts resting on the Boulder Clay are overlain by Hoxnian deposits (see p.56). However, near Kennett, where Boulder Clay overlies the Glacial Silt, a Devensian age is ruled out, since the former is pre-Hoxnian. Elsewhere, the intimate association of the Glacial Silt and the chalky Boulder Clay indicates a close relationship between the two. As the faunas come from the top of the silt, immediately beneath River Terrace Deposits, it is more probable that a certain amount of reworking of Anglian Glacial Silt took place in Devensian times. For convenience, however, the whole of the sequence is described in this chapter. CRB, BSPM

Details

Kennett valley and associated valley

Yellow to buff silt has been worked in a pit adjacent to Kennett Church [7005 6832]. Eastwards, the silts become buried under gravelly Head. A borehole [7025 6820], sited on Head, probably penetrated the maximum thickness of silt in this area:

	Depth m
Top soil	0.3
HEAD	
Sand and gravel	4.7
GLACIAL SILT	
Clay, silty, yellow, small flints	6.7
Silt, clayey, grey, alternating with silty, grey, clay containing small flints	17.8
Sand, silty, grey	21.8
Clay, silty, grey, laminated	25.6
Sand, silty, grey	26.5
Clay, grey, fissured	27.4
Sand, silty, grey	30.5
MIDDLE CHALK	
Chalk, rubbly	31.4

Pits and a borehole in a disused gravel pit [700 680] south of Kennett Church proved buff silts under Fourth River Terrace Gravel. In the deepest borehole [7007 6804], 2.8 m of silt with a thin chalky gravel lens were proved under 3.2 m of terrace sand and gravel. The silt is buff and laminated, with lenses of disturbed (?cryoturbated) coarse-grained sand, and contain gastropods and bivalves. The silt becomes fine grained with increasing depth and the sand lenses die out. Towards the base of the pit, sandy silt bands (7 to 8 cm thick) are interbedded with clayey silt (2–3 cm thick generally, but in places up to 7 cm). CRB

A sparse suite of fresh-water or oligohaline ostracods was recovered and includes: *Candona ?neglecta*, the dominant species, *Ilyocypris gibba* and *Limnocythere inopinata*. The limited assemblage is of little palaeoecological or chronological value. Such ostracods are fairly eurythermal, and *C. neglecta*, at least, can withstand drying out. Two of these species are recorded also from the Cavenham pit (p.56). DMG

Another borehole [7000 6796] in the pit proved 6.1 m of silts, lying on 0.6 m of slightly chalky, very sandy, silty clay with scattered flints. The clay rests on coarse-grained sand, which in turn rests on soft redeposited chalk. Eastwards, old workings in the terrace [7060 6815] proved buff to grey, slightly chalky silts, underlying gravel. The eastward continuation of the silts is indicated by a well [7086 6810] east of the Kennett valley which proved 14.2 m of drift on Chalk. Slightly farther east [7130 6804], brown silt was augered beneath a thin terrace gravel.

Silt, under terrace gravels, occurs also in a gravel pit [7175 6750] in the bottom of the valley about 1 km north-east of Kentford Church. There, the underlying buff-grey silts, containing small chalk pellets and scattered small flints, have an irregular upper surface. At one point [7163 6742] they rest on Chalk.

South-eastwards, there is a tongue of Boulder Clay in the floor of the valley [725 667], and a borehole [7239 6676] proved 3 m of made ground and 3.1 m of brown clay with chalk pebbles and Jurassic shell debris, resting on 18.9 m of silt above Chalk. The silt, brown at the top, was much greyer below 15.2 m and contained variable amounts of chalk pellets and scattered small patinated flints. A second borehole [7264 6667], a little to the east, proved 3 m of terrace gravels on 14.7 m of alternating silt and clay, with a band of flinty sand between 6.1 and 7.9 m. The silts are buff-yellow and contain scattered chalk pellets and some sand. The clays are more chalky than the silts and contain some angular flints. Farther south, another borehole [7316 6576] proved 11.1 m of brown, possibly laminated, silt with chalk pellets, below 1.2 m of chalky sand and Boulder Clay. Southwards, Glacial Silt extends along a narrow drift-filled channel under a cover of Boulder Clay.

Lark valley and tributary valley

In the extreme north, a well [7218 7498] north of Barton Mills recorded 13.41 m of 'clay' (possibly silt) beneath sand and gravel. There are, however, better-known sections in Mildenhall brickyard [718 752], now built over, but recorded by Skertchly (*in* Whitaker and others, 1891). A sketch shows sandy soil overlying thin Boulder Clay, which in turn overlies grey laminated loam. The Boulder Clay appears to rest in a depression in the loam; sandy soil rests on the loam towards the margin of the depression. From the eastern side of the yard, Skertchly recorded: bedded sand and gravel, 2.1 m; light bluish loam, 3.7 m; Chalk. He also noted that 'a goodly number of rudely fashioned tools' had been found in the loam.

Upstream, much of the loam lies below river gravel. A well [7326 7514], north-east of Barton Mills, proved 18.5 m of 'white clay' beneath terrace sand and gravel. This 'white clay' has been interpreted as Middle Chalk by Holmes (1971), who also interpreted the overlying sand and gravel as glacial, but it may be a mixture of silt, Boulder Clay and redeposited chalk, filling a continuation of the Lark buried channel.

South of the Lark, the Glacial Silt emerges from beneath the Second River Terrace Deposits north and east of Tuddenham. Augering has proved a variation from chalky, buff, grey and fawn silt or silty clay, to chalky, silty, fine-grained sand. BSPM

The Cavenham pit [761 710] is floored by bluish grey clayey silt with scattered angular flints and small rounded chalk gravel. Continuous flight auger holes in the pit [7620 7079; 7616 7096; 7613 7083: 7593 7097] proved an interbedded sequence of bluish grey silts and clayey silts with varying amounts of chalk and rare flints. From here the base of the silts descends north-eastwards from 2 m above OD to 0.85 m below OD. TEL, CRB

The top of the silt is locally shelly, and also contains wood and moss debris. Although the sample from this locality was one of the largest examined (3.95 kg), the fauna was sparse and of low diversity (Table 6). Among the bivalves are a number of specimens of *Pisidium obtusale lapponicum*, a cold-water species that is found today in arctic Europe and North America, but has been recorded in Britain only in Pleistocene deposits. Coupled to the impoverished nature of the remainder of the fauna, its presence points to an unfavourable environment. The association of *Pupilla muscorum* with *Succinea oblonga* and other fully aquatic molluscs may indicate a marshy situation at the edge of a lake or slow-flowing river. Whilst the succineids normally live on or amongst waterside plants, *P. muscorum* is essentially a land-snail indicative of open habitats, but it could easily have been introduced into an aquatic assemblage by flooding or the collapse of river banks. Moreover, Kerney and others (1964, pp.160–161) have indicated that in colder episodes of the Pleistocene, a form of *P. muscorum* occurred in marsh assemblages and was more common in wet places than it is today. DKG

Ostracods from this same level included *Candona neglecta* and *Limnocythere inopinata*. These two species have also been recorded from silt at Kennett. DMG

A sample of the moss from the top of the silt has yielded a mid-Devensian date of 26 870 + 260 BP (see also Lackford Pit below), though this date does not necessarily apply to the whole of the deposit.

West of the tributary valley running from Cavenham to Icklingham, the silt crops out beneath a thin wash of gravel [765 704 to 7725 7155], but the outcrop ends where the River Terrace Deposits thicken abruptly south-west of Cavenham Mill. East of the valley, the silt rises slightly up the valley side, and the junction of the silt and Boulder Clay follows a slight depression north of Bunker's Barn [7747 7029]. The junction is marked by a deeper depression where the silt is banked against Chalk south of Lackford [792 701]. There, the upper part of the Glacial Silt varies between greyish fawn mottled silty clay, grey stiff clayey silt, and grey soft clayey silt, all with abundant small chalk pellets. A well [7985 7046] at Lackford Manor House proved a minimum of 13.5 m of silt beneath terrace deposits. Another [7938 7004], west-south-west of Lackford Church, which commenced within 60 m of the Chalk outcrop, proved nearly 11 m of silt, overlying 0.6 m of gravel.

A borehole [7928 7101] in the Lackford Bridge pit proved soft saturated silt to a depth of 48.6 m, and this was underlain by gravel and redeposited chalk to a depth of 55 m, where the Chalk was reached. The lithology varies between a bluish grey well-sorted, chalky silt and a poorly sorted clayey silt. Sand-sized chalk grains are scattered throughout, and the poorly sorted silt characteristically contains subangular to subrounded chalk pebbles and worn subangular flints. Samples from depths of 21.6 and 40.4 m showed lamination. TEL

The surface of the silts was seen in the floor of the Lackford pit [800 707]. Locally, the bluish grey silts were shelly and also contained wood fragments. The fauna is included in Table 6. The ostracod *Candona neglecta* is locally abundant. In an unpublished report (August, 1982) by G R Coope and B J Taylor, the following beetles were identified: *Patrobus assimilis* (2), *P. septentrionis* (1), *Trechus rivularis* (2), *Bembidion guttula* (2), *Agonum fuliginosum* (1), *Helophorus grandis* (1), *Helophorus* (small species) (2), *Ochthebius minimus* (2), *Olophrum fuscum* (4), *Pycnoglypta lurida* (32), *Arpedium brachypterum* (39), *Acidota quadrata* (4), *Boreaphilus henningianus* (3),

Stenus sp., (6), Boletobiinae gen. et sp. indet. (1), Aleocharinae gen. et sp. indet. (17), *Simplocarea metallica* (3), *Byrrhus sp.* (17), *Cateretes pedicularis* (1), *Otiorhynchus nodosus* (1) and *Notaris aethiops* (1).

Coope and Taylor reported that the local environment indicated by the coleopteran assemblage is that of an open site with *Carex* and wet moss and very small puddles of standing water. A suite of small staphylinids (*Pycnoglypta lurida*, *Arpedium brachypterum*, *Acidota quadrata* and *Boreaphilus henningianus*) are often found together under plant debris, commonly dwarf willow leaves, in alpine or tundra environments, where they occur even at the margins of melting snow. The assemblage indicates much colder climatic conditions than those of the present day, but it is not possible on so limited a sample to quantify the climatic parameters. The coleoptera species are found together in numerous sites that range from the end of the Windermere Interstadial to the beginning of the Loch Lomond Stadial. In particular, *Pycnoglypta lurida* and *Acidota quadrata* are always common in British faunas of this time, but are notably rare in mid-Devensian deposits. Furthermore, *Trechus rivularis* was very common throughout England during the latter half of the Windermere Interstadial (the Allerød Chronozone), but then died out in Britain and is unknown during the intense cold-episode of the Loch Lomond Stadial. This species is unknown in the mid-Devensian (in spite of over 50 insect assemblages of this age so far investigated), though it was abundant in Britain during the early Devensian Chelford Interstadial. The presence of this species and the nature of the faunal assemblage would, as a whole, seem to preclude a mid-Devensian age for this sample, but a radiocarbon age determination on shell fragments from this level gave a date of 25 030 + 1430/ − 1210 BP, whilst moss debris gave a date of 28 880 + 520/ − 480 BP. Both dates, and also that from Cavenham, are in close agreement in indicating a mid-Devensian age for the top of the silts. Possibly the coleoptera come from a small amount of sediment at the very top of a composite deposit, but the results remain anomalous.

The silts were poor in pollen; they yielded the tree pollen *Pinus* and one grain of *Alnus* that was probably reworked. Dr M J Tooley, who identified the pollen, comments that the presence of *Selaginella* spores indicates open and rather cool, moist conditions.

Kerney (1976, p.74) described a section in the Glacial Silt in an old brickyard [798 719] north of the Lark. He recorded 0.25 m of mottled orange and pale grey, calcareous silt with scattered flints and chalk fragments, and with shells, including *Pomatias elegans* in the uppermost 5 cm; this overlies 0.2 m + of orange-brown chalky silt with abundant chalk fragments, and is covered by 0.55 m of soil and 0.4 m of shelly calcareous tufa. Mr T E Lawson estimates that the underlying Boulder Clay is here about 2 m thick and rests on Chalk. A rich interglacial molluscan fauna was obtained from the overlying tufa. CRB

South-east of Flempton, the Glacial Silt underlies the Second River Terrace Deposits. It crops out as yellowish to grey-brown silt north of Grange Farm, Hengrave [8225 6928]. Towards the north of this outcrop, the boundary between Glacial Silt and chalky Boulder Clay has been taken arbitrarily where the silt becomes much more clayey. A borehole [8185 6973] just north of this outcrop proved (Hawkins, 1981):

	Depth m
Soil	0.7
RIVER TERRACE DEPOSITS	
Sand, pebbly	0.9

* Non-British species

GLACIAL SILT
Silt, unlaminated, mottled orange-brown and pale grey 2.0
Silt, as above, but laminated, sandy at 2.5 m 4.5
Silt, poorly laminated, grey 5.5
Silt, unlaminated, dark grey, becoming stiff downwards 6.0
Silt, clayey, unlaminated, dark grey, with abundant subrounded chalk clasts up to fine gravel grade, and subangular to subrounded flints up to fine gravel grade; some red chalk 8.0
Silt, clayey, unlaminated, dark grey 16.0

BOULDER CLAY
Clay, orange-brown, with abundant subrounded chalk clasts, iron-stained fine gravel and sand, flints, and red chalk 18.4

Adjacent to Hengrave Hall, the Glacial Silt was formerly dug [8260 6855] as a 'brickearth'. Bennett (in Whitaker and others, 1891) described the deposits as 'stiff clean grey loam'; augering in the banks of the flooded pits now shows only buff silt. On the south side of Hengrave Park, the outcrop of Glacial Silt abuts against that of the chalky Boulder Clay, but their relationship is not clear.

Silts occur widely beneath Second River Terrace Deposits between Flempton and Bury St Edmunds. No borehole in this tract has reached bedrock (Hawkins, 1981), but the minimum thicknesses of silt (and silty clay and clay) are given in Table 5. Two boreholes [8247 6944; 8326 6851] sited on Alluvium proved 12.2 + and 8.3 + m respectively of silts below alluvial gravel (Hawkins, 1981).

At the old barracks in Bury St Edmunds, two wells [8424 6458; 8431 6452] record 1.2 and 18.3 m of 'boulder clay' on Chalk, respectively; since a temporary section [8424 6450] across the Newmarket Road from the barracks was in 3 m of sandy silt, the boreholes may have been in Glacial Silt rather than Boulder Clay. In any event, the deposits appear to occupy a steep-sided circular depression cut in Chalk. BSPM

In the tributary valley leading from Livermere Park, yellow, grey and brown silts occur beneath River Terrace Deposits north of Ingham Dairy [around 854 698]. One borehole [8520 6977] proved 2.3 m of pale greyish brown silt, beneath 2 m of River Terrace Deposits, resting on chalky till (Hawkins, 1981). It is possible that 0.9 m of 'Lacustrine Deposits', encountered between depths of 7.3 and 8.2 m within 'Glacial Sand and Gravel' in a borehole [8537 6913] to the south-south-east, may also be Glacial Silt, although its fauna (see p.61) gives no evidence that temperatures when it was laid down differed significantly from those of the present day. Provisionally this deposit, and a similar one at Fornham St Martin [8504 6747], are regarded as interglacial deposits (see p.61).

Farther south near Westfield Farm [868 660], and away from the valleys, grey silty clay occurs at the base of the Boulder Clay; about 1 km farther east [8805 6592], at least 1.5 m of buff silt overlies Boulder Clay. A borehole [8800 6589] in this spread proved 1.1 m of buff-grey silt with scattered grains of chalk, beneath Cover Sand and ?Head, and resting on chalky Boulder Clay. There is a slightly more extensive and thicker occurrence of silts about 1 km south of Great Barton [89 66]. A borehole [8898 6589] proved 1.6 m of Cover Sand, above 5.8 m of grey, buff and brown silt, silty clay and sandy silt with 1.2 m of gravel in its middle; the silt is underlain by 2 m of chalky till, which in turn rests on Chalk (Hawkins, 1981). Khaki silts were augered beneath Cover Sand at a third locality [8870 6564], but their extent beneath Cover Sand is unknown. All the lithologies are similar to those known to occur in channels, but they may, nevertheless, be of a different origin.

Black Bourn valley and tributaries

At Hunston [978 685], silt appears to occur within a channel otherwise filled by Boulder Clay. At the surface, yellow, brown and grey clayey silt can be augered. The silts, which are poorly laminated and orange-brown, becoming grey with depth, were proved to a depth of 18.7 + m.

Peaty silt has been encountered between depths of 2.8 and 3.5 m in a borehole [9533 6604] in the valley at Norton. The silt, which is greenish grey and shelly, underlies Second River Terrace Deposits and rests on Boulder Clay. A radiometric age determination of 34 380 + 510/ − 730 BP on the peaty material is only slightly older than the mid-Devensian ages obtained at Lackford and Cavenham (p.56) (Clarke and Auton, 1982). Another borehole [9552 6460], 1.4 km to the south, proved a dominantly peaty sequence to 3.6 m, above 2.9 m of greenish grey silt and silty sand, locally shelly, which in turn rests on 0.9 m of peaty silt, and Boulder Clay. The peaty silt has been dated at 26 010 ± 230 years BP (Clarke and Auton, 1982), a date similar to that obtained from the top of the silt at Lackford (p.56). CRB

Between the depths 6.7 and 6.9 m, the silts yielded a molluscan fauna listed in Table 6 (Col.17). Additionally, the ostracods *Candona neglecta* and *Metacypris cordata*, which indicate temperatures similar to those of the present day, were found at all levels from the Alluvium to the basal peat. DKG, DMG

WOOLPIT BEDS

'Brickearth' at Woolpit has been worked at least since the 16th century (Whitaker and others, 1881; Northeast, 1972) and was the source for the locally famous bricks known as Woolpit or Suffolk Whites. The name Woolpit Beds has recently been given to this high-level brickearth (Bristow and Gregory, 1982). The Woolpit Beds (Table 4, Plate 5) overlie chalky Boulder Clay and are apparently overlain locally by Glacial Sand and Gravel or chalky till, or both. Sparse marine Pleistocene foraminifera, together with Jurassic and Cretaceous species, have been obtained from the Woolpit Beds, which occupy a depression approximately 1 km across in the Boulder Clay surface. The beds are at their highest around the margin of the depression where they attain a maximum height of 60 above OD. Numerous pits have been opened in the 'brickearth', and poor exposures of up to 2 m of buff laminated silt, fine-grained sand, silty clay and clayey silt can still be seen on the western side [9815 6225] of the last pit to be worked. Woolpit No. 3 Borehole [9820 6238] proved 23.25 m of Woolpit Beds, consisting dominantly of fine-grained silty sand, together with clayey silt and silty clay; two seams of chalky till are present towards the base. Some beds are laminated, whilst others are bioturbated.

The macrofauna includes fragments of *Balanus*, crinoid columnals, bryozoa, gastropods and bivalves (including a mytilacean fragment) of uncertain origin. The sparse foraminifera have been listed and discussed by Bristow and Gregory (1982); *Elphidium clavatum* is by far the commonest species. Isolated specimens, for example *Elphidiella hannai* and *Cibicides lobatulus*, are probably derived from the Crag, in which they are more abundant; the presence of other species in the Woolpit Beds, for example *Protelphidium anglicum* and *P*. cf. *orbiculare* and their absence from the Crag, indicates that, even though they may also be derived, the Crag was not their source. Indeed, the dominance of *Elphidium clavatum*, and the virtual absence of *Elphidiella han-*

Plate 5 Finely laminated silty clay and fine-grained sand of the Woolpit Beds, Woolpit Brickworks. (A13042)

nai in the Woolpit Beds set this fauna apart from Crag faunas at Ludham (Funnell, 1961), Easton Bavents (Funnell and West, 1962) and Bramerton (Funnell and others, 1979).

Many other post-Anglian deposits from the district have been examined for microfauna, but none contains Pleistocene foraminifera. Gregory (1922, reproduced in Boswell, 1929), however, recorded Pleistocene foraminifera from Boulder Clay in Ballingdon Grove brickpit, Sudbury, and concluded that the Boulder Clay had been deposited from melting ice in sea-water. (The Ballingdon Grove pit is also of interest since 'brickearth', locally overlain and underlain by chalky Boulder Clay, was formerly exposed there (see Boswell, 1929, fig. 11).

The local presence of both chalky Boulder Clay and Upper Glacial Sand and Gravel above the Woolpit Beds, means that the Woolpit Beds must be wholly of Anglian age. It is possible that the Woolpit Beds represent a local deposit of ice-transported early Pleistocene sea-bed material deposited in a hollow on the surface of the Boulder Clay, or that the sediment and fauna have been washed out of ice surrounding this hollow. The possibility that they are in-situ marine deposits seems unlikely in view of their apparent interdigitation with Boulder Clay, their height (60 m above OD) and their distance both from the coast (35 km) and from the nearest known marine Middle Pleistocene deposits in the Nar Valley (45 km). The contained fauna is presumably slightly earlier than, or approximately contemporaneous with, the Anglian ice-advance. The presence of *Elphidium clavatum* is indicative of cold, shallow-water conditions, although *Protelphidium anglicium* indicates some moderating influence.

Details

The Woolpit Beds are best known from Woolpit No. 3 Borehole [9820 6238], where 23.25 m of silty clay, clayey silt and silty fine-grained sand were proved. The detailed log is given by Bristow and Gregory (1982). In Woolpit No. 1 Borehole [9814 6228], 70 m distant, the Woolpit Beds were more than 19.5 m thick. In No. 2 Borehole [9844 6217], some 270 m farther east-south-east, 18 m of silty clay and clayey fine-grained sand were proved above chalky Boulder Clay. All three of the boreholes have yielded a sparse foraminiferal fauna, recorded in tabular form by Bristow and Gregory (1982). South and east of the last locality, the Woolpit Beds apparently pass beneath Upper Glacial Sand and Gravel. They were absent in a borehole [9847 6194] 230 m south of No. 2 Borehole.

All three Woolpit boreholes were sunk in the floor of the last large-scale brickpit to have been worked. According to Mr O Baker, the present owner of the restored pit, 'brickearth' was worked to a depth of about 7.5 m in the centre of the pit, and a well dug for another 8 m was still in the 'brickearth'. There are numerous old pits round the periphery of the deposit, but most of the deposit has been dug away, leaving depressions floored with the chalky till. In the banks of the main pit, up to 2 m of laminated silty clay and fine-grained sand can still be seen [9810 6225], Plate 5. Some 2.5 m of buff laminated silt were seen in another old pit [9810 6262] north of the old road. In general, augering in the Woolpit Beds proves buff, yellow or grey silts.

In a spread of 'brickearth' now detached from the main crop, Whitaker and others (1881, p.13) recorded a section at Cranmore

Bridge [?9905 6235] where 1.5 m of chalky Boulder Clay rests on 1.2 m of dark bluish grey clay, which in turn overlies 3 m of laminated, buff brickearth. In another pit 'half a mile east of the church' [?983 625], the same authors referred again to Boulder Clay above the 'brickearth'. At a third pit at Crossways, 'half a mile north-east of Woolpit' [?9790 6285], they noted 3.6 m of brown brickearth resting on 0.6 m of black earth consisting of much carbonaceous matter, including leaves and pieces of wood, together with pieces of bones including *Bos* and *Cervus*, which in turn overlies a shell marl containing *Planorbis*, *Limnaea* and *Valvata piscinalis*. Fine-grained sand overlies the 'brickearth' hereabouts. The fresh-water and terrestrial fauna marks the silting of a shallow pool occupying the basin, and may be much more recent than the underlying silts.

The Upper Glacial Sand and Gravel overlies Woolpit Beds near the Cranmore Bridge pit [9905 6235], near an old pit [9885 6275] 1.5 km east-north-east of Woolpit Church, and also at another nearby pit [9910 6245], now back-filled. CRB

CHAPTER 6

Quaternary Drift: Hoxnian to Flandrian

Those deposits that postdate the melting of the Anglian ice are in general thin and limited in outcrop. When the ice melted, it exposed an irregular land surface on which the present drainage developed. Many of the evolving valleys followed the line of the old tunnel-valleys, though their irregular long-profiles led initially to the formation of ephemeral lakes in the deeper depressions that slowly filled with sediments. Knowledge of these lacustrine deposits tends to be fortuitous. At Sicklesmere, however, such deposits have been identified with certainty as being of Hoxnian age (Table 4).

There is no evidence in the district to establish that any of the post-Hoxnian deposits belong to the Wolstonian and Ipswichian stages; all appear to be of Devensian and Flandrian age (Table 4). The valley sides and floors are mantled with Head (and locally Head Gravel), which formed by solifluction in a periglacial climate, presumably during the Devensian. Possibly concurrently, sand and gravel aggradation took place in the river valleys to produce a suite of River Terrace Deposits. Cryoturbation structures and fossils within these gravels show that they formed in a cold climate; radiocarbon dates establish that at least some levels are mid-Devensian in age. The late Devensian ice-sheets did not spread to this part of England, but thin sheets of Cover Sand occur widely in the central and northern parts of the district.

Finally, Alluvium and Peat formed in the bottoms of many of the valleys during the Flandrian, and locally are still slowly accumulating.

LACUSTRINE DEPOSITS

At Sicklesmere [8745 6092], lacustrine clays resting in a hollow on the surface of the Anglian Boulder Clay have yielded a Hoxnian flora (West, 1981). These are the only proved interglacial lacustrine deposits in the district, though a probable Hoxnian molluscan fauna has been obtained from calcareous tufa overlying Glacial Silt and Boulder Clay at Icklingham [798 719] (Kerney, 1976; Holyoak and others, 1983).

There are other sites where lacustrine clay and silt contain molluscs and flint implements (p.69), but the faunas are not age-diagnostic, although they indicate that the climate was no colder than it is at present. The stratigraphical position of these deposits is not everywhere clear; at several sites they overlie Boulder Clay, and at one [8504 6747] at Fornham St Martin, lacustrine silt is overlain by Fourth River Terrace Deposits. It is, however, possible that separate lacustrine deposits formed at different times.

Details

The only lacustrine deposits of proved age are at Oak's Kiln, Sicklesmere [8745 6092]. There, Bennett and Blake (1886, p.17) recorded 4.2 m of stiff brownish grey loam, greenish at the bottom, overlying more than 0.9 m of black peat with bits of wood. A more detailed section is given by West (1981) who made pollen analyses of several samples from this site, and concluded that Hoxnian sediments were locally present in the bottom of the pit. The pit is now overgrown, but peat can be consistently augered in the bottom. The following section [8744 6094] was revealed in 1977:

	Thickness m
Topsoil and made ground; buff, clayey, fine-grained sand	0.8
Clay, grey, slightly mottled brown	0.9
Silt, mottled orange and grey, with a gradational basal contact	0.3
Clay, mottled orange and grey	0.5
Clay, light grey, plastic, with modern rootlets	0.2
Peat, black, woody	0.9
CHALKY BOULDER CLAY	0.1

The Hoxnian clay-mud proved in West's boreholes 1 and 2 appears to be absent in the above section. The basal peat, which is barren, may correspond with West's 'detritus-mud with wood', and the overlying clays may correspond with West's 'grey and brown clays'. The uppermost 0.8 m in the above section probably correspond, in part, to brickearth. West demonstrated that the surface of the Boulder Clay dipped steeply north-westwards, and it was only in the north-western part of the pit that the Hoxnian deposits occurred. The surface of the Boulder Clay must also rise steeply north-westwards beyond the limit of the pit, as chalky Boulder Clay can be augered some 30 m beyond the northern edge of the pit. The deposits thus appear to occupy a channel. Possibly this channel continues south-west of Sicklesmere, where a borehole [8754 6044] proved 2.4 m of pale yellowish brown, silt with scattered chalk and flint sand, above 7.9+ m of grey, poorly laminated silt, and beneath 7.2 m of River Terrace Deposits (Hawkins, 1981).

Another brickpit [8760 6115] some 250 m north-east of Oak's Kiln, has now been backfilled. Bennett and Blake (1886, p.17) recorded 4.5 m of reddish brown clay (Head), resting on an irregular surface of Boulder Clay in part of the pit, and elsewhere on a dark green clay in which flint implements have been found. Gravel is said to occur underneath this latter clay, which in turn rests on Boulder Clay. The origin of the clay with implements is not known, but it presumably formed during an interglacial.

About 1 km north-west of the above pit, there is the ploughed-over site of another clay pit [8690 6213]. Boulder Clay and some gravel was augered at many points around the pit, but a borehole [8690 6200] close by proved, in descending sequence: Made Ground, 1.2 m; clay and gravel (?Head), 0.8 m; creamy silt, becoming bluish grey in the bottom 0.3 m, 12.8 m; silt, orange-brown with chalk pebbles, 0.7 m; Chalk. These deposits appear to occupy a local steep-sided depression, and their similarity to those near Oak's Kiln suggests that they may also be interglacial.   CRB

Another borehole [8618 6193] near Nowton Court encountered silt at two levels: the upper, beneath 2.5 m of Head, occurred between the depths of 2.5 and 14.8 m; the lower, beneath gravel, lay between 21.5 and 23.0 m (the base of the borehole). The upper silt contained a limited molluscan fauna (mainly between depths of 9 and 10 m) (Table 6, Col. 13) which included *Pisidium* sp., *Bithynia tentaculata*, *Valvata cristata* and *Sphaerium* sp.. *B. tentaculata* and *V. cristata* favour slow-flowing rivers and lakes, but the scarcity of shells, apart from the relatively durable opercula of *B. tentaculata*, coupled with the poor preservation and restricted diversity of the fauna, suggest that it may be partially reworked. DKG

A black peaty seam, 0.15 m thick, with flint implements underlay some 5.9 m of River Terrace Deposits at the former Grindle Pit [8593 6324] (Bennett and Blake, 1886, p.16). CRB

Another possible lacustrine site is at Fornham St Martin, where a borehole [8504 6747] proved 6.9 m of dominantly grey silt, locally laminated and with scattered shells and plant fragments, which rest on gravel above chalky Boulder Clay and are overlain by 5.6 m of River Terrace Deposits. Molluscan faunas were obtained at depths of 5.6 to 6.5 m, 7.5 to 8.0 m and 8.0 to 9.0 m (Table 6). All three faunas point to a slow-flowing or stagnant aquatic environment. Terrestrial species are completely absent from the top sample, and are represented by only a single specimen of *V. pulchella* and a vertiginid fragment in the middle one. *Cochlicopa lubrica* is terrestrial, but can live in damp or even saturated sites. None of the species present indicates temperatures different from those prevailing today. DKG

Another locality where shelly silts have been encountered is near Timworth Green. There, a borehole [8537 6913] proved:

	Thickness m	Depth m
Topsoil Sand, brown, with scattered flint pebbles	0.4	0.4
COVER SAND Sand, brownish orange, with scattered flint pebbles	1.7	2.1
?HEAD (or ?BOULDER CLAY) Clay, buff-brown, with chalk pebbles	3.4	5.5
?RIVER TERRACE DEPOSITS Gravel, coarse, dominantly flinty	1.8	7.3
?LACUSTRINE INTERGLACIAL SILT Clay, silty, pinkish brown	0.7	8.0
Silt, sandy, dark grey, organic, poorly laminated	0.2	8.2
GLACIAL SAND AND GRAVEL Sand, orange, with scattered flints	2.3	10.5
Gravel, 'Bunter' and flint pebbles	2.0	12.5
MIDDLE CHALK Chalk	0.5	13.0

The exact stratigraphical position of these deposits is uncertain. Cover Sand obscures much of the surface in this area, though chalky Boulder Clay has been augered west of the borehole site, River Terrace Deposits occur to the north, and Glacial Sand and Gravel crops out to the east. Of critical importance is the 3.4 m of brown-buff chalky clay encountered in the upper part of the borehole. If this is Boulder Clay, it is the only record in the Bury St Edmunds district of Boulder Clay overlying fossiliferous Quaternary deposits; alternatively, it is Head made up of solifluced Boulder Clay CRB

The fauna (Table 6) comprises both aquatic and terrestrial species. *Lymnaea truncatula* favours shallow, well-aerated water, but is amphibious and can resist periods of drought. *Zonitoides nitidus*, although terrestrial, is common on marshes, river banks and wet places. *Cochlicopa lubrica* and *Carychium* cf. *minimum* also prefer damp sites, while the Succineids live in marshes or river and lakeside banks amongst waterside plants. On balance, the fauna suggests a marshy, lakeside or riverside environment. There is no evidence that temperatures differed significantly from those of the present day. DKG

Kerney (1976) recorded a rich molluscan fauna from a calcareous tufa overlying silt and Boulder Clay in Beeches Pit [798 719], 2.5 km east-south-east of Icklingham Church, and it is convenient to describe this site together with the above, possibly interglacial ones. The assemblage indicates that the tufa formed in a temperate forest in association with pools fed by springs. Various aspects of the fauna resemble those from a tufa of supposed Hoxnian age at Hitchin and from Hoxnian deposits at Barnfield Pit, Swanscombe, but Kerney pointed out that, in the absence of supporting pollen evidence, no firm conclusions as to the age of the deposit could be made. Holyoak and others (1983) added several molluscs to Kerney's list, together with a tooth of the wood mouse *Apodemus* cf. *sylvaticus*. Many of the additional molluscs are not age-significant, as most of them have also been recorded from the Alluvium and Peat of the district (Table 6), but one, *Laminifera pauli*, is known only from the Hitchin deposit in Britain, and indicates a probable close correlation between the tufas at both sites. The above authors attempted to obtain uranium-series dates on the tufa matrix; dates indicated an age greater than 300 000 years BP. CRB

HEAD AND HEAD GRAVEL

Those heterogeneous deposits that do not fall into specific genetic divisions have been grouped under the term Head. They result from down-hill movement, partly by solifluction, of weathered surface material from a variety of lithological units: soil creep and minor mass movements probably still contribute to their accumulation. The various lithologies of the Head thus reflect the source material upslope. For example, Head derived from Boulder Clay is usually a chalk-free, orange-brown, stony clay; elsewhere, where Glacial Sand and Gravel or River Terrace Deposits occur, the Head is dominantly sandy and gravelly. In many cases, it is impossible to distinguish Head from its parent body; similar difficulty is experienced in separating Head from weathered in-situ deposits. The Head is generally confined to valleys, but locally it spreads out to form extensive sheets. Its recorded thickness varies between less than 1 and 9 m; only deposits generally thicker than 1 m have been shown on the geological map.

Within the district, no Head has been recognised lying beneath Boulder Clay and the Glacial Sand and Gravel, whilst Head overlies Hoxnian deposits in the Lark valley at Sicklesmere. The relationship of Head to the younger drift deposits, principally the River Terrace Deposits and Cover Sand, is less certain. There are few localities where undoubted solifluction deposits have been recognised resting on River Terrace Deposits, although the back margins of some of the terraces have been degraded by soil creep which has spread sediment a short distance over the terrace.

Head is associated with 'Hummocky ground' at a number of localities, as it is in the Cambridge district to the west (Worssam and Taylor, 1969). 'Hummocky ground' consists of a number of oval or rounded hollows up to 2 m deep and 50 m diameter. Worssam and Taylor (1969, p.99) recorded that the intervening ridges are of Chalk and that the hollows contain sand; this is not always so in the Bury St Edmunds district (see p.70). All the areas of 'hummocky ground' within the present district are low-lying and generally occur where the drift cover does not exceed 2 m in thickness. The origin of 'hummocky ground' was discussed by Worssam and Taylor (1969) who suggested that it was due either to solution or to Pleistocene periglacial conditions; possibly it formed by a combination of both processes.

Three areas of poorly sorted, unbedded, dominantly coarse gravel near Great Barton, Ampton and Honington have been mapped as Head Gravel. They probably originated largely by solifluction processes, but some transport and sorting by water may have taken place. Thicknesses of up to 5 m have been proved in the Great Barton area.

Details

Lark valley

Small patches of sandy clay and clayey fine-grained sand occur in the valley bottom of the headwaters of the Lark near Whepstead [830 580]. Around Pinford End [850 597], deposits of Head are more extensive. For the most part they consist of clayey fine-grained sand, locally chalky and gravelly [848 598]. Coarse-grained sand and gravel was encountered at two points [8493 5960; 8545 5974] and may include soliflucted River Terrace Deposits.

Head, associated with the small valley which flows through Hawstead, is gravelly close to the confluence with the Lark; nearby River Terrace Deposits probably constituted the source material. Silt and silty clay, which were noted within the Head at a number of points near Hawstead [8575 5976; 8660 5932; 8558 5805], are also probably derived from River Terrace Deposits.

The sides of the tributary valley to the Lark, which descends from Bradfield Combust to the confluence at Sicklesmere, are extensively mantled with Head. For the most part, this is sandy and gravelly, and much of the contributory material has been derived from the Upper Sand and Gravel. Locally, thin dark brown sandy clay and stones overlie gravel, which rests on the weathered top of the Boulder Clay [8920 5910]. The Head is particularly gravelly southeast of the Windmill [8845 5960], and has been worked for gravel north and north-east of the Windmill [8793 6025; 8812 6017]. It is probably derived from River Terrace Deposits.

A section at the old brick pit [876 815] at Sicklesmere was recorded by Bennett and Blake (1886, p.17). They saw up to 4.5 m of reddish brown clay (here regarded as Head), resting on an irregular surface of Boulder Clay; other workers recorded up to 9 m of this clay. On the opposite side of the valley, however, the Head is dominantly sand with minor amounts of gravel.

One of the best sections [880 618] is in a minor tributary valley: it shows 1.5 m of brown sand with scattered flints, the basal 0.3 m being more pebbly, with angular and nodular flints and scarce, rounded, brown quartzite pebbles; this rests on 1.5 m of chalky sand. Lower down the same valley [8781 6185], nodular flints at the base of the Head rest on Chalk.

About 500 m north of Bridge Farm, another tributary valley joins the Lark, and the Head, 2.6 m thick, seems to be chalky sand and gravel [8739 6239]. Farther upstream, a borehole [8829 6288] proved the following sequence:

	Thickness m
Topsoil	
Sand, brown, fine-grained, with scattered flints	0.7
HEAD	
Sand, pebbly and gravelly, orange-brown, fine- to medium-grained, with scattered angular to subrounded flints up to cobble grade; scarce rounded brown quartzites	0.7
Sand, pebbly, orange, with scattered angular to subrounded flints	1.4
Sand, medium-grained, orange	0.9
Sand, as above with scattered black, angular to subrounded flints	1.3
Chalk paste, white to pale orange, with rounded and subangular flints	0.3
UPPER CHALK	—

Clayey sand, locally up to 2.5 m thick [8618 6193], with minor amounts of gravel, is dominant along the left-bank tributary which flows north of Nowton Park. Similar deposits mantle the lower valley sides of the valley system east of Bury St Edmunds [around 869 654]. CRB

Extensive Head occurs along the southern flanks of the Linnet valley. Trial pits have proved up to 3.7 m of variable deposits that range from clayey coarse-grained sand, to sandy clays, and to silty clays with chalk and flint pebbles. BSPM

Much farther north, in the higher reaches of the valley that rises near Culford Heath [860 749] and extends through Troston and Great Livermere, the Head consists of gravelly sand, locally with many rounded quartzites [863 748]. At Black Hill, rounded 'Bunter' quartzites and angular flints are the dominant component [887 743], and farther down the valley [890 742], the deposit is sufficiently gravelly to have been worked for gravel. Near Troston Mount [885 741], the Head is peaty, but close by [895 740], it is very gravelly with 'Bunter' quartzites and large, white, patinated, fresh flints. Southwards to Slades Covert [around 890 726], the Head is dominantly a clayey gravel. On Troston Heath [887 741], south of Honington Airfield, there is much angular patinated flint debris on the surface, which has been called Head Gravel. Its thickness is unknown, but exceeds 1.3 m. CRB

In the tributary valley that joins the above valley near Slades Covert, up to 3 m of clayey sand and gravel overlie orange clay in an old pit [8704 7339]. Lower down the valley, there is a mixture of clayey sand and gravel, while near Great Livermere, a reticulate patterning shown on aerial photographs [892 717] suggests that up to 1.5 m of clayey sand and gravel may overlie chalky Boulder Clay. CRB, TEL

Downstream, the Head is very gravelly west of Timworth Hall [867 695], but westwards it appears to become more sandy [862 691]; there are up to 1.5 m of gravelly sand in the tributary valley to the south which passes through Springhill Covert [8720 6755].

Between The Plains [865 703] and The Holmes [872 702], south of Ampton, sand and gravel, up to at least 2 m thick, rests irregularly on chalky Boulder Clay and has been classified as Head Gravel. Its irregular nature is evidenced by a faint reticulate pattern visible on aerial photographs. Locally [8713 6991; 8712 7048], springs issue from its base. CRB

It is difficult to distinguish soliflucted chalk from in-situ Chalk in the absence of good sections. A pit [7880 6933] on the northern side of Risby Poor's Heath showed 2 m of chalky sand and chalk gravel, but the area has been mapped as Upper Chalk rather than Head. In the extreme north-west, Head covers an area of extremely hummocky relief, where the hummocks consist of Chalk and the hollows are filled with sand and gravelly sand. Patches of Head occur about 1 km west of Chalk Hill near Barton Mills, and near Herringswell Manor [722 711].

Kennett valley and tributaries

Head, varying from a clayey flinty silt to gravel, occurs along the lower flanks of much of the Kennett valley and its tributaries. In some of the valley bottoms, the clayey gravel has probably been derived from now degraded terraces.

Head also occurs along the valley north of Denham, where up to 2 m of silty sands with local concentrations of angular flints are exposed [7527 6300 to 7544 6353]. BSPM

Tributaries of the Gipping

Two unnamed streams in the extreme south-east drain eastwards to the Gipping. Head, consisting dominantly of clayey sand with minor amounts of gravel, is present along the larger stream which flows through Rattlesden. In general, it does not appear to exceed 1.5 m in thickness, but a well [9754 5893] at Rattlesden passed through 4.9 m of 'loam and stone', here regarded as Head, before entering Crag.

The Black Bourn and its tributaries

Head is present in the upper reaches of The Black Bourn north-east of Freecroft Wood. The deposits consist of sandy clay, clayey sand, and sand and gravel, and are locally chalky.

Clayey sands, with minor amounts of gravel, are predominant along the valley to Drinkstone [96 62] and Broadgrass Green [969 633]. Just beyond Broadgrass Green, The Black Bourn is joined by a north-west-flowing tributary; the surface indications along this tributary valley suggest that the Head is quite gravelly, although the only borehole [9775 6322] into the deposit proved 2+ m of brown sandy and silty clay.

Lower down the main valley, where Glacial Sand and Gravel crops out on the valley sides, the Head is correspondingly gravelly. At Norton [955 664], in particular, surface indications are of a very gravelly deposit.

The valley that runs westwards from Hunston is mantled with Head. At the eastern limit of the district, the Head consists of up to 1.4 m of sand with a thin gravelly base. In a subsidiary tributary near Mill Hill, Hunston, fine- to medium-grained clayey sand exceeds 2 m in thickness.

There is a fairly wide expanse of Head near Bridge Farm where the Hunston tributary joins The Black Bourn. It appears to have a high gravel content, and a borehole [9491 6847] close to the farm proved 1.7 m of brown clayey sand and gravel, above 0.6 m of more clayey and slightly chalky sand and gravel; this rests on sand and gravel which is thought to be River Terrace Deposits.

A major tributary enters The Black Bourn at Grimstone End. Along this valley, the Head is dominantly fine-grained sand on the west bank of Pakenham Fen. South of Pakenham, where the valley divides, fine-grained sand predominates southward as far as Thurston, but locally, gravel lies beneath it. The sand is 2.2 m thick in a borehole [9321 6413] at Thurston Planch, and 3.8 m thick in boreholes for the Beyton By-pass [around 932 638]. In the branch that continues westwards through Barton Mere, surface indications are of a locally very gravelly Head [914 668], and 2.1 m of sandy clay, clayey sand and gravel have been proved above the Mere.

Head deposits in a shallow subsidiary valley north of Great Barton are particularly gravelly and have been distinguished as Head Gravel. The gravel has been worked in several pits in the woods south-west of the Bunbury Arms. The westernmost pit [899 674], about 5 m deep and mostly overgrown, has about 1 m of coarse unsorted gravel still visible at its top. An exposure on the south side of a second pit [9015 6735] shows 2 to 3 m of unbedded, unsorted, coarse gravel resting on Chalk. The junction with the Chalk is in general planar, but pockets of gravel appear to be piped down to at least 1.5 m below the contact.

North of the main road, the Head Gravel rests on Boulder Clay, and a borehole [8984 6807] proved 5.5 m of very clayey sandy gravel.

Similar deposits have been referred to Head Gravel north of Upper Town, where sections in the old chalk pit [9170 6795] show up to 3.5 m of coarse, unsorted, knobbly flints above Chalk. One section had 2 m of brown sand and pebbly loam at the top, resting on decalcified, unsorted and unbedded gravel with included pockets of chalk-rich gravel. The fields to the east are covered with huge knobbly flints [920 683], but the Head Gravel seems to be thin and a borehole [9240 6808] proved only 1.4 m of it.

Southward, east of East Barton, fine-grained sand, gravelly sand and sandy gravel occupy the bottom of another tributary [912 652], and the deposits are sufficiently gravelly to have been worked for sand and gravel [9180 6483].

At Blackthorpe, the valley system splits into several broad valleys, all of which have extensive Head deposits on their sides and bottoms. Some 2 to 3 m of clayey sand and gravel have been recorded at several localities [9095 6350; 9140 6345; 9190 6347]. CRB

RIVER TERRACE DEPOSITS

The River Terrace Deposits were probably formed episodically by meltwaters emerging from waning ice sheets or snow-fields, at a time when river-flow was greater than it is now and larger bed-loads were carried. Cryoturbation structures have been noted in the Fourth and Third River Terrace Deposits (see p.66; Worssam and Taylor, 1969, p.95), and ice-wedge casts in the Second River Terrace Deposits, indicating cold climatic conditions. Molluscs and pollen from the First River Terrace Deposits also indicate temperatures lower than at present, while the fauna of large vertebrates in several of the terraces, with the exception of one record of *Hippopotamus*, is also indicative of cooler conditions than those of the present-day.

At Lackford and Cavenham (Plate 6), First and Second River Terrace Deposits overlie deposits which have been dated at 25 030 + 1430/ − 1210 BP and 28 880 + 520/ − 480 BP (Lackford), and 26 870 + 260 BP (Cavenham) (see pp.56 and 57). In The Black Bourn valley, Second River Terrace Deposits overlie silts which have been dated at 34 380 + 510/ − 730 years BP. Consequently, these terraces are no older than the mid-Devensian; the higher ones are presumably older.

Lark valley

Four terraces have been recognised within the Lark valley.

Fourth River Terrace Deposits are restricted to a small outcrop near Fornham St Martin [850 675] where they have a surface level of about 35 m above OD, some 10 m above the floodplain. The only borehole [8504 6747] to penetrate the deposits proved them to be 5.6 m thick, including 2.1 m of clayey, sandy and pebbly silt. Mean grading figures show 23 per cent 'fines', 71 per cent sand and 6 per cent gravel (Hawkins, 1981).

Third River Terrace Deposits have been recognised only at Timworth Green [860 692] where they have a surface level of about 29 m above OD, about 5 m above the floodplain. They have been proved in only one borehole [8590 6923], where they were 3.6 m thick. The deposits vary markedly in grade, but have a mean of 5 per cent 'fines', 55 per cent sand and 40 per cent gravel (Hawkins, 1981)

Second River Terrace Deposits occur as scattered patches [876 605; 866 630] between Sicklesmere and Bury St Edmunds, and as a more or less continuous spread from just north of Bury St Edmunds to Tuddenham. Spreads also occur along the stream which flows westwards from Great Livermere.

Plate 6 Ice-wedge cast within Second River Terrace Deposits, Cavenham. (A13063)

Along the Lark valley, the surface of the deposits falls from 43 m above OD at Sicklesmere, about 2 m above the floodplain, to 41 m above OD south of Bury St Edmunds, to 29 m above OD north-west of Bury St Edmunds, and to about 20 m above OD at Tuddenham.

The thickness of deposits below Bury St Edmunds varies from 1.7 m [8309 6981] north-east of Hengrave, to 13.3 m [7636 7316] near Icklingham. The mean grading figures given by Clayton (1983, table 2) erroneously include some samples from the First River Terrace Deposits; they show, nevertheless, that the deposits are dominantly of sand (76 per cent) with 17 per cent of gravel and 7 per cent of 'fines'. At Sicklesmere, Second River Terrace Deposits have a total thickness of 6.8 m, but this includes a 1.1 m bed of silt in the middle. Mean grading figures show 20 per cent 'fines', 42 per cent sand and 38 per cent gravel (Hawkins, 1981).

At Sicklesmere, bones of *Rhinoceros tichorhinus* and *Elephas primigenius*, both indicative of cool climatic conditions, have been found in the Second River Terrace Deposits (Bennett and Blake, 1886), and ice-wedge casts occur in them at Cavenham [7642 7090] (Plate 6).

There are small outcrops of First River Terrace Deposits near Hawstead [862 585; 860 596], Bury St Edmunds [856 646], Lackford [800 705], and from Icklingham [770 725] to the margin of the district north of Mildenhall. The terrace surface falls from about 60 m above OD at Hawstead, some 1 to 2 m above the floodplain, to 31 m above OD at Bury St Edmunds, c.23 m above OD at Lackford, and 8 or 9 m OD on Tuddenham Heath where the terrace rises southwards away from the river to about 11 or 12 m above OD. In addition, a large, flat, low-lying tract of sand and gravel extends northwards from Barton Mills to the Fens (just outside the district); this was previously regarded as Glacial Sand and Gravel (Holmes, 1971), but has now been reinterpreted as First River Terrace Deposits. This interpretation suggests that, during the accumulation of these deposits, the Lark flowed northwards along this line and not along its present westward course, a suggestion supported by the absence of terraces along the Lark west of Barton Mills.

The thickness of the First River Terrace Deposits varies from 0.2 m at Lackford [8175 6973] to 8 m east of Mildenhall [7286 7457]. Mean grading figures show 6 per cent 'fines', 86 per cent sand, and 8 per cent gravel; fine-grained (46 per cent) and medium-grained (36 per cent) sand are dominant.

A shelly fauna has been obtained from First River Terrace Deposits at Lackford (Table 6; see also p.70). The presence of the cold-water bivalve *Pisidium obtusale lapponicum* and the relative abundance of *Pupilla muscorum* indicate temperatures lower than at present, as does the presence of spores of *Selaginella*. Bones of *Bos*, *Mammuthus* and a large cervid have been found in the gravel (see p.70).

A peat-filled channel associated with Second and First River Terrace Deposits runs from the present Lark valley just south of Mildenhall, westwards towards Worlington. A slight rise along this channel divides the present drainage. It is possible that the Lark formerly flowed westwards along this course before adopting its present more northerly route. An alternative explanation, which is supported by the distribution of the terraces between the Snail valley and Mildenhall, is that the River Snail, which lies just beyond the Bury St Edmunds district, flowed eastwards from its present course and entered the Lark valley via this channel.

Kennett Valley

Four terraces have also been recognised in the Kennett valley. With the exception of the First, which occurs only in the extreme west, all the deposits have been worked extensively for gravel. Locally, extraction and restoration have made it impossible to differentiate between the Second and Third terraces.

In the higher reaches [720 596] of the Kennett, the surface of the Fourth River Terrace Deposits is at about 60 m above OD. The surface falls to about 42 m above OD near Moulton Bridge [695 647; 702 655]. At Kentford, the surface falls northwards from about 43 m [706 663] to about 32 m [707 671]. Farther north-west [70 68], the surface lies at about 30 m above OD, some 8 m above the floodplain (see Worssam and Taylor, 1969, fig. 7). In a trial pit [7007 6804], up to 7.6 m of sand and gravel have been proved. Mean grading figures for one borehole [7140 6799] show 23 per cent 'fines', 66 per cent sand and 11 per cent gravel (Clayton, 1983). Elsewhere, the deposits appear to have a higher gravel content, but commonly include much chalk. A mixed vertebrate fauna includes both cool (*Rhinoceras*) and warm-loving (*Hippopotamus*) forms (Whitaker and others, 1891). Wright (1886) recorded flint implements in terrace deposits in the Kentford area, although their exact provenance is uncertain (see below).

Third River Terrace Deposits, with an upper surface between 55 and 58 m above OD, flank the River Kennett near Ousden. Near Moulton Bridge, the upper surface falls to about 37 m above OD (see Worssam and Taylor, 1969, fig. 7). In places [e.g. 706 634], the deposits are at least 6 m thick.

Second River Terrace Deposits are most extensive below Kentford. In addition to the terraces along the present Kennett, an extensive spread occupies the low which passes through Tuddenham. The thickness of these deposits varies from 1.1 m [7303 7121] to 4.5 [7137 7010] (Clayton, 1983, p.50). Mean grading figures show 5 per cent 'fines', 80 per cent sand and 15 per cent gravel. Fine-grained (54 per cent) and medium-grained (23 per cent) sands are the dominant constituents, while the gravel content varies markedly from 0 to 38 per cent.

Small areas of First River Terrace Deposits are preserved near Kennett Hall [7007 6880]. The maximum thickness proved is 4.6 m [7024 6842], but no figures are available for the grade of the deposit. BSPM

The Black Bourn and its tributaries

River Terrace Deposits occur at three levels within the valley of The Black Bourn, though those of the Third Terrace, which is the highest, is limited to a small spread near Grimstone End [934 696] where its upper surface is at about 35 m above OD, some 5 to 6 m above the floodplain.

The Second River Terrace Deposits have a surface level of about 38 m above OD near Norton, some 2 m above the floodplain. The surface falls to between 30 and 31 m above OD near Ixworth [93 70], and to about 25 m above OD near Honington [913 745]. Second River Terrace Deposits also occur along the stream which flows through Stowlangtoft. At Stowlangtoft, their surface level is at about 35 to 36 m above OD, some 2 to 3 m above the floodplain. The deposits vary in thickness from 2.6 m [9533 6604] at Norton to 15.2 m [9359 7422] at Bardwell. Mean grading figures show 10 per cent 'fines', 46 per cent sand and 43 per cent gravel. A radiometric age determination of 34 380 + 510/ – 730 years BP has been obtained from peaty silt underlying terrace deposits at Norton (Clarke and Auton, 1982).

The First River Terrace Deposits near Woolpit fall northwards from c.52 m above OD [960 624] to c.45 m above OD [966 638], and lie about 2 m above the floodplain. Lower downstream, deposits of this terrace form low islands about 1 m high within the peaty floodplain [around 954 651]. The maximum thickness proved is 2.4 m [9474 6787]. Mean grading figures show 8 per cent 'fines', 48 per cent sand and 44 per cent gravel, very similar to those of the Second Terrace. CRB

Details

Kennett valley

FOURTH TERRACE: Fourth River Terrace Deposits, consisting of an unknown thickness of angular to subrounded, commonly patinated flint gravel, lie at 60 m above OD west of Ousden [around 720 596].

Further remnants occur downstream just north of Moulton Bridge [696 646], where two patches of gravel occur, with surfaces at about 42 m above OD. On the more southerly patch [696 647], flints in the soil were mainly 5–8 cm across, subrounded, and with a brown patina. BCW

South-south-west of Kentford Church, a small flat [702 655] is underlain by Fourth River Terrace Deposits, subangular flints in a sandy matrix occur in the soil. Around Kentford [7093 6678], a more extensive outcrop occurs, which has been worked extensively for gravel; many of the pits have been backfilled or landscaped. A degraded face [7177 6689] in old workings east of Kentford Church revealed 4+ m of mainly subangular, patinated, flint gravel. A 5.5 m section was described by Whitaker and others (1891) and showed: 'Gravel, and rolled flints, with a few boulders of quartzite, obscurely bedded in places, up to 10 feet (3.05 m) thick, overlying gravel, almost wholly of chalk pebbles, with layers of chalky false bedded sand passing into pipe clay'. Wright (1886) recorded flint implements, both worn and fresh, in the pit, and Whitaker and others (1891) collected fragmentary bones of *Bos*, *Cervus*, *Elephas primigenius*, *Equus*, *Hippopotamus*, and *Rhinoceras*. Bennett (*in* Whitaker and others, 1891) noted that the elephant teeth and flint implements came from the upper gravel, which he thought was deposited at 'different times and under different conditions' to the lower, and older gravel.

Variation within the Fourth River Terrace Deposits is shown by two boreholes close to the above exposure. One [7175 6684] proved 1.5 m of fine- to coarse-grained sand and subangular to rounded flint gravel with scattered small flint cobbles, on stiff structureless 'remoulded' chalk. The other [7187 6685] proved 2 m of calcareous silt and chalky sandy silt on 1+ m of chalky sand. Augering in a disused gravel pit [7134 6650], now landscaped, south of the old A45, proved about 2 m of gravel on rather soft Chalk.

There are small gravel workings [7070 6695] north of Kennett Church, but no face remains. Boreholes alongside the A45 have proved up to 4.3 m of calcareous, slightly silty, fine- and medium-grained sand, with some fine to coarse flint gravel, resting on structureless 'remoulded' chalk. A section [7125 6741] east of Cock and Bull Farm, Kentford, revealed:

	Depth m
Gravel, poorly bedded, with mainly nodular and subrounded flints of cobble size; also some rounded quartzite and some well-rounded flints in a brown, medium- and coarse-grained sandy matrix; probably decalcified	3.3
Gravel, mainly chalk, but also some small angular and subangular flints, in pale grey buff, sandy, silty matrix	seen to 3.9

The operator reported that up to 5 m of sand and gravel were dug from this pit.

A discontinuous, largely overgrown section [7128 6830 to 7163 6802], about 1 km east of Kennett Church, showed up to 4 m of sand and gravel. BSPM

Terrace gravel caps the ridge that extends from Dane Hill, in the adjacent Cambridge district, eastwards through Kennett village [697 682]. At Dane Hill, the terrace overlies a Boulder Clay-filled channel. To the north-east, yellowish silts that underlie the terrace deposit crop out, and sandy fine-grained gravel overlies at least 1.8 m of buff or yellow laminated silt in a small, largely overgrown pit [697 682] between 5 and 6 m deep.

Some 300 m south of Kennett Church, a gravel pit [700 679] showed 4.5 m of gravel, much disturbed by frost action. The lowest 1.5 m was gravel with a sandy matrix, crowded with chalk pebbles and with scattered grey flints; this passed up into rather less chalky gravel which rose in places to within 0.6 m of the surface, and was overlain along a sharp junction by brown decalcified gravel, consisting of closely packed, mostly slightly worn, small, angular flints in a matrix of sand and flint chips.   BCW

A trial pit [7007 6804] dug in 1978 into the northern end of the eastern face proved:

	Depth m
Gravel, mainly of angular to subangular patinated flints up to 4 cm diameter, with a sandy matrix and no obvious bedding	1.3
Sand, medium-grained, orange-brown, containing some small flints between depths of 1.5 and 1.6 m; horizontally bedded with much iron staining along bedding; a few flint pebbles	3.1
Gravel, mainly of subangular flints, with some rounded chalk clasts up to 5–10 cm diameter; coarse-grained sand matrix	3.2
Silt, buff, laminated, containing bivalves and gastropods; lenses of interbedded coarse-grained sand in upper part show distortion, possibly due to cryoturbation; thin gravel lens at 4.1 m; the silt becomes finer grained with increasing depth and consists of interbanded sandy silt bands (7–8 cm thick) and clayey silt bands (2–3 cm thick generally, but up to 7 cm thick)	6.0

Another pit [7007 6794], in the south-east corner of the gravel pit, proved a similar sequence of 4 m of decalcified, contorted sand and gravel in the upper part, resting on laminated shelly silt.

About 200 m to the east, a face [7038 6809] in a landscaped gravel pit exposed up to 2 m of dominantly coarse and well-sorted flint gravel with interbedded clean medium- to coarse-grained sand, overlying much more poorly sorted chalky gravel and sand, with less well-defined bedding. The junction between the two gravels was sharp with a slight northward dip. The upper gravels thinned southwards against the rising hill-side. An older pit [7010 6815] nearby appears to have worked only the upper cleaner gravels; these may represent a younger deposit banked against Fourth River Terrace Deposits, but their height suggests that both the gravels fall within the Fourth Terrace.   BSPM

THIRD TERRACE: Third Terrace gravels occur on both sides of the River Kennett about 2 km west of Ousden, at heights of between about 55 and 58 m above OD. The gravels, which consist mainly of angular flints, with subordinate subangular to subrounded flints, have been worked in two small pits [7215 5945; 7225 5933], about 2 m deep, on either side of the Ousden to Ashley road.

For 1 km southwards from Moulton Bridge, a strip of Third Terrace gravel, 150 m wide, with a surface about 37 m above OD, flanks the west side of the Kennett floodplain. A pit [706 634] proved between 4.5 and 6 m of gravel, of which the top 0.6 to 1 m is decalcified. The gravel is characterised by large, only slightly worn flints, many of them 0.1 to 0.15 m across, and abundant chalk pebbles of about 1 cm diameter with small angular flints and sand in the matrix. Some sarsens approaching the size of boulders occur in the gravel.

A section [694 686] in a pit about 800 m north-west of Kennett Church in the Cambridge district exposed about 2 m of gravel, chalky at its base, resting on at least 0.3 m of buff clayey silt. About 100 m north-west, another section in the same pit revealed rubbly Chalk beneath gravel. In a separate pit [693 688] just to the north, about 2 m of well-bedded flint gravel with seams of sand were exposed; there was a slight festooning of flints in the upper 0.6 m.

SECOND TO THIRD TERRACE: Along the sides of the stream that flows north-westwards 1.5 km west of Lower Green [744 657], there are small patches of degraded terrace gravels associated with Head. A borehole [7275 6648] about 1 km west of Seven Mile Bridge encountered more than 4 m of silty, fine- and medium-grained sand, and fine to medium, patchily clayey, flint gravel.

Extensive sand and gravel workings occur on either side of the railway 1 km east-north-east of Kentford Church. In the southernmost pit [7130 6650], a degraded section showed up to 1 m of mainly angular patinated flints with some rounded quartzites and vein quartz. Below this, the section was obscured, but Chalk was augered in the base of the pit. A borehole [7128 6694] about 200 m north of this pit proved:

	Depth m
Topsoil, brown, sandy, clayey, with a little fine to coarse flint gravel	0.2
Sand, fine- and medium-grained, brown, clayey, and flint gravel with scattered cobbles	2.4
Sand, silty, fine- to medium-grained, brown, with some fine to coarse flint gravel and a little fine to medium chalk gravel	5.5
Middle Chalk	6.7

North of the railway line, a section [7151 6711] revealed up to 5 m of gravel on Chalk. The gravel consists mainly of angular and subangular patinated flints with some bedded sand lenses. A well [7189 6716], sunk in one of the old gravel pits, recorded 5.5 m of sand and 'ballast' on Chalk. Approximately 300 m farther north, very poorly sorted chalky gravel, up to 1.5 m thick, overlies soft puggy Chalk. The Chalk surface is very irregular, and in places the Chalk has been squeezed up to form lumps up to 1 m in diameter in the gravel; subrounded and rounded chalk pebbles are also present. The gravel consists mainly of angular and subangular flints, together with some quartzite and rounded sandstone pebbles, and is overlain, along a sharp horizontal junction, by much cleaner, well-bedded gravel and interbedded sand. The distinction between the two gravels is not so clear at the northern end of the pit [7180 6768]. There is channelling within the upper gravel towards the north-eastern corner, and buff to grey silt, with an irregular upper surface, underlies the gravel beneath much of the pit.

A section [717 683] near the edge of the terrace, on the north-east of Kentford Heath, revealed up to 2 m of subangular flint gravel on an irregular Chalk surface.

SECOND TERRACE: There is a group of old pits 300 m east of Kennett Hall. North-east of these pits, a large tract of terrace stretches as far as Tuddenham [740 725]. Over most of this area, fine-grained sand has been augered to depths of 1.4 m. A well [7135 6946] proved 2.4 m of sand, on 2.1 m of gravel, on Chalk. Several metres of sand have been dug in two overgrown pits [7155 6993; 7157 6985] just west of Herringswell church. In the Woodlands area [7215 6970] of Herringswell, the flat-lying spread of fine-grained sand at the surface is remarkably free of flints, and is very similar to Cover Sand.

A trial pit [7123 7007] south of Park Farm, Herringswell, proved:

	Depth m
Topsoil, dark	0.3
Gravel, mainly angular flints, and sand, medium- to coarse-grained	2.1
Silt, clayey and sandy, with rounded chalk pebbles	3.0

Some 400 m north-east, within shallow gravel workings, another pit [7153 7033] revealed:

	Depth m
Topsoil, sandy	0.3
Sand, medium-grained	1.3
Gravel, sandy	2.3
Sand, medium-grained	2.8
Gravel and sand, clayey	3.0

North-east of Hall Farm [724 704], Herringswell, the surface of the terrace is very irregular, with peat in some of the depressions.

FIRST TERRACE: First River Terrace Deposits are limited in extent, occurring only south of Kennett Hall [7007 6880] on both sides of the river at about 1 m above alluvium level. Boreholes south of the river proved between 3.2 and 4.6 m of sand and gravel on Chalk. One [7024 6842], proved 2.3 m of fine, medium, and coarse sandy flint gravel, resting on 2.3 m of medium- to coarse-grained sand with chalk and flint pebbles up to 5 cm in diameter. BSPM

Lark Valley

FOURTH TERRACE: A small spread of sand and gravel with a surface level of about 35 m above OD (some 10 m above alluvium level) occurs north of Fornham St Martin. A borehole [8504 6747] north of the crossroads proved 5.6 m of fine- to medium-grained, orange-brown sand with rare scattered flints resting on shelly silt (see p.57) at 29.6 m above OD.

THIRD TERRACE: In the tributary valley of the Lark at Timworth, Third River Terrace Deposits, with a surface level of about 30 m above OD, are more gravelly than Fourth River Terrace Deposits. At one point [8590 6923], they consist of 3.8 m of sandy gravel.

SECOND TERRACE: Second River Terrace Deposits at Sicklesmere have a surface level of about 46 m above OD, some 5 m above the alluvium. In one borehole they consist of 3.6 m of clayey sand, pebbly sand and clayey sand and gravel, locally chalky [8754 6044]. Bennett and Blake (1886) recorded the following section in a pit at Sicklesmere: soil, 0.3 m; gravel with a chalky matrix, 1.8 m; clean coarse gravel, bedded with fine gravel, and with bones of *Rhinoceros tichorhinus* and *Elephas primigenius* at the bottom, 3.7 m.

At Southgate Bridge, the terrace deposits on either side of the river have been extensively worked for sand and gravel, but most of the pits have been backfilled. A small pit [8665 6305] alongside the railway line, showed 4 m of coarse, poorly sorted, crudely bedded, flint gravel. At the former Grindle Pit [8600 6325], Bennett and Blake (1886) recorded: loam, sandy and gravelly, 2.1 m; brown loam or brickearth, 2.1 m; buff sand and gravel, 1.2 to 1.8 m; black peaty seam containing flint implements, 0.15 m; gravel, unstratified and coarse, thinning out westwards, 2.1 m; on Glacial Sand and Gravel. They also recorded a 4.3 m section in sand and flint gravel at the old Botanic Garden [c.859 642]. This must be a very small deposit, for no undisturbed sand and gravel was noted during the present survey.

At Timworth, the surface of the Second Terrace is about 26 m to 27 m above OD, about 2 m higher than the Alluvium [856 694]. A borehole [8520 6977] north of the river proved 2 m of medium-grained sand with scattered flints resting on Glacial Silt. CRB

Sand, gravelly sand and gravel form a continuous spread along the south-west side of the Lark valley from Bury St Edmunds to just south of Flempton. The terrace, which attains a maximum width of just over 700 m, ranges in height from 30 m above OD near Bury St Edmunds, to about 23 m near Flempton, and 22 m at West Stow. Although generally flat, there are irregularities in the surface.

Several boreholes have been drilled through the terrace deposits (Hawkins, 1981); the abbreviated results are given in Table 5 below:

Table 5 Thicknesses of Second River Terrace Deposits between Fornham All Saints and Hengrave

Borehole	TL 86 NW 118	TL 86 NW 117	TL 86 NW 116	TL 86 NW 115	TL 86 NW 110
NGR	8393 6728	8328 6783	8326 6851	8291 6841	8238 6910
Terrace deposits	to 4.7 m	3.8 m	4.2 m	5.3 m	2.1 m
Glacial Silt	to 21.4 m+	20.2 m+	12.5 m+	8.0 m+	20.3 m+

In general, the boreholes show that the upper part of the River Terrace Deposits consists of fine-grained sand, with scattered subangular flints. At depth, this is replaced by sandy gravel or gravel consisting of angular and subangular patinated flints.

Near Hengrave, several brick pits [8260 6855] have been dug through the terrace deposits, which are generally less than 1.5 m thick, into silty clays and silts (see p.57). A borehole [8414 6976] east of South Wood proved 2.8 m of sand, with a variable content of subangular to subrounded flint, above 1.2 m of fine and coarse gravel with subangular to subrounded flints, which rests on Boulder Clay.

Between South Wood and Dixon's Covert, a borehole [8309 6981] proved 2.5 m of yellow-brown, medium-grained sand with scattered subrounded to subangular flints. The sand, which is clayey towards its base, overlies Boulder Clay. BSPM

North-west of Cavenham, there is a spread of Second River Terrace Deposits about 8 km^2 in extent. The sequence comprises an upper sand and a lower coarse gravel, which rests on Glacial Silt. One section [7632 7085] in the south-east corner of Cavenham pit, showed:

	Depth m
SUBSOIL (topsoil has been stripped off) Sand, brown, fine- to medium-grained	0.2
SECOND RIVER TERRACE DEPOSITS Sand, fine-grained, yellowish fawn, with abundant dark mineral grains; stringers of small, subangular, white, patinated flint gravel with scattered larger nodular flints; locally, chalk pellets form up to 25 per cent of the gravel content; sedimentary structures include graded bedding and channel cross-bedding; small channels with gravel stringers fining into the centre, with a lateral persistence of between 4 to 20 m	3.7
Gravel, coarse to fine, with angular to subangular flints and shattered nodular flints up to 0.2 m; fine gravel fraction is largely rounded chalk pellets; matrix is a fawn, fine-grained sand; some lenses of fine-grained sand	5.9
GLACIAL SILT Silt, dark grey, clayey, chalky	6.1

Another section [7642 7090] at the eastern end of the face showed:

	Depth m
RIVER TERRACE DEPOSITS	
Sand, fine- to medium-grained, well-sorted, well-bedded, bedding generally horizontal; local small-scale cross bedding, local stringers of fine-grained sand; several ice-wedge casts; gravel more abundant in basal 1 m above a sharp base	4.8
?HEAD GRAVEL	
Gravel, coarse to fine, compact, poorly sorted, in clayey medium-grained sand with scattered gravel; irregular lobate base	5.8
Gravel, melange of clayey sand and gravel, chalky sand and gravel; silt stringers and balls; generally very disturbed, possibly cryoturbated	c.7.2
GLACIAL SILT	
Silt, sandy, light reddish brown, laminated, compact, calcareous, with numerous comminuted shell fragments; interbedded with gravel, light reddish brown, structureless, with clayey sand matrix and some pockets of clean sand; sharp irregular base	9.2
Silt, sandy, compact, light to medium bluish grey, laminated, with stringers of sandy fine gravel which pass laterally into beds of structureless, poorly sorted, sandy gravel	10.7

A broad, curving, roughly north–south channel, about 3 m deep, is cut into Glacial Silt and filled with River Terrace Deposits in the eastern part of the pit.

North and north-east of Tuddenham, the surface of the Second Terrace drops northwards from about 20 m to 10 m above OD. The surface deposits consist mainly of brown fine-grained sand with scattered flints; locally, a gravelly sand or sandy gravel has been augered. Generally, the gravel consists of subangular and angular patinated flints, but some concentrations of rounded quartzite and vein quartz pebbles occur [e.g. 748 711].

Within the main outcrop of the River Terrace Deposits, patches of Glacial Silt are present beneath up to 1 m of sand about 1 km east of Tuddenham [747 714] and about 700 m east of Glebe Farm [738 730]. The occurrence of silt at shallow depths indicates that the terrace deposits thin markedly between the area of gravel to the east and Tuddenham in the west.

A trial pit [7404 7405] in the terrace south of Mildenhall Warren exposed 2.9 m of unstratified clean, buff, fine-grained, sand, with scattered small flints; another [7330 7422] proved 3.1 m of slightly pebbly medium-grained sand, with small flints and quartzites. Farther downstream, boreholes at Mildenhall Upper School [721 746] indicate a rapid thinning of the terrace from 6 m in the east [7217 7456] to about 2 m in the west [7212 7465] over a distance of just over 100 m. North of the school, a well [7218 7498] close to the edge of the terrace proved: sand, 3.7 m; 'shingle', 0.6 m; sand, 3.65 m; 'stone' gravel, 1.5 m; clay, 13.4 m; Chalk, soft (reconstituted), 5 m; Chalk, 0.9+ m.

Skertchly (in Whitaker and others, 1891) noted that sections in the Mildenhall Brickworks [719 752] changed markedly during the working of the pit. In 1875, the eastern face revealed 2.4 m of bedded sand and gravel on 2.7 m of light bluish loam, which in turn rested on Chalk. Further north, at Mildenhall Second Upper School [714 757], pits and boreholes have proved up to 2 m of sand with scattered gravel, resting on soft white Chalk; the sand and gravel is chalky and contains large lumps of soft chalk up to 1 m in diameter.

On the eastern margin of the Second Terrace, a well [7326 7514] north of Woodcock Covert proved brown sand to 6.7 m, on 6.7 m of 'pea shingle', resting on 32 m of 'white clay'; farther north, a second well [7296 7593] proved 'sand and stone' to 2.1 m on 5.2 m of gravel, on Chalk.

At Mildenhall Golf Course [701 734], there is a patch of flinty sand that is locally gravelly. A well [6959 7341] in an adjacent patch of Second Terrace south of Worlington proved 10.4 m of sand on Chalk.
BSPM

FIRST TERRACE: Spreads of a low terrace are present at Hawstead Green [862 585] at about 55 m above OD, and south of Hawstead Hall [862 596] at about 50 m above OD. Surface indications are of a sandy deposit overlying a flint gravel, locally chalky.

On the north-east side of Bury St Edmunds there is a low spread of sand and gravel at about 31 m above OD, approximately 1 m above alluvium level. A well [8565 6467] proved the following descending sequence: sandy soil, 1 m; coarse-grained sand, 1 m; sand and gravel, 4.5 m; grey silt.
CRB

First River Terrace Deposits have been extensively worked north and north-west of Ash Carr, Lackford. The following section was measured in the middle of the north face [7988 7091] in 1977:

	Thickness m	Depth m
?MADE GROUND		
Sand and gravel	0.60	0.60
RIVER TERRACE DEPOSITS		
Sand and gravel, bedded, with wood fragments at the top (sample g)	2.90	3.50
Sand, fine-grained	0.15	3.65
Clay, dark grey, silty (sample f)	0.08	3.73
Sand, fawn	0.15	3.88
Silt, greyish buff	0.10	3.98
Sand and gravel, with angular flints and rounded quartzites, and 10 cm of fine-grained sand at base (sample e)	0.53	4.51
Interbedded clay, silt and coarse-grained chalky sand, with lenses of gravel (sample d)	0.72	5.23
Silt, buff-khaki, fine-grained sand, and 7 cm of black organic silty clay (sample c)	0.26	5.49
Gradational passage downwards into Sand, coarse-grained, with angular and sub-angular flints (sample b)	0.24	5.73
GLACIAL SILT		
Silt, bluish grey (sample a)	0.80	6.53

Samples c and f yielded the molluscs listed in Table 6 (Col. 6). The only noticeable differences between the samples are that 'f

Localities referred to in Table 6

1 Bridge Farm [948 683], Peat
2 Pakenham Fen [930 681], Peat
3 Timworth Farm [857 697], Peat and calcareous tufa
4 Borehole TL 86 NW/109 [8247 6944], Alluvium; 0.8–1.3 m
5 Borehole TL 86 NW/109 [8247 6944], Alluvium; 1.3–2.0 m
6 Lackford Pit [7988 7091], First River Terrace Deposits
7 Lackford Pit [7969 7076 and 7991 7074], Glacial Silt
8 Cavenham Pit [7641 7088], Glacial Silt
9 Borehole TL 86 NE/83 [8537 6913] ?Glacial Sand and Gravel
10 Borehole TL 86 NE/101 [8504 6747], ?Glacial Silt 5.6–6.5 m
11 Borehole TL 86 NE/101 [8504 6747], ?Glacial Silt 7.5–8.0 m
12 Borehole TL 86 NE/101 [8504 6747], ?Glacial Silt 8.0–9.0 m
13 Borehole TL 86 SE/166 [8618 6193] ?Glacial Silt
14 Borehole TL 86 SE/168 [8706 6265], Alluvium
15 Borehole TL 96 SE/133 [9552 6460], Alluvium, 0.5 m
16 Borehole TL 96 SE/133 [9552 6460], Alluvium, 3.6–3.7 m
17 Borehole TL 96 SE/133 [9552 6460], ?Glacial Silt 6.7–6.9 m

Table 6 Distribution of Pleistocene and Holocene freshwater molluscs in the Bury St Edmunds district

Locality (see p.68)	1	2	3	4	5	6	7	8	9	10	11	12	13	14	15	16	17
Acroloxus lacustris (Linné)	6			11	19											4	
Aegopinella pura (Alder)		9															
Ancylus fluviatilis Müller											1						
Anisus leucostoma (Millet)		3		2	12	8	120										
A. vortex (Linné)			3	1													
Armiger crista (Linné)	3		15	4				2			3				2	255	1
Bathyomphalus contortus (Linné)			3							5	2				1		
Bithynia tentaculata (Linné)		128	78	66	149					175	27	5	103			26	16
Carychium minimum Müller									12								
C. tridentatum (Risso)		1	3	3	11									19			
Cepaea nemoralis (Linné)		11															
Cochlicopa lubrica (Müller)		8		1					6			1					
Gyraulus albus (Müller)	111		5	27	44											19	
G. laevis (Alder)						2											
Hippeutis complanatus (Linné)	34		2	2	9											27	
Leucophytia bidentata (Montagu)				1													
Lymnaea palustris (Müller)		42	13				4										
L. peregra (Müller)	58	9	18			4			1							14	
L. stagnalis (Linné)		2	1														
L. truncatula (Müller)		1	5			28	112		13					3			
L. sp.			5														
Menetus dilatatus (Gould)	1		2														
Oxyloma pfeifferi (Rossmässler)			13		14			2									
cf. *O. sarsi* (Esmark)		22															
Physia fontinalis (Linné)					1											2	
Planorbarius corneus (Linné)			3														
Planorbis carinatus (Müller)		11	3														
P. planorbis (Linné)	1	33	25		3												
P. sp.	1																
Pupilla muscorum (Linné)	3				34	200	230	9									
Succinea oblonga Draparnaud						33	104	2	2								
S. putris? (Linné)				2	1												
S. sp.	34		1	1				29									
Trichia hispida (Linné)		59	5											1			
T. striolata (Pfeiffer)		1															
Vallonia excentrica Sterki			2			2											
V. pulchella (Müller)		4				2				3	1			5			
Valvata cristata (Müller)			96	13		5	1			26	10		1			238	5
V. macrostoma Mörch																9	
V. piscinalis (Müller)	69			6	196	8	1				4			4		18	5
Vertigo pygmaea (Draparnaud)			2	1	2												
Vitrea crystallina (Müller)		2															
Viviparus contectus (Millet)			9														
Zonitoides excavatus (Alder)		1		23	17												
Z. nitidus (Müller)										30							
Pisidium amnicum (Müller)																	1
P. casertanum (Poli)							99	4									
P. henslowanum (Sheppard)				2	11						1						
P. milium Held			13		45												
P. nitidum Jenyns			140	164	400+	1				5	4	3				62	
P. obtusale lapponicum (Clessin) Favre & Jayet						9		5									
P. obtusale (Lamarck)						79	1	1?									
P. pulchellum Jenyns			2	2	16												
P. subtruncatum Malm			15	8	42												
P. sp.			18	22				16									
Sphaerium corneum (Linné)	11	1				1									5		

contained far more *Pisidium* and was the only one with the cold-water indicator *P. obtusale lapponicum*.

The fauna, although rather more diverse than that of the underlying mid-Devensian silts (see Table 6, Col. 7), affords no good evidence of environmental change. Interestingly, *Pupilla muscorum*, the dominant species in both sample *a* from the Glacial Silt and samples *c* and *f* from the River Terrace Deposits, was absent from sample *b* at the base of the terrace. *Succinea oblonga* and unidentifiable succineid fragments are common throughout. Faunal dominance by drought-resistant species, such as *A. leucostoma* and *P. muscorum*, in association with significant numbers of succineids, which favour marshes or planty waterside situations, suggests a marsh environment, which possibly dried out intermittently. No direct indication of age is available from the molluscs, but the presence of a number of valves of *Pisidium obtusale lapponicum* in sample *f* points to a colder climate than at present. DKG

Pollen from sample *b* included *Pinus*, *Selaginella* and *Lycopodium*; the last two taxa indicate a cool open habitat. Sample *c* was poor in pollen, whereas sample *d* contained a little pollen of open boreal aspect; single grains of *Abies* and *Picea* were recovered. The presence of *Selaginella* again indicates cool, humid conditions.

An organic horizon was noted about 2.6 m above the base of the terrace deposits in the north-east of the pit [8002 7074], but it contained only incomplete succineids and unidentifiable gastropod fragments. In the south-east [8000 7066], there were 80 cm of cross-bedded, fine-grained, organic shelly sand and silty and sandy clay; the molluscan fauna recovered comprised *Succinea oblonga* and *Sphaerium corneum*. This bed rested on 2 m of coarse sandy gravel, and was overlain by c.40 cm of cross-bedded, fine-grained sand with angular gravel stringers, which in turn was overlain by an alternating sequence of angular gravel and sand. Another section [7969 7076] showed 4 to 5 m of gravel, resting on shelly and peaty silts which rise towards the south-west.

Vertebrate remains are commonly found in this pit, although their exact provenance in most cases is not known; some appear to have come from the base of the terrace gravels. Bones collected by the author from the top of the gravels included a tibia and metacarpal fragment of a large cervid (probably *elaphas*). Mr J Wymer, who made the identification, also notes that various bones of *Bos*, and teeth and a pelvic bone of *Mammuthus*, have been collected from this pit. CRB

In the northern part of Tuddenham Heath, the First Terrace surface is about 1 to 2 m above the present flood plain. It rises from between 8 to 9 m above OD near the river, to about 11 to 12 m above OD in the south, where there is a strong back-feature against the Second Terrace. West of Tuddenham Heath, a small patch of buff silt crops out in ditches [7385 7300] beneath a thin gravel, but ditches mostly reveal up to 2 m of sand or angular to subangular flint gravel. Generally, the First River Terrace Deposits are more gravelly than the Second (Clayton, 1983).

South-west of Mildenhall, an area of rather hummocky sandy gravel has been mapped as First River Terrace Deposits. A ditch within this terrace [7065 7373] showed up to 2 m of sand and angular to subangular patinated flint gravel. BSPM

The Black Bourn and its tributaries

THIRD TERRACE: A small spread [934 696] of Third River Terrace Deposits occurs at Grimstone End near Ixworth.

SECOND TERRACE: The surface of the terrace deposits near Norton are at about 38 m above OD. A borehole [9533 6604] sited close to their margin proved 2.8 m of sandy gravel above 0.7 m of greenish grey, shelly, peaty silt. A radiometric age determination of 34 380 + 510/ − 730 years BP has been obtained from the peaty silt beneath the terrace (Clarke and Auton, 1982).

At Grimstone End [94 69], the Second River Terrace Deposits have been largely quarried away. Pits at the southern margin of the terrace formerly exposed 2+ m of poorly bedded and poorly sorted gravel with interbedded thin bands of fine- to medium-grained clayey sand. The gravel contains well-rounded quartzite pebbles and angular and subangular flints. Pits [936 692] farther north are about 2.5 m deep; small poor exposures are similar to those above.

A borehole [9368 6956] in the terrace spread north of Pakenham Fen proved a total of 8.1 m of sandy gravel, resting on Chalk; possibly some of this is Glacial Sand and Gravel.

Scattered remnants of Second River Terrace Deposits occur along the stream which flows through Stowlangtoft. The most eastern is at about 35 to 36 m above OD, some 2 to 3 m above the Alluvium. A borehole [9642 6865] in this spread proved 3 m of sandy gravel above Boulder Clay.

To the north, in a borehole [9359 7422] near Bardwell, Second River Terrace gravels are 15.2 m thick, while boreholes proved thicknesses of 8.3 m [9129 7456] and 9.4 m [9151 7486] farther downstream at Honington.

FIRST TERRACE: West of Woolpit, The Black Bourn is flanked by terraces some 1 to 3 m above the floodplain. Locally [9605 6235], these have been worked for sand and gravel. A borehole [9661 6290] downstream proved 2 m of sandy gravel above Boulder Clay. North of the railway line, First River Terrace Deposits form low features, about 1 m high, within and bordering the Alluvium. Farther north, a borehole [9474 6787] near Bull Bridge encountered 2.4 m of sandy gravel above Boulder Clay. CRB

COVER SAND

'Cover Sand' was introduced by Straw (1963) as a replacement term for 'Blown Sand', a deposit that occurs over extensive areas of north Lincolnshire, because he considered that the sands were not wholly aeolian. Catt (1977, fig. 16.1) has summarised the distribution of Cover Sand and loess in Britain. There is an extensive spread of Cover Sand in the Breckland, which extends into the northern part of the Bury St Edmunds district; more patchy occurrences lie to the west and east of that town. The southernmost outcrop is near Rougham [90 62], but even farther south, Cover Sand is preserved in pipes ('gulls' or 'gaults') and involutions within Boulder Clay. Thicknesses of up to 3 m are known, but involutions can produce marked variations over short distances.

Where Cover Sand is widespread, thick, and overlies a markedly different lithology, it can be mapped easily. Problems arise, however, where Cover Sand overlies Glacial Sand and Gravel or River Terrace Deposits; in such cases its presence cannot everywhere be satisfactorily determined. Moreover, towards its feather edge, the Cover Sand is commonly cryoturbated into the underlying deposits—usually Chalk (Plate 7) or Boulder Clay—and an intricate pattern of polygons and stripes of sand occur within the host rock (see p.74), making the mapped limit of the Cover Sand somewhat arbitrary. Generally, the patterned ground is readily apparent on aerial photographs, but, except in a few favoured conditions and localities, it is rarely clear on the ground. In those areas, the Cover Sand can occupy up to 40 per cent of the surface, but its thickness within the stripes and polygons is usually less than 1 m, although thicknesses of 1.7 m have been recorded.

Plate 7 Cryoturbation of Cover Sand into Chalk, Kentford. (A13064)

Another problem associated with Cover Sand is its mobility. In many areas it appears to have moved down slope, and it is not everywhere possible to separate Cover Sand from Head derived from it. Moreover, it is extremely susceptible to present-day wind transport. Extensive re-afforestation of much of the Breckland has minimised this problem; nevertheless, there are still 'blows' across bare fields on dry windy days, moving sand up to the widely spaced hedgerows which serve as wind breaks and sediment traps.

The Cover Sand is dominantly a fine-grained sand, the commonest particle sizes falling between 0.06 and 0.3 mm (Maarelveld, 1960; Williams, 1964; Chorley and others, 1966; Strong, 1978), though Chorley and others demonstrated an overall fining in the grain size of the Cover Sand south-westwards across the Brecklands. Williams regarded the well-sorted sands of Thetford Heath as typical of a dune sand; he noted that some grains in the small fraction of coarse-grained sand were well-rounded and had frosted surfaces, and that some flint pebbles within the Cover Sand had highly polished surfaces suggestive of wind blasting. However, examination of seven samples from the Woolpit-Tostock-Elmswell area by Mr G E Strong shows that the sands are dominantly fine or very fine grained, moderately to poorly sorted, and have a symmetrical to positively skewed particle-size distribution (Figure 13).

The mineral composition of the Cover Sand has been investigated by Watt and others (1966) who found the following overall percentages of minerals to be present: quartz, 87; flint 1.5; orthoclase and minor amounts of other felspars, 11; and heavy minerals 0.5 to 1. These percentages, however, vary with grain size; for example the percentage of flints, usually subangular and strongly weathered, increases markedly with increased particle diameter.

The coarser sands contain larger amounts of well-rounded quartz grains, some of which are frosted, and many fractured flints. The problem of the occurrence of the latter within the sand is discussed by Williams (1964), who considered that the flints were expelled from the adjacent till and Chalk by frost action, prior to the deposition of Cover Sand. He could not, however, be certain of the mechanism that then incorporated the flints into Cover Sand, although he suggested that frost and burrowing animals were possible agents.

Some workers (for example Perrin, 1957; Chorley and others, 1966) have claimed that Cover Sand is produced by the decalcification of chalky drift—the so-called Gipping Till (see Bristow and Cox, 1973). Watt and others (1966) discounted such an origin and concluded that the bulk of the Cover Sand resulted from periglacial modification of an aeolian deposit. They did not suggest a source for the sand, but argued against its derivation from the Sandringham Sands, as had been proposed by Rastall (1912). In Lincolnshire, Straw (1963) suggested that Cover Sand was derived from Triassic sandstones.

In the present district, there is a similarity between the gradings of the Cover Sand in the easternmost localities and those of the Crag (Figures 11 and 13), suggesting that the latter may provide the source of the local Cover Sand.

The exact age of the Cover Sand cannot be determined. The sand post-dates the Anglian Boulder Clay, and its absence beneath the mid-Devensian River Terrace Deposits of the Lark valley suggests, though does not prove, that it may post-date the terrace deposits. The widespread, thin, fine-grained sandy topsoil on the surface of the terraces may represent partially reworked or cryoturbated Cover Sand. Catt (1977) suggested that the Cover Sand was late Devensian (c.11 000 BP) in age: it would thus be equivalent to the Younger Cover Sand of the Netherlands. West and others (1974), however, thought that the Cover Sand was of early Devensian age.

Details

Cover Sand

Icklingham – The King's Forest area

Much of this area is covered with an irregular thickness of Cover Sand involuted into Chalk or Boulder Clay. It is only near Bernersfield Farm [around 79 75] that thicknesses of sand consistently in excess of 1 m have been found and, consequently, where the Cover Sand has been mapped. The widespread, but discontinuous extent of Cover Sand beyond the mapped area is, however, readily evident from the patterned ground visible on aerial photographs (e.g. Watt and others, 1966, fig. 1).

Culford Heath – Honington

Patterning caused by thin Cover Sand cryoturbated into Chalk or Boulder Clay is common on most air-photographs of this tract. The sections of several trial pits recorded by Mr T E Lawson suggest that Cover Sand was deposited in two episodes.

A pit [8583 7165] 0.5 km south-south-west of Folly Grove revealed the following section:

	Depth m
Topsoil	0.3
Cover Sand	
Sand, fine- to medium-grained, reddish brown to fawn, gravelly, with numerous shattered flints	0.7
?Head	
Sand, fine- to medium-grained, clayey, reddish brown, gravelly, with pockets of chalky clay up to 20 cm across	1.4
Cover Sand	
'Balls' up to 20 cm diameter of fine-grained sand in bed below; three such 'balls' seen in 1.3 m horizontal section	3.0
Boulder Clay	
Clay, grey, chalky and flinty	3.1

In another pit [8187 7175] just north of the previous section, the following section was exposed:

	Depth m
Topsoil	0.3
Cover Sand	
Sand, fine- to medium-grained reddish brown to fawn,	

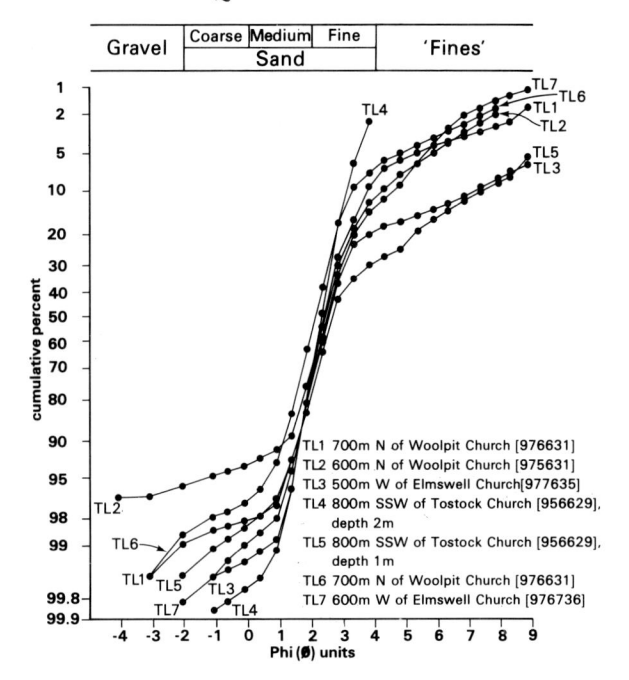

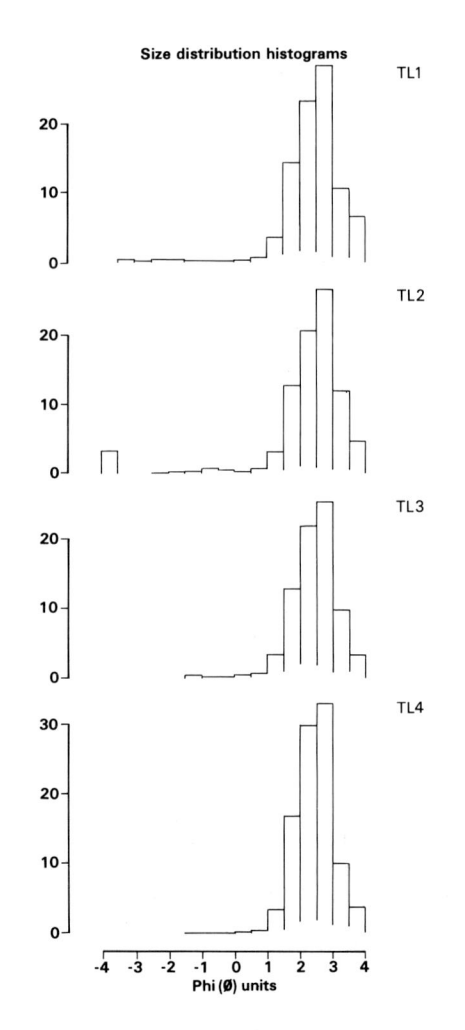

Figure 13 Grading curves and size distribution histograms for samples of Cover Sand around Woolpit, Elmswell and Tostock

	Depth m
with scattered flints and some chalk pellets	1.0
?HEAD	
Sand, fine- to medium-grained, yellowish brown, with pockets of chalky clay and some scattered flints	1.6
COVER SAND	
Sand, fine- to medium-grained, yellowish brown, with a few angular flints: some flints up to 0.3 m diameter and rest on an irregular surface of	1.9
BOULDER CLAY	
Clay, chalky and flinty, slightly sandy	3.1

A third pit [8592 7203] showed:

	Depth m
Topsoil	
COVER SAND	
Sand, fine- to medium-grained	0 to 0.8
?HEAD	
Clay, chalky and flinty, sandy, silty	1.3
COVER SAND	
Sand, fine- to medium-grained, clayey, especially towards base; some chalk fragments	1.8
BOULDER CLAY	
Clay, grey, very chalky	2.4

A fourth pit [8631 7458] 1.1 km south-east of Lodge Farm, revealed:

	Depth m
Topsoil	0.30
COVER SAND	
Sand, fine- to medium-grained, slightly clayey, fawn, with scattered rounded 'Bunter' quartzites and angular flint,	0.70
HEAD	
Sand, gravelly, clayey, locally very clayey; white patinated flints up to 0.2 m across abundant in the east face	1.20
COVER SAND	
Sand, fine- to medium-grained, clayey, with scattered angular flints	1.75
?BOULDER CLAY	
Clay, slightly sandy, mottled fawn and grey	1.85
GLACIAL SAND AND GRAVEL	
Gravel, medium, in a clayey, coarse-grained sand matrix; dominantly rounded 'Bunter' quartzites, with only a few flints; band of clay, 8 cm thick, at base	3.20
CHALK	touched

A fifth pit [8616 7495] 400 m north-west, however, encountered only one layer of Cover Sand which extended down to a depth of 2.3 m.

The Chalk inlier [88 75] at Honington has thin Cover Sand over its surface; this gives a pattern of stripes and polygons. CRB

Risby–Flempton

Extensive areas of Cover Sand occur near Risby [80 66], where it generally overlies Boulder Clay and locally [788 665] passes on to Chalk. A ditch section [796 656], about 1 km south-west of Risby Church, exposed up to 1 m of fine-grained sand with scattered flints over a length of 200 m; locally, there are patches of Boulder Clay beneath it, and the Cover Sand becomes clayey adjacent to the Boulder Clay. Williams (1964, fig. 2c) figured a cross section of a pit [777 678] on Risby Poor's Heath in which Cover Sand is complexly involuted into Chalk. It varies in thickness from 0.3 to only 1 m, and so has not been shown on the 1:50 000 map.

A borehole [8035 6866] near Brakey Pin, Flempton, proved:

	Depth m
Clay, sandy, pebbly, orange-brown, and sand, fine- to medium-grained, with scattered flints	1.0
Sand, clayey, becoming more sandy and orange, with scattered flints	2.1
BOULDER CLAY	4.2

A large area of permanent pasture at Hengrave Park [820 783] is thought to be on Cover Sand. Several small areas [827 635] of Cover Sand have been mapped south of Westley Bottom, where the distinction between it and the underlying Glacial Sand and Gravel is based largely on the presence or absence of gravel; where flints were common, the deposit has been mapped as Glacial Sand and Gravel. A borehole [8266 6342] proved:

	Depth m
Soil	
Sand, fine-grained, brown, with scattered flints	0.5
COVER SAND	
Sand, fine-grained, orange-brown, with scattered flint pebbles; becoming increasingly clayey towards base	1.5
GLACIAL SAND AND GRAVEL	
Gravel, sandy and clayey, brown to orange-brown, with angular to subrounded flints, and some chalk pebbles	2.6
CHALK	touched

Fornham St Martin and Timworth Green

Three patches of Cover Sand occur north of Fornham St Martin. The northernmost [845 690] is dominantly a fine-grained sand which consistently exceeds 1.2 m in thickness; locally, some gravel is associated with the sand. A borehole [8539 6844] in the spread to the south proved: brown, medium-grained sand with scattered flint pebbles (Topsoil), 0.3 m; orange-brown sand with flints (Cover Sand), 2.2 m; orange-brown silty clay with scattered flints (Boulder Clay). The southernmost deposit [854 680] appears to consist of fine-grained sand which becomes more clayey downwards.

Rushbrooke to Stowlangtoft

Much of the surface of the old Bury St Edmunds airfield [88 64] is covered with Cover Sand which, at least locally, is cryoturbated into Boulder Clay, as in a temporary exposure [8747 6390]. Site investigation boreholes north-west of Eldohouse Farm proved up to 4 m of fine-grained sand, clayey sand and sandy clay above Boulder Clay. A borehole [8788 6387] just south-south-east of the farm proved 0.5 m of sandy topsoil above 1 m of fine-grained, orange-brown sand with scattered flint pebbles, which overlies Glacial Sand and Gravel. Eastwards and north-eastwards from the farm, the general sequence is fine- to medium-grained sand above clayey sand.

On the spread at Cattishall [885 653], the Cover Sand contains much fine-, medium- and coarse-grained chalk sand. A borehole [8898 6589] near Great Barton Church proved 0.5 m of sandy topsoil, above 1.1 m of buff-orange, fine- to medium-grained clayey sand, with scattered flint, chalk and rare 'Bunter' quartzite pebbles, which rest on Glacial Silt. North-west of the church, the Cover Sand is also locally chalky and generally passes down into a more clayey deposit.

A similar sequence was observed in the spread east of Great Barton, where a borehole [9025 6682] passed through 0.3 m of sandy topsoil, then 0.7 m of yellowish orange, chalk-rich, fine- to medium-grained sand with flint and chalk pebbles, into Chalk. Near East Barton, the Cover Sand consists of up to at least 1.3 m of fine-grained sand, locally chalky and generally not becoming clayey downwards, at least within augered depth. However, a borehole [9043 6564] sited close to the margin of the deposit, proved 0.3 m of topsoil above 0.8 m sand, which becomes increasingly clayey and pebbly downwards, and which rests on Boulder Clay. Much of the ground to the east [around 908 655] and south of East Barton [around 902 653] is hummocky. Similar hummocky ground was noted [910 645] north of Newhall Covert, where the succession is: sandy soil, 0.1 m; clayey sand, 1.4 m; clayey pebbly sand, 0.2 m; Boulder Clay [9125 6447].

West of Manor Farm, Pakenham, a borehole [9118 6756] proved topsoil, 0.2 m; fine- to medium-grained, orange-brown sand, 0.7 m; clayey sandy silt (Cover Sand), 0.2 m; Boulder Clay. Augering suggests that fine-grained sand is dominant and only rarely becomes clayey downwards. A similar spread of fine-grained sand north of the main road is up to at least 1.2 m thick.

In the Stowlangtoft chalk pit [947 689], 'balls' of Cover Sand are involuted into Chalk at the top of the face. CRB

Seven samples of Cover Sand, which were cryoturbated into the Boulder Clay, were collected from the Woolpit By-Pass. The results of particle size analyses show (Figure 13) that the samples are dominantly fine-grained sand with a small amount of medium- and coarse-grained sand; the samples have a significant percentage (up to 30) of 'fines' (material below 0.06 mm), which may indicate some contamination by Boulder Clay. CRB, GES

PATTERNED GROUND

Patterned ground, as stripes, was first recorded in East Anglia by Watt (1955) on Thetford Heath. Since that time, the study of aerial photographs has shown patterned ground to be extensive over much of the Breckland, as well as elsewhere in the British Isles (Perrin, 1963; Williams, 1964; Watt and others, 1966; Evans, 1976). The patterns are best seen on aerial photographs of arable areas taken in late spring and early summer, or of areas with well-differentiated natural vegetation that reflects the small-scale changes in drainage and alkalinity that are responsible for the soil characteristics.

In East Anglia, the distribution of patterned ground is closely related to that of Cover Sand; it is absent both where the sand is absent and where it is more than 2.5 m thick, and best seen where it is between 0.5 and 1.5 m thick. The patterns were caused by thermal contraction under periglacial conditions; this formed cracks which were then filled by Cover Sand. Annual freeze-thaw dilated and deepened the cracks, which continued to fill with sand. The patterns express the juxtaposition of Cover Sand with Chalk (Plate 7) or Boulder Clay, the sand forming stripes, reticulations or polygons within these last two deposits. The resulting soil contrasts are usually readily evident in ploughed fields; less evident are the vegetational patterns produced by adjacent calcicole and calcifuge plant assemblages (see, for example, Watt and others, 1966). On aerial photographs, the patterning is usually evident at most times of the year in areas of natural vegetation, but is generally obscured in fields of ripened cereals. A typical pattern is produced by *Calluna* (heather) or *Ulex* (Gorse) growing within *Agrostis-Festuca* grassland; Corbett (1971, fig. 7) has a sketch-diagram of such patterning.

Watt and others (1966) described a possible mechanism for polygon formation. In areas of shallow permafrost, frost scars are formed by differential heaving; the vegetation is destroyed over the heaves and bare soil results, while peat accumulates in the adjacent lower areas. The bare frost-heaved ridges become ice-free during the summer, but heaving again occurs during the following autumn and enlarges the bare area. As freezing continues, cryostatic pressure from the top and sides forces unfrozen material upwards along the frost scar, and irregular polygons form as the scar grows. The active zone of freeze/thaw is thought by the above authors, and also by Williams (1964), to be limited to a depth of 2 m.

The type of pattern varies with the surface gradient, there being a lateral passage from polygons on the plateaux, to anastomosing stripes at the plateau edges, and to subparallel stripes elongated normal to the contours along the slopes (Watt and others, 1966). Moreover, the nature of the underlying material affects the form of the pattern. On Chalk, there are polygons and stripes, with repeat intervals of 10 and 7.5 m respectively; on Boulder Clay there is a tighter, reticulate pattern. Perrin (1963) noted that patterning occurred on all slopes, but considered that it was commonest on south-facing ones. Evans (1976), however, thought patterns were commonest on south-east- and north-west-facing slopes.

Williams (1968, fig. 27) has described the polygons in detail. Basically, the centre of each polygon is convex with little or no cover of sand, and the margins of the polygons are followed by broad, flat-bottomed, sand-filled troughs; this characteristic shape distinguishes these polygons from those formed by ice-wedges.

The ridges have been described by Perrin (1963), who noted that, where composed of Boulder Clay, they contain angular chalk clasts. These clasts have a varying alignment of long axes, which change from near horizontal at the base to near vertical towards the top, though locally there is a flattening at the top. Watt (1955) recorded the aggregation of flints, many with their long axes vertical, along the centre line of the stripes. CRB

ALLUVIUM

Alluvium is present in all the major and many of the minor river valleys, and commonly includes an upper clayey unit and a lower gravelly one. This lower unit has been referred to as First River Terrace Deposits by Hawkins (1981), Clayton (1983) and Clarke (1983) for convenience when assessing sand and gravel resources. The gravels are confined to the floodplain and everywhere underlie the alluvial clay, even where First River Terrace Deposits are absent and the rivers are flanked with Chalk. They are better regarded as part of the present-day floodplain deposits for the purposes of geological description.

The upper unit varies from a stiff mottled orange and greyish brown clay to a highly organic shelly clay. Along the River Lark, the Alluvium is commonly closely associated with peat and is locally richly fossiliferous (Table 6). On faunal evidence it would appear that the environment resembled that of the present day. No datings have, however, been obtained from the deposit, though peat beneath the Alluvium near Langham [9796 6873] has been dated as 4720 ± 40 years BP (Clarke and Auton, 1982).

The thickness of the Alluvium of the Lark varies from 1.7 to 9 m with an average of 4.6 m. The upper clay varies in recorded thickness from 0.3 to 4.7 m with an average of 1.9 m, and the lower gravel from 0.8 to 5.3 m with an average of 3.2 m. The thickest occurrences of alluvial gravel are in the lower reaches of the Lark below West Stow, where thicknesses range between 3.6 and 5.3 m, with an average of 4.5 m. Grading figures for alluvial gravels show them to have a mean gravel content higher (37 to 58 per cent) than the mean of either the River Terrace Deposits or the Glacial Sand and Gravel.
CRB

Details

Lark Valley (Whepstead to Flempton)

The Lark rises near Plumpton House [around 814 587]. Alluvium is present downstream from Stonecross Green [825 580] and forms a narrow tract, varying in width from 20 to 80 m, across which the river meanders gently as far as Pinford End [849 597]. For some 500 m downstream [851 597–856 599] the Lark has a number of closely spaced meanders incised into Alluvium by up to 4.5 m [8545 5980]. A similar feature is present in the tributary valley that enters the district [87 57] west of Bradfield Combust; this has a fairly broad (up to 100 m wide) alluvial tract with a straight stream bed, but has a number of closely spaced meanders downstream [870 582].

North of Sicklesmere, the Alluvium consists of more than 1.2 m of clayey sand [8787 6100]; downstream, up to 1.2 m of soft, brown, organic clay overlies peat.

The Alluvium broadens north of Bridge Farm, where a borehole [8706 6265] has proved the following descending sequence: brown silty fine-grained sand (topsoil), 0.3 m; silt and clayey silt, mottled rust-brown and grey, shelly, with scattered flint sand and pebbles, 0.6 m; clayey gravel, locally with a silty matrix, 0.8 m; silt, grey and brown mottled, with common chalk sand and pebbles, and some flints, 0.3 m; Chalk. Molluscs from the silt and clay include: *Carychium tridentatum*, *Vallonia pulchella*, *Vertigo pygmaea*, *Sphaerium corneum* and fragments of *?Pisidium*. The fauna indicates a marshy environment, probably draining into a nearby river or pond.

A borehole [8589 6359] in the flood plain of a tributary valley south of Bury St Edmunds proved 1.5 m of topsoil and yellow clay with chalk stones, resting on 1.4 m of dark alluvial gravel, 1.4 m; overlying clays and sands, which are probably glacial.

Downstream, boreholes [8591 6394; 8576 6434] proved more than 3 m of clayey alluvium with peaty lenses. However, a nearby borehole [8585 6441] proved 3.1 m of dominantly sand and gravel (beneath 1.7 m of made ground) resting on Chalk. Another borehole [8590 6453] encountered little sand and gravel, and proved: made ground, 1.4 m; soft to firm olive-brown slightly sandy clay, 0.35 m; slightly clayey sandy gravel, 0.55 m; dark grey, brown and black silty organic clay, 1.2 m; soft brown peat, 0.7 m; Chalk. Near Tollgate Bridge, boreholes [8511 6610; 8516 6604; 8516 6612] establish that the Alluvium, which is up to 4.6 m thick, is again dominantly gravelly, but with interbeds of silt and peat up to 1.1 m. North of Tollgate Bridge, two more boreholes [8491 6668; 8490 6682] proved similar sequences, but with up to 2.1 m of alluvial gravel beneath peat.
CRB

At Kingsburyhill Wood, Fornham St Genevieve, a small pit [833 689] exposed 0.5 m of dark grey alluvial silt on 3 m of bedded flint gravel, which rests on Boulder Clay. There is a similar sequence in a borehole [8247 6944] north-east of Grange Farm, Hengrave. Two samples collected from the alluvial silt, at depths between 0.8 and 2 m, contained a molluscan fauna comprising mainly aquatic freshwater species, together with a small proportion of terrestrial species (Table 6). Both faunas are relatively diverse and indicate temperate conditions, with slow flowing or standing shallow water. East of Hengrave [826 686] and Flempton [813 698], alluvial gravel again underlies silt at shallow depths.

The peat within the Alluvium at Lackford [800 708] has been radiometrically dated by the Department of Geological Sciences, University of Birmingham, at 430 ± 50 to 540 ± 100 years BP (Birm-1060A, B and C). It yielded a rich fauna of beetles very like the present-day local ones. The full faunal list identified by Drs G R Coope and B J Taylor, is as follows (numbers in parentheses are numbers of individuals): *Notiophilus sp.* (1), *Blethisa multipunctata* (1), *Clivina collaris* or *fossor* (1), *Trechus quadristriatus* (1), *Bembidion assimile* (3), *Pterostichus minor* (1), *P. nigrita* (3), *P. strenuus* (1), *Amara sp.* (1), *Chalenius sp.* (1), *Noterus clavicornis* (1), *Hybius sp.* (1), *Hydroporus sp.* (3), *Heleophorus sp.* (1), *Coelostoma orbiculare* (4), *Cercyon melanocephalus* (1), *C. pygmaeus* (5), *C. sternalis* (1), *C. tristis* (3), *Megasterum obscurum* (1), *Cryptopleurum minutum* (2), *Hydrobius fuscipes* (1), *Laccobius sp.* (1), *Chaetarthria seminulum* (13), *Ochthebius minimus* type (3), *Carpelimus sp.* (2), *Platystethus nodifrons* (4), *Anotylus nitidulus* (2), *A. rugosus* (1), *Stenus sp.* (8), *Lathrobium sp.* (2), *Gyrohypnus punctulatus* (1), *Xantholinus* cf. *longiventris* (4), *Philonthus sp.* (3), *Trachyporus sp.* (2), Aleocharinae gen. et sp. indet. (13), *Aphodius sp.* (13), *Cetonia aurata* (1), *Cytilus siriceus* (3), *Byrrhus sp.* (1), *Porcinolus murinus* (1), *Dryops sp.* (5), *Elmis aenea* (1), *Atomaria* cf. *mesomela* (1), *Donacia cinerea* (1), *D. sp.* (1), *Plateumaris* cf. *descolor* (1), *Hydrothassa* cf. *aucta* (1), *Prasocuris plellandrii* (1), *Apion sp.* (4), *Bagous sp.* (2), *Limnobaris pilistriata* or *talbum* (2).
BSPM

Livermere tributary of the Lark

Below the lake at Livermere, the floodplain of this unnamed tributary is floored by peat, which rests on dominantly gravelly Alluvium to the north of Timworth [8576 6972]. South-westwards, patches of peat, shelly silt and calcareous clay, up to 1 m thick, rest on alluvial gravel. A rich molluscan fauna was obtained from one of these patches [857 697] (see Table 6). West of the old railway line, the Alluvium, which is up to 400 m wide, appears to consist entirely of sand and gravel.
CRB

Kennett valley

A narrow belt of Alluvium, up to 200 m wide, extends along much of the Kennett valley. It consists of dark organic silty clay or clayey silt, commonly less than 1 m thick, overlying gravel. Small patches of alluvial gravel are present at the surface just west of Kentford Church [7045 6681]. Boreholes south of the railway proved 1.4 m of alluvial clay above 2.9 m of alluvial gravel. A borehole south of Kennett Hall encountered 2.1 m of alluvial clay resting on 1.2 m of alluvial sand and gravel.
BSPM

The Black Bourn and its tributaries

The Black Bourn rises near Bradfield St George [c.915 590]. Near the headwaters [9410 5977], the Alluvium consists of 0.6 m of greyish brown clay above 0.6 m of coarse gravelly clay, which in turn rests on chalky Boulder Clay. Farther downstream [9485

6048], 1 m of greyish brown clay overlies an undetermined thickness of alluvial sand and gravel.

Some gravel is locally intercalated in the clay, for a borehole [9668 6318] at Broadgrass Green proved: topsoil, 0.15 m; brown, slightly sandy silty clay, 0.6 m; brown clayey gravel and sand with scattered boulders and thin beds of clay, 1 m; soft grey-brown mottled, slightly organic, silty clay, 0.45 m; brown slightly organic clay, 2+ m. Downstream, another borehole [9676 6389] proved: 6.7 m of sand and gravel resting on Boulder Clay; there were, however, pockets of silty clay throughout.

North of Tostock, the Alluvium passes into a wide expanse of peaty and organic chalky clay [around 955 648]. At Norton, the belt of peat narrows to 20 m and merges into Alluvium. Northwards, the alluvial clay consists of 1 m of grey clay resting on gravel [9541 6640], and of 0.7 m of sandy clay overlying 0.7 m of firm black peat, which rests on sand and gravel [9530 6680].

Alluvial gravel has been dredged out of The Black Bourn [9476 6768] south of Bull Bridge. Some 0.8 m of clayey silt overlies 0.6 m of gravel at one point [9480 6826]; a little to the north-west [9455 6835], between 0.5 and 1.2 m of peaty sand overlies alluvial gravel.

Farther downstream, west of Bridge Farm, between 0.3 and 1.5 m of peat overlies alluvial gravel [9440 6864 to 9495 6818]. Within this tract, the peat is patchy and has been mapped as Alluvium to distinguish it from the nearby, but higher peat which has formed where springs issue from the Glacial Sand and Gravel.
CRB

At one point [around 948 683], the alluvial peat and associated grey clay is highly fossiliferous. In addition to the molluscan assemblage (Table 6, Col.1), the following ostracod fauna was recoverd: *Cypridopsis aculeata*, *Cypria ophthalmica*, *Cyclocypris laevis*, *Candona neglecta*, *C. albicans* and *Candonopsis sp*. It implies fresh water to oligohaline conditions, though *C. aculeata* is rarely found in completely fresh water: most of the ostracods are eurythermal. One fresh-water acritarch, *Micrhystridium penkridgensis*, was also found. The assemblage as a whole suggests a weedy, shallow-water lake or other permanently aquatic environment which existed when temperatures were close to those of the present day. DKG, DMG

A borehole [9796 6873] in the floodplain of the unnamed stream which flows through Stowlangtoft and Hunston, proved a similar general sequence: peaty topsoil, 0.2 m; clay, silty, mottled grey and brown, 0.5 m; peat with wood fragments, 2.3 m; silt, shelly, greenish grey, 1.9 m; clayey gravel (alluvial gravel), 1 m; silty clay (?Boulder Clay), 0.7 m, Chalk. The peat has been dated at 4720 ± 40 years BP (Clarke and Auton, 1982).

In the main valley, boreholes [9377 6966; 9364 6999] proved the now familiar sequence, as did another [9242 6666] above Pakenham. CRB

Between Ixworth and Bardwell, the Alluvium is dominantly a peaty silt, though north of Bardwell, gravel has been locally dredged out from beneath this [940 745]. Peaty silt and sand overlies alluvial gravel downstream as far as Ixworth Thorpe and near Sapiston.
CRB, TEL

PEAT

The main spreads of Peat lie along the River Lark and the tributaries of The Black Bourn. Near Tuddenham, this alluvial peat occupies hollows on the surface of the River Terrace Deposits. Alluvial peat commonly passes into highly organic silty Alluvium, and locally into calcareous tufa. It is usually richly fossiliferous, with a molluscan fauna indicative of a climate similar to that of the present. Peat also occurs locally along spring-lines, such as those south of Sicklesmere [876 600] on the south bank of the River Lark, and west of Stowlangtoft [950 682]. Faunas are similar to those from the alluvial peat. In places, peat has been proved under alluvial clay. One such occurrence, at a depth of 3 m in a borehole [9796 6873] near Stowlangtoft, has been dated radiometrically at 4720 ± 40 years BP. (Clarke and Auton, 1982). Locally, peat has been recorded beneath River Terrace Deposits (gravel), and such occurrences are presumably substantially older. CRB

Details

Lark and tributary valleys

Upstream from Sicklesmere, along the south bank of the River Lark, there is a long narrow strip of Peat generally more than 1.4 m thick [8765 6022 to 8675 5928]; locally, however, it is thin, for a borehole [8749 5995] proved only 0.3 m of peat. The peat is associated with copious springs issuing from the Boulder Clay, which forms the back margin to the peat.

The crescent-shaped mere north of Sicklesmere, which reputedly gave its name to the village, is now drained. Locally [8664 6153 to 8780 6147], there is up to 1 m of peat at the surface; elsewhere [8700 6145; 8750 6155] up to 1.2 m of soft brown or black alluvial clay overlies peat.

Two boreholes [8559 6357; 8511 6358] along the River Linnet proved 1.3 m of peat beneath 1.8 m of topsoil and dark clay, and 1.5 m of 'soft dark clay' beneath 0.8 m of topsoil, respectively. Two peat beds were noted (1.7 to 2.8 m and 4.6 to 4.8 m) in a borehole [8598 6378] just north of St Botolph's Bridge, Bury St Edmunds, and peat and associated organic clay and silt have been proved in several other holes [8591 6394; 8511 6610; 8581 6416] in this general tract. CRB

There is an extensive area of alluvial peat in the Livermere tributary upstream from Timworth Church. The peat is generally up to 1.5 m thick, though there are irregular pockets of peat south-west of the church which are less than 1 m thick and too small to map separately. The westernmost locality where peat has been identified is close to the old railway embankment [8565 6960], where there are patches of shelly peat and calcareous tufa up to 1 m thick. The diverse fauna is included in Table 6, Col.3; it indicates temperate climatic conditions. CRB, DKG

Peat occupies hollows in the sandy soil along the valley which runs from Herringswell [729 700] north-eastwards into the Lark valley. More than 2 m of peat was cut in a ditch [7345 7122] south of Tuddenham, and 3 m of peat resting on Chalk was reported from footings [7382 7091] at Old Hall Farm. Over much of the valley, however, gravel underlies peat at a depth of about 1 m. The largest area of peat in the district flanks the Lark and extends up the Herringswell tributary for almost 7 km west of Temple Bridge [758 728]. BSPM

The Black Bourn and its tributaries

There is a wide expanse of peat south-west of Norton [953 650], where a borehole [9552 6460] has proved 0.1 m of peaty topsoil on 0.4 m of mottled clayey silt, on 2.6 m of peat; the molluscs *Armiger crista*, *Bathyomphalus contortus* and *Lymnaea truncatula* were obtained from the interbedded shelly silt (Clarke and Auton, 1982). Over 1 m of peat has been proved [9548 6485] hereabouts and along the western margin of this spread.

Peat flanks both sides of the Alluvium north of Bull Bridge; east of The Black Bourn it is more than 1 m thick [950 682] and is associated with calcareous tufa.

Peat, associated with organic sands, also occurs [956 684] along the stream which flows through Stowlangtoft. A sample of peat [9796 6873] at a depth of 3 m has been radiometrically dated at 4720 ± 40 years BP (Clarke and Auton, 1982). Farther upstream [around 982 682], there is an extensive peaty alluvial flat that continues north-eastward into the adjacent Eye (190) district.   CRB

Pakenham Fen lies on a west-bank tributary. The peat is generally more than 1.2 m thick, and is locally richly fossiliferous (Table 6, Col.2). The fauna points to a temperate marshy environment.

CRB, DKG

CHAPTER 7

Economic geology

SAND AND GRAVEL

This account draws on the results of four surveys carried out by the Industrial Minerals Assessment unit of BGS. These surveys together cover some two-thirds of the Bury St Edmunds district (see Figure 14). They are based on sampling from boreholes sunk at a frequency of, ideally, one in each square kilometre of sand and gravel, and the results have been published as descriptive reports containing 1:25 000-scale resource maps, in the Mineral Assessment Reports of the BGS (Hawkins, 1981; Corser, 1982; Clarke, 1983; Clayton, 1983). For the purposes of these resource surveys, sand and gravel are regarded as potentially workable (and are described therefore as 'mineral') if the following four arbitrary limiting criteria are broadly met:

1 The deposit should average at least 1 m in thickness
2 The ratio of overburden to sand and gravel should be no more that 3:1
3 The proportion of 'fine' (particles passing the 0.063 mm sieve) should not exceed 40 per cent by weight
4 The deposit should lie within 25 m of the surface

In the Bury St Edmunds district, the major resources of sand and gravel aggregates are found in the extensive spreads of Glacial Sand and Gravel and River Terrace Deposits. Kesgrave Sands and Gravels, Ingham Sand and Gravel, Cover Sand, Head and Head Gravel represent minor resources; the Crag forms a possible resource for a more limited range of applications (Clarke, 1983, pp.8, 9).

Crag

The Crag is restricted to the southern and eastern parts of the district. Over parts of this area, the deposit is deeply buried beneath an overburden of Boulder Clay and does not meet the depth and overburden criteria for 'mineral'. In and adjacent to the major valleys, however, the Boulder Clay is thinner, or has been completely removed by erosion, and the Crag can be classified as 'mineral'. Generally, the Crag is 4 to 8 m thick, although locally over 10 m have been encountered. A contoured map of Crag thickness for the area around Woolpit is shown in Clarke (1983), and for the whole of the Bury district by Bristow (1983).

Within the district, the Crag sands generally contain 10–20 per cent 'fines' and about 5 per cent of gravel by weight. The sand fraction fairly consistently comprises fine- and medium-grained sand, with a little coarse-grained sand. The gravel fraction is present as thin pebbly stringers within the sands, and also as a pebble bed, usually less than 1 m thick, at the base of the deposit. Flint is the dominant component of the gravel, with some vein-quartz, quartzite, shell debris and iron-pan fragments.

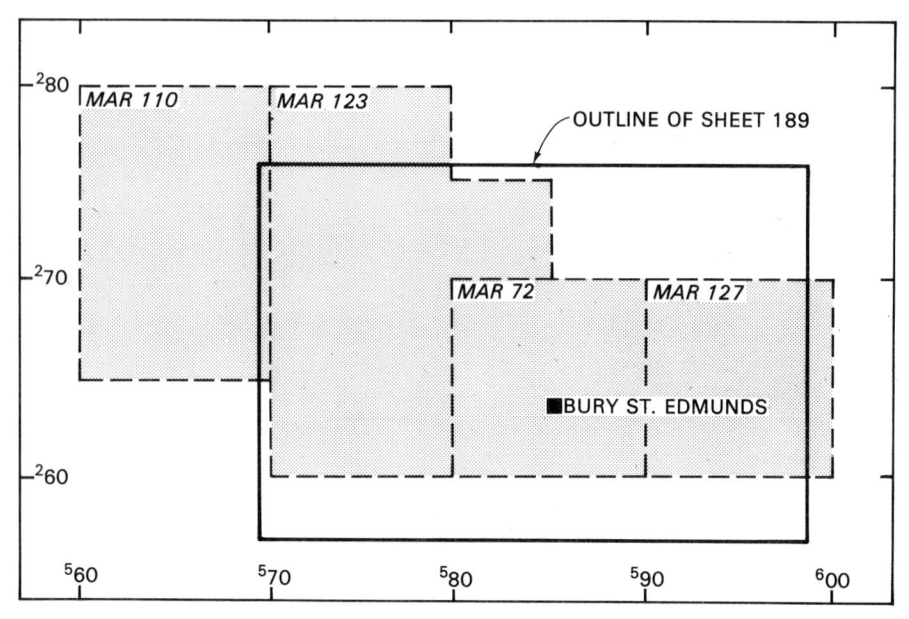

Figure 14 Incidence of 1:25 000 sand and gravel resource maps in and around the Bury St Edmunds district

Whilst the Crag is predominantly sand, in general it is too fine grained to meet the specifications for building sand (BS 882/1201), though locally it may meet the broadest classification of a Zone 4 sand. The high content of glauconite probably makes the unweathered sands unsuitable for certain other applications, though where they have been oxidised and leached, they may possibly prove useable as a source of foundry or wearing coarse (asphalt) sand (Clarke, 1983).

Kesgrave Sands and Gravels

The Kesgrave Sands and Gravels are preserved in the northeast of the district where they rest on Crag or Upper Chalk. Outcrops are restricted to the area around Bardwell [940 737] and Stanton [970 733], although the deposits have been proved at depth in several boreholes to the south in the adjacent Woolpit resource sheet area (Clarke, 1983). There, the deposit is generally 3–5 m thick, with a maximum recorded thickness of 8.4 m in a borehole [9676 6489] near Norton.

In general, the deposits contain about 25 per cent gravel, 70 per cent sand and 5 per cent 'fines'. Medium-grained sand dominates within the sand fraction, but fine- and coarse-grained sand is also present. The gravel-sized clasts comprise subangular to subrounded flints, with quartz, quartzite and well-rounded flint pebbles.

Ingham Sand and Gravel

Sand and gravel deposits rich in well-rounded, brown 'Bunter' quartzite and vein-quartz pebbles occur in a pit [851 713] at Ingham, and have been mapped at outcrop in the north-eastern part of the district where they form a fairly continuous sheet, up to about 3 m thick, beneath Boulder Clay and resting on Upper Chalk.

Glacial Sand and Gravel

Glacial Sand and Gravel deposits are widely distributed throughout the district; they most commonly occur in close association with Boulder Clay and Glacial Silt. Over much of the area, they occur as lensoid layers or irregular masses beneath, within and above the regional sheet of Boulder Clay. The thickest developments, including over 23 m recorded in borehole [7432 7118] near Tuddenham, are located within drift-filled channels.

In the south-west, patches of Glacial Sand and Gravel occur beneath the Boulder Clay sheet, for example around Denham Castle [749 629]. Locally, these occurrences exceed 10 m in thickness and may be workable. The deposits are more extensive beneath the Boulder Clay in the central and eastern parts of the district, where they range from less than 1 m up to 22 m thick. In the south, there is an irregular sheet of sand and gravel up to 9 m thick beneath the Boulder Clay. Within and above the Boulder Clay, further sand and gravel is present, especially in the south-east of the district. Lithologically, the deposits are poorly sorted and extremely variable, ranging from very clayey sand to coarse gravel. On the whole they comprise about 60 per cent sand, 25 per cent gravel and 15 per cent 'fines'. The sand is mainly of quartz with a little flint, although locally, chalk is abundant. The gravel fraction is dominated by clasts of subangular to subrounded flint, with some chalk, vein-quartz, quartzite and more exotic components. Where the deposits occur close to the surface, decalcification has commonly reduced or even entirely removed chalk clasts.

Glacial Sand and Gravel has been extensively worked in the Hessett [935 615], Drinkstone [960 615], Tostock [955 635] and Woolpit [975 625] areas where it forms a sheet several metres thick overlying the Boulder Clay.

River Terrace Deposits

River Terrace Deposits form the principal aggregate resources of the district. They are most extensive in the north-west along the valley of the River Lark and its tributaries. Smaller scale deposits are present in the east along the valley of The Black Bourn. Sand and gravel occurring beneath a thin overburden of clayey Alluvium was conventionally regarded as First River Terrrace Deposits during the aggregate assessment surveys of the district, but they are classified with the Alluvium in this memoir.

The sand fraction of the River Terrace Deposits is of fine and medium grade, and is overwhelmingly composed of quartz. The gravel fraction is dominated by subangular to subrounded flints, with subordinate amounts of well-rounded flint, quartz, quartzite and sandstone pebbles.

In the Lark drainage system, some four terrace levels have been distinguished. The upper two (Fourth and Third terraces) generally consist of pebbly sand, 2–4 m in thickness; the lower two (Second and First terraces) comprise sand and gravel, locally greater than 10 m thick, but more generally less than 6 m thick (Clayton, 1983). The deposits have been worked extensively, principally around Kentford [710 670] and Lackford [790 705].

The deposits of The Black Bourn valley are classified mainly as those of the Second and First terraces. In general they are between 2 and 3 m thick, but locally attain 5 m. These deposits are probably richer in gravel than most others in the district, containing an average gravel content of about 35 per cent by weight. Small workings are present at Grimstone End [935 690].

Head and Head Gravel

Although deposits of Head and Head Gravel are considered to be generally too variable in grade, composition and thickness to be potentially workable, locally they nevertheless satisfy the criteria for 'mineral'. The deposits generally range between 1 and 4 m in thickness and form thin superficial spreads at the bottom of slopes, where they have accumulated by solifluction. They are predominantly poorly sorted pebbly sands which commonly contain over 20 per cent of 'fines'. The composition of the deposits is strongly influenced by their older source deposits.

Cover Sand

Cover Sand forms thin superficial spreads, principally in the

80 CHAPTER 7 ECONOMIC GEOLOGY

central and northern parts of the district. The deposits comprise pebbly sands, in which common cryoturbation has led to some mixing with the underlying deposits, mainly Boulder Clay. As a result, the Cover Sand deposits are commonly very clayey, and in many areas they average barely 1 m in thickness; regionally they are not regarded as potentially workable, although locally they may fulfil the arbitrary resource criteria quoted at the beginning of this chapter.   SJM

CHALK

Chalk was formerly extensively worked for lime in and around Bury St Edmunds. Some of the workings were open pits [e.g. 8500 6385; 8636 6475; 8450 6454; 8476 6380; 837 628], from some of which Chalk was subsequently abstracted from underground galleries. The existence of the Horringer Court Galleries [837 628] has been known for over 100 years (Bennett and Blake, 1886), and the plan of the galleries published (Pearman, 1976). Pearman also produced a map of the Jacqueline Close underground workings [848 639] (Plate 8), together with a brief outline of the rediscovery of the galleries in the 1950's and 1960's. He noted that the pit was extended northwards by galleries in the latter part of the nineteenth century; the first edition (1886) of the 25-inch Ordnance Survey map shows an air shaft at this site. The date of closure of these workings is unknown.

Farther east, another large pit [8500 6385] has been in existence from at least 1750, as shown by the presence of a lime-kiln on that site on Warren's town map; another is shown farther north [c.8515 6415]. Manuscript notes in the Bury St Edmunds Record Office record that Chalk was worked to a depth of a 30- to 40-rung ladder until about 1893 or 1894. Another pit [8450 6454] which was extended northwards by galleries (MS record BGS) has been partially filled and built over. No detail of the extent of the workings or of their closure is available. On the east of the town, there is a series of chalk pits at The Glen [8645 6465], one of which [8648 6466] was extended horizontally by radiating tunnels up to 200 m in length. The pit and the tunnels have now been designated a Special Site of Scientific Interest by the Nature Conservancy Council.   CRB

There are now only two active workings within this district, both in Middle Chalk, at Red Lodge and Barton Mills. They produce calcium carbonate for agriculture which is sold as 'agricultural lime', although it is not calcined, but only screened in order to control the particle size and to remove flints.

Because Chalk absorbs up to about 25 per cent water, working it in open pits is difficult in rain, and subsequent treatment is impossible unless the raw material is artificially dried before crushing and screening. Artificial drying has become prohibitively expensive because of high fuel costs and, consequently, extraction and processing are now economic only in dry weather. Thus, extraction at Red Lodge and Barton Mills takes place only in the summer, and production is restricted.   PMH

BRICK-CLAY

Glacial Silt, the Woolpit Beds, Hoxnian Lacustrine Deposits and the more loamy Boulder Clay have been used for brickmaking (Whitaker and others, 1881; Whitaker and

Plate 8 Subsidence above old chalk mine workings, Jacqueline Close, Bury St Edmunds. (A12816)

others, 1891). Most of the operations were small and probably few survived into the twentieth century. An exception is the brickworks at Woolpit [982 622], where 'Brickearth' has been worked since at least the 16th century (Northeast, 1972) and which was the source of the locally famous bricks known as Woolpit or Suffolk Whites. Extensive pits have been dug over all the outcrop of the laminated silts, silty clays and fine-grained sand of the Woolpit Beds. Even here, brickmaking ceased in about 1934.   CRB

WATER SUPPLY

The district lies within the Great Ouse River Division of the Anglian Water Authority and comprises Hydrometric areas 33, 35 and 36. It is intensely farmed, and agricultural irrigation is becoming increasingly important. Average annual precipitation (based on the standard 35-year period 1916–1950) varies from less than 551 mm at Beck Bridge [662 733], just outside the district, to 633 mm at Bury St Edmunds [850 643]. There are no storage reservoirs because the geology of the area does not readily permit their construction. The only stream gauging station is at Temple Weir [758 730] on the River Lark, where a mean discharge of 1.24 m^3/sec was registered over the period 1960–1973. There are a number of publications on the hydrogeology of the district, the more important of which include those of Whitaker (1906) and Woodland (1942).

The greater part of the district is covered by Boulder Clay and Glacial Sand and Gravel. Chalk, the principal aquifer, is exposed primarily in the north and west; in the south-east, Chalk is overlain by Crag. Parts of the Drift and the Lower Greensand also yield groundwater, although at present no borehole taps groundwater from the latter formation.

LOWER GREENSAND: This is a highly permeable, loosely cemented sandstone with local clay beds, and it commonly contains glauconitic and ferruginous material. It does not crop out within the district, but was encountered in the Culford Borehole [831 710] (Figure 1) and in all of the Ely-Ouse Water Transfer Scheme boreholes north of Kentford (Figure 6). The Culford Borehole, now partly silted up, formerly yielded 2.5 l/s.

CHALK: This is the main aquifer. It is a pure, fine-grained, high porosity (commonly 40–50 per cent) limestone. Because the pore sizes are minute, as low as 1 μm, the flow of water through the saturated zone depends on the presence of fissures. The number and nature of these is largely dependent upon the precise lithology, including the distribution of flints, the structure and the geomorphological history. In particular, the yield of a Chalk borehole is almost entirely dependent upon the number and nature of the fissures it intersects.

All three divisions (Upper, Middle and Lower) of the Chalk are present in the district. Generally, the Upper Chalk produces the highest yields.

The highest recorded yield of 120 l/s is at Bury St Edmunds, where a 760 mm diameter borehole penetrated 45.26 m of Upper Chalk. A 530 mm diameter borehole through Upper and Middle Chalk at Rushbrooke [873 623] yielded 53 l/s; another borehole of 250 mm diameter at Barton Mills [709 712] yielded 25 l/s. The efficiency of some wells has been increased by treating with acid. At Ixworth [940 697], two connected boreholes treated with acid yielded 55 l/s. At a site in Bury St Edmunds [850 642], five shafts and boreholes yielded 115 l/s from Upper Chalk.

The alignment of drift-filled channels cut in Chalk may be controlled by lines of structural weakness, which in turn increase the degree of fissuring. In addition, the higher infiltration capacity of the essentially gravelly fill of the channels may lead to enlargement by solution of fissures in the underlying Chalk, enhancing yields. Yields are generally good where Chalk is overlain by a thin layer of glacial deposits. At Mildenhall [729 759], Chalk overlain by 7.3 m of sand and gravel (River Terrace Deposits), yielded 35 l/s.

Groundwater from Chalk is used for many purposes. The Anglian Water Authority abstracts up to 105 l/s at Barrow Heath [779 654] for public water supply; at Bury St Edmunds [856 656 and 861 656], the British Sugar Corporation has a licence to abstract 40 l/s for industrial use. Groundwater is also abstracted for spray irrigation and other agricultural purposes.

CRAG AND DRIFT: Quaternary deposits, consisting of Crag sands and unconsolidated chalky clay, sand, silt and gravel of glacial and fluviatile origin, are generally considered to be in hydraulic continuity with the Chalk. Local supplies can be obtained from these unconsolidated deposits, although yields may suffer during droughts and the groundwater is liable to pollution. More important from the hydrogeological point of view, most of these deposits allow a significant proportion of infiltration to percolate to deep storage in the Chalk.

CHEMICAL CHARACTERISTICS OF GROUNDWATERS: Chemical analyses of different water samples are shown in Table 7, from which it can be seen that there is some correlation between the total dissolved solids (TDS) content and the total hardness. It is also apparent that boreholes Nos 2 and 3 (Table 7), lying close to the River Lark, and No. 6, near the River Kennett, show higher TDS values. Total hardness ranges between 170 and 395 milligrams/litre (mg/l), although the total hardness of water samples from Upper and Middle Chalk mainly ranges between 325 and 395 mg/l. Chalk water from beneath a thick mantle of Boulder Clay and sand and gravel shows a higher carbonate hardness as indicated, for example, by analyses Nos 2 and 4 (Table 7) of waters from boreholes where the Chalk is overlain by 6.4 m of mottled clay, peat, sand and gravel, and by 57 m of Boulder Clay and Glacial Sand and Gravel respectively. The high values are probably due to a high carbon dioxide content in the heavier soils. Where Chalk is overlain by clay-free sand and gravel only, the carbonate hardness is low (for example, No. 7 of Table 7, which is an analysis of water from Chalk overlain by 7.3 m of sand and gravel). The chloride content in all the formations is low.   PKM

Table 7 Analyses of groundwater (expressed in milligrams/litre)

Borehole No.	1	2	3	4	5	6	7
Location	West Stow [8207 7538]	Bury St Edmunds [8491 6668]	Bury St Edmunds [8500 6420]	Bradfield St George [9096 5996]	Rushbrooke [8730 6230]	Moulton [6994 6456]	Mildenhall [7296 7592]
Analyst*	3	1	2	4	2	1	1
Date	1948	1961	1969	1939	1969	1969	1969
Aquifer †	UCk/MCk	MCk	UCk/MCk	UCk	UCk/MCk	MCk	S & G/LCk
Total dissolved solids (at 180°C)	—	435	550	—	395	450	240
Total hardness ‡	170	340	370	395	325	355	190
Non-carbonate hardness ‡	—	40	110	55	35	120	30
Carbonate hardness ‡	—	300	260	340	290	235	160
pH	8.0	6.9	7.2	7.2	7.05	7.2	7.4
Free carbon dioxide	—	70	26	—	34	32	15
Calcium	—	127	—	—	—	136	74
Magnesium	—	5	—	—	—	3	1
Sodium	—	14	—	—	—	10	6
Potassium	—	3.9	—	—	—	3	1
Carbonate	—	180	—	—	—	141	96
Sulphate	—	29	—	—	—	60	7
Chloride	12	24	32	38	22	27	13
Nitrate nitrogen	—	3	15.5	—	2.5	11	5.8
Fluoride	—	0.3	—	—	—	0.1	0.1
Silica	—	28	—	—	—	11	11
Iron	0.1	0.04	0.15	—	—	—	0.4

* 1 The Counties Public Health Laboratories, London 2 Lincolne Sutton & Wood Ltd, Norwich 3 The Dept. of Govt. Chemist, London 4 County Laboratory, Ipswich
† S & G sand and gravel, UCk Upper Chalk, MCk Middle Chalk, LCk Lower Chalk
‡ As calcium carbonate

REFERENCES

ALLSOP, J M. 1985. Geophysical investigations into the extent of the Devonian rocks beneath East Anglia. *Proc. Geol. Assoc.*, Vol. 96, 371–379.

BADEN-POWELL, D F W. 1948. The Chalky Boulder Clays of Norfolk and Suffolk. *Geol. Mag.*, Vol. 85, 279–296.

— and OAKLEY, K P. 1952. Report on the re-investigation of the Westley (Bury St Edmunds) Skull site. *Proc. Prehist. Soc.*, New Series, Vol. 18, No. 1, 1–20.

BAILEY, H W, GALE, A S, MORTIMORE, R N, SWIECICKI, A, and WOOD, C J. 1983. The Coniacian–Maastrichtian stages of the United Kingdom, with particular reference to southern England. *Newsl. Stratigr.*, Vol. 12, 29–42.

BALSON, P S. 1980. The origin and evolution of Tertiary phosphorites from eastern England. *J. Geol. Soc. London*, Vol. 137, 723–729.

BARKER, R D, and HARKER, D. 1984. The location of the Stour buried tunnel-valley using geophysical techniques. *Q. J. Eng. Geol., London*, Vol. 17, 103–115.

BENNETT, F J. 1884. The geology of the country around Diss, Eye, Botesdale, and Ixworth (explanation of Quarter-sheet 50 N.W.). *Mem. Geol. Surv. G.B.*

— and BLAKE, J H. 1886. The geology of the country between and south of Bury St Edmunds and Newmarket (explanation of Quarter-sheet 51 SE). *Mem. Geol. Surv. G.B.*

BERTRAM, H, and KEMPER, E. 1971. Das Alb von Hannover. *Beih. Ber. Naturh. Ges.*, Vol. 7, 27–47.

BLACK, M. 1972–1975. British Lower Cretaceous coccoliths, 1. Gault Clay. *Monogr. Palaeontogr. Soc.*, 1–142.

BOSWELL, P G H. 1929. The geology of the country around Sudbury (Suffolk). *Mem. Geol. Surv. G.B.*

BRISTOW, C R. 1977. *In discussion of* Middle Pleistocene stratigraphy in south east Suffolk. ROSE, J, and ALLEN, P. 1977. *J. Geol. Soc. London*, Vol. 133, 83–102. *J. Geol. Soc. London*, Vol. 134, 94–95.

— 1980. The geology of the country around Walsham-le-Willows. *Open-file Rep. Inst. Geol. Sci.*, No. 1980/6.

— 1981. Geology of the country around Felsham and Rattlesden. Explanation of 1:10 560 geological sheets TL 95 NW and 95 NE. *Open-file Rep. Inst. Geol. Sci.*, No. 1981/1.

— 1983. The stratigraphy and structure of the Crag of mid-Suffolk, England. *Proc. Geol. Assoc.*, Vol. 94, 1–12.

— 1985. Geology of the country around Chelmsford. *Mem. Br. Geol. Surv.*, Sheet 241 (England and Wales).

— 1986. *Geological notes and local details for 1:10 000 sheets TM 07 NW and NE (Botesdale and Wortham)* (Keyworth: British Geological Survey.)

— and COX, F C. 1973. The Gipping Till: a reappraisal of East Anglian glacial stratigraphy. *J. Geol. Soc. London*, Vol. 129, 1–37.

— and GREGORY, D M. 1982. Notes on the high-level, (?marine), Late-Anglian Woolpit Beds, Suffolk. *Trans. Suffolk Nat. Soc.*, Vol. 18, 310–317.

BROMLEY, R G, and GALE, A S. 1982. The lithostratigraphy of the English Chalk Rock. *Cret. Res.*, Vol. 3, 273–306

BULLARD, E C, GASKELL, T F, HARLAND, W B, and KERR-GRANT, C. 1940. Seismic investigation of the Palaeozoic floor of east England. *Philos. Trans. R. Soc. London*, A, Vol. 239, 29–94.

CASEY, R. 1959. Field meeting at Wrotham and the Maidstone By-pass. *Proc. Geol. Assoc.*, Vol. 70, 206–209.

— 1961. The stratigraphical palaeontology of the Lower Greensand. *Palaeontology*, Vol. 3, 487–621.

CATT, J A. 1977. Loess and coversands. 221–229 in *British Quaternary studies*. Shotton, F W (editor). (Clarendon Press.)

CHORLEY, R J, STODDART, D R, HAGGETT, P, and SLAYMAKER, H O. 1966. Regional and local components in the areal distribution of surface sand facies in the Breckland, eastern England. *J. Sed. Petrol.*, Vol. 36, 209–220.

CHROSTON, P N, and SOLA, M A. 1982. Deep boreholes, seismic refraction lines and the interpretation of gravity anomalies in Norfolk. *J. Geol. Soc. London*, Vol. 139, 255–264.

CLARKE, M R. 1983. The sand and gravel resources of the country around Woolpit, Suffolk. Description of 1:25 000 sheet TL 96. *Miner. Assess. Rep. Inst. Geol. Sci.*, No. 127.

— and AUTON, C A. 1982. The Pleistocene depositional history of the Norfolk-Suffolk borderland. *Rep. Inst. Geol. Sci.*, No. 82/1, 23–29.

— and CORNWELL, J D. 1983. The buried glacial channels of the Woolpit (Suffolk) area—a preliminary report. *Rep. Inst. Geol. Sci.*, No. 83/10, 31–36.

CLAYTON, A R. 1983. The sand and gravel resources of the country between Mildenhall and Barrow, Suffolk: description of 1:25 000 sheets TL 76, TL 77 and part of TL 87. *Miner. Assess. Rep. Inst. Geol. Sci.*, No. 123.

CORBETT, W M. 1971. Soil surveying in Norfolk and Suffolk. *Bull. Geol. Soc. Norfolk*, No. 19, 2–31.

CORNWELL, J D. 1985. Applications of geophysical methods in mapping unconsolidated sediments in East Anglia. *Modern Geology*, Vol. 9, 187–205.

— and CARRUTHERS, R M. 1986. Geophysical studies of a buried valley system near Ixworth, Suffolk. *Proc. Geol. Assoc.*, Vol. 97, 357–364.

CORSER, C E. 1982. The sand and gravel resources of the country north of Newmarket. Description of 1:25 000 sheet TL 67 and part of TL 66. *Miner. Assess. Rep. Inst. Geol. Sci.*, No. 110.

DIMITROVA, N. 1974. Crétacé Inferieur (gastropoda et bivalvia). 9–258 in *Les fossiles de Bulgarie*, IV. TZANKOV, V (editor). (Sofia.)

DONOVAN, D T, HORTON, A, and IVIMEY-COOK, H C. 1979. The transgression of the Lower Lias over the northern flank of the London Platform. *J. Geol. Soc. London*, Vol. 136, 165–173.

ETIE, BEN AKPAN, FARROW, G E, and MORRIS, N. 1982. Limpet grazing on Cretaceous algal-bored ammonites. *Palaeontology*, Vol. 25, 361–367.

EVANS, P. 1971. Towards a Pleistocene time-scale. 123–356 in The Phanerozoic time-scale: a supplement. *Spec. Publ. Geol. Soc. London*, No. 5, part 2.

EVANS, R. 1976. Observations on a stripe pattern. *Biul. Peryglac.*, Vol. 25, 9–22.

FUNNELL, B M. 1955. Notes on the geology of the country around Ingham near Bury St Edmunds. *Trans. Suffolk Nat. Soc.*, Vol. 9, 227–236.

— 1961. The Palaeogene and early Pleistocene of Norfolk. *Trans. Norfolk & Norwich Nat. Soc.*, Vol. 19, 340–364.

— NORTON, P E P, and WEST, R G. 1979. The Crag at Bramerton, near Norwich, Norfolk. *Philos. Trans. R. Soc. London, B*, Vol. 287, 489–534.

— and WEST, R G. 1962. The Early Pleistocene of Easton Bavents, Suffolk. *Q. J. Geol. Soc. London*, Vol. 118, 125–141.

GALLOIS, R W. 1978. The Pleistocene history of west Norfolk. *Bull. Geol. Soc. Norfolk*, Vol. 30, 3–38.

— and COX, B M. 1977. The stratigraphy of the Middle and Upper Oxfordian sediments of Fenland. *Proc. Geol. Assoc.*, Vol. 88, 207–228.

— and MORTER, A A. 1982. The stratigraphy of the Gault of East Anglia. *Proc. Geol. Assoc.*, Vol. 93, 351–368.

GAUNT, G D, FLETCHER, T P, and WOOD, C J. In press. Geology of the country around Kingston upon Hull and Brigg. *Mem. Br. Geol. Surv.*, Sheets 80 and 89 (England and Wales).

GREGORY, J W. 1922. *Evolution of the Essex rivers and of the lower Thames.* (Colchester: Benham & Co.)

HARMER, F W. 1902. A sketch of the later Tertiary history of East Anglia. *Proc. Geol. Assoc.*, Vol. 17, 416–439.

HAWKINS, M P. 1981. The sand and gravel resources of the Bury St Edmunds (Suffolk) area. Description of 1:25 000 sheet TL 86. *Miner. Assess. Rep. Inst. Geol. Sci.*, No. 72.

HEWITT, H D. 1924. Notes on some Chalk sections in the district around Thetford, Norfolk. *Proc. Geol. Assoc.*, Vol. 35, 220–244.

— 1935. Further notes on the Chalk of the Thetford District, Norfolk. *Proc. Geol. Assoc.*, Vol. 46, 18–37.

HEY, R W. 1967. The Westleton Beds reconsidered. *Proc. Geol. Assoc.*, Vol. 78, 427–445.

— 1980. Equivalents of the Westland Green Gravels in Essex and East Anglia. *Proc. Geol. Assoc.*, Vol. 91, 279–290.

HOLMES, S C A. 1971. The geological mapper and the employment of his results, as illustrated in some areas of southern England. *Proc. Geol. Assoc.*, Vol. 82, 161–186.

HOLYOAK, D T, IVANOVICH, M, and PREECE, R C. 1983. Additional fossil and isotopic evidence for the age of the interglacial tufas at Hitchin and Icklingham. *J. Conchol.*, Vol. 31, 260–261.

HUMPHREYS, B, and BALSON, P S. 1985. Authigenic glauconite in the East Anglian Crags. *Proc. Geol. Assoc.*, Vol. 96, 183–188.

INSTITUTE OF GEOLOGICAL SCIENCES. 1981. 1:250 000 Series, Bouguer gravity anomaly map, Sheet 52°N–00°, East Anglia. (Keyworth: Institute of Geological Sciences.)

— 1982. 1:250 000 Series aeromagnetic anomaly map, Sheet 52°N–00°, East Anglia. (Keyworth: Institute of Geological Sciences.)

JEANS, C V. 1973. The Market Weighton Structure: tectonics, sedimentation and diagenesis during the Cretaceous. *Proc. Yorkshire Geol. Soc.*, Vol. 39, 409–444.

— 1978. Silicifications and associated clay assemblages in the Cretaceous marine sediments of southern England. *Clay Miner.*, Vol. 13, 101–126.

— 1980. Early submarine lithification in the Red Chalk and Lower Chalk of Eastern England: a bacterial control model and its implications. *Proc. Yorkshire Geol. Soc.*, Vol. 43, 81–157.

— MERRIMAN, R J, MITCHELL, J G, and BLAND, D J. 1982. Volcanic clays in the Cretaceous of southern England and Northern Ireland. *Clay Miner.*, Vol. 17, 105–156.

JELETZKY, J A. 1980. New or formerly poorly known biochronologically and palaeobiogeographically important gastroptinid and cleaniceratid (Ammonitida) taxa from the Middle Albian rocks of mid-western and Arctic Canada. *Pap. Geol. Surv. Canada*, 79–122.

JUKES-BROWNE, A J. 1903. The Cretaceous rocks of Britain, 2. The Lower and Middle Chalk of England. *Mem. Geol. Surv. GB.*

— 1904. The Cretaceous rocks of Britain, 3. The Upper Chalk of England. *Mem. Geol. Surv. GB.*

KELLY, S R A. 1971. A new section in the Upper Greensand near Erdington, Wiltshire. *Proc. Geol. Assoc.*, Vol. 82, 445–448.

KEMPER, E. 1984. Unter-Cenoman in Nordwestdeutschland. *Geol. Jahrb.*, Vol. A75, 465–487.

KERNEY, M. 1976. Mollusca from an interglacial tufa in East Anglia, with the description of a new species of *Lyrodiscus* Pilsbry (Gastropoda: Zonitidae). *J. Conchol.*, Vol. 29, 47–50.

— BROWN, E H, and CHANDLER, T J. 1964. The late-glacial and post-glacial history of the Chalk escarpment near Brook, Kent. *Philos. Trans. R. Soc. London, B*, Vol. 248, 135–204.

LAKE, R D. 1977. In discussion of Middle Pleistocene stratigraphy in south-east Suffolk. ROSE, J, and ALLEN, P. 1977. *J. Geol. Soc. London*, Vol. 133, 83–102. *J. Geol. Soc. London*, Vol. 134, 94.

— ELLISON, R A, AND MOORLOCK, B S P. 1977. In reply to ROSE, J, ALLEN, P, and HEY, R W. 1976. Middle Pleistocene stratigraphy in southern East Anglia. *Nature, London*, Vol. 263, 492–494. *Nature, London*, Vol. 265, 663–664.

— YOUNG, B, WOOD, C J, and MORTIMORE, R N. 1987. Geology of the country around Lewes. *Mem. Br. Geol. Surv.*, Sheet 319, (England and Wales).

LAWSON, T E. 1982. *Geological notes and local details for 1:10 000 sheets TM 28 NW, NE, SW, SE (Harleston, Norfolk).* (Keyworth: Institute of Geological Sciences.)

LINSSER, H. 1968. Transformation of magnetometric data into tectonic maps by digital template analysis. *Geophys. Prospect.*, Vol. 16, 179–207.

MAARLEVELD, G C. 1960. Wind directions and coversands in the Netherlands. *Biul. Peryglac.*, Vol. 8, 49–58.

MCRAE, S G. 1972. Glauconite. *Earth Sci. Rev.*, Vol. 8, 397–440.

MERRIMAN, R J. 1983. The origin of glauconitic material in Crag deposits from East Anglia. *Proc. Geol. Assoc.*, Vol. 94, 13–16.

MITCHELL, G F, PENNY, L F, SHOTTON, F W, and WEST, R G. 1973. A correlation of Quaternary deposits in the British Isles. *Spec. Rep. Geol. Soc. London*, No. 4, 99 pp.

MORTER, A A, and WOOD, C J. 1983. The biostratigraphy of Upper Albian–Lower Cenomanian *Aucellina* in Europe. *Zitteliana*, Vol. 10, 515–529.

MORTIMORE, R N, and WOOD, C J. 1986. The distribution of flint in the English Chalk, with particular reference to the 'Brandon Flint Series' and the high Turonian flint maximum. In *The scientific study of flint and chert: papers from the Fourth International Flint Symposium*, Vol. 1. SIEVEKING, G, and HART, M B (editors). (Cambridge University Press.)

MURRAY, K H. 1986. Correlation of electrical resistivity marker bands in the Cenomanian and Turonian Chalk from the London Basin to East Yorkshire. *Rep. Br. Geol. Surv.* Vol. 17, No. 8.

NORTHEAST, P. 1972. *Woolpit Brick*. MS document (4pp), Local Studies Collection, Suffolk Record Office, Bury St Edmunds.

OWEN, H G. 1971a. Middle Albian stratigraphy in the Anglo-Paris Basin. *Bull. Br. Mus. Nat. Hist. (Geol.)*, Suppl. 8, 1–164.

— 1971b. The stratigraphy of the Gault in the Thames Estuary and its bearing on the Mesozoic tectonic history of the area. *Proc. Geol. Assoc.*, Vol. 82, 187–207.

— 1973. Ammonite faunal provinces in the Middle and Upper Albian and their palaeogeographical significance. 145–154 in *The Boreal Lower Cretaceous*. CASEY, R, and RAWSON, P F (editors). *Geol. J. Spec. Issue*, No. 5. (Liverpool.)

— 1976. The stratigraphy of the Gault and Upper Greensand of the Weald. *Proc. Geol. Assoc.*, Vol. 86 (for 1975), 475–498.

PEARMAN, H. 1976. Caves and tunnels in south-east England. *Rec. Chelsea Speleol. Soc.*, Vol. 7, Pt. 1. 42 pp.

PERRIN, R M S. 1957. The clay mineralogy of some tills in the Cambridge district. *Clay Minerals Bull.*, Vol. 3, 193–205.

— 1963. The use of air photographs in the study of patterned ground in East Anglia. *Int. Arch. Photogrammetry*, Vol. 14, 183–188.

— 1971. *The clay mineralogy of British sediments*. (London: Mineralogical Society.)

— DAVIES, H, and FYSH, M D. 1973. Lithology of the Chalky Boulder Clay. *Nature, London, Phys. Sci.*, Vol. 245, 101–104.

RANCE, C E DE. 1868. On the Albian, or Gault, of Folkestone. *Geol. Mag.*, Vol. 5, 163–171.

RASTALL, R H. 1912. The mineral composition of some Cambridgeshire sands and gravels. *Proc. Cambridge Philos. Soc.*, Vol. 17, 132–143.

READ, W A. 1977. *In discussion of* Middle Pleistocene stratigraphy in south-east Suffolk. ROSE, J, and ALLEN, P. 1977. *J. Geol. Soc. London*, Vol. 133, 83–102. *J. Geol. Soc. London*, Vol. 134, 94.

RICHARDSON, J B, and LISTER, T R. 1969. Upper Silurian and Lower Devonian spore assemblages from the Welsh Borderland and South Wales. *Palaeontology*, Vol. 12, 201–252.

ROSE, J, and ALLEN, P. 1977. Middle Pleistocene stratigraphy in south-east Suffolk. *J. Geol. Soc. London*, Vol. 133, 83–102.

— — and HEY, R W. 1976. Middle Pleistocene stratigraphy in southern East Anglia. *Nature, London*, Vol. 263, 492–494.

— — and WYMER, J J. 1978. Weekend field meeting in south east Suffolk, 15–17 October 1976. *Proc. Geol. Assoc.*, Vol. 89, 81–90.

SKERTCHLY, S B J. 1879. On the manufacture of gun flints. *Mem. Geol. Surv. G.B.*

SPAETH, C. 1971. Untersuchungen an Belemniten des Formenkreises um *Neohibolites minimus* (Miller 1826) aus dem Mittel- und Ober-Alb Nordwest-deutschlands. *Beih. Geol. Jb.*, Vol. 100, 1–127.

— 1973. *Neohibolites ernsti* and its occurrence in the Upper Albian of northwest Germany and England. 361–368 in *The Boreal Lower Cretaceous*. CASEY, R, and RAWSON, P F (editors). *Geol. J. Spec. Issue*, No. 5.

STRONG, G E. 1978. Particle size analysis of seven coversands from Suffolk (Sheet 189). *Rep. Petrol. Unit, Inst. Geol. Sci.* No. 126.

STRAW, A. 1963. Some observations on the 'Coversands' of North Lincolnshire. *Trans. Lincolnshire Nat. Union*, Vol. 15, 260–269.

— 1979. The geomorphological significance of the Wolstonian glaciation of eastern England. *Trans. Inst. Br. Geogr. New Series*, Vol. 4, 540–549.

SUMBLER, M G. 1983. A new look at the type Wolstonian glacial deposits of Central England. *Proc. Geol. Assoc.*, Vol. 94, 23–31.

SUTCLIFFE, A. 1975. A hazard in the interpretation of glacial-interglacial sequences. *Quaternary Newsl.*, No. 17, 1–3.

TRIPLEHORN, D M. 1966. Morphology, internal structure and origin of glauconite pellets. *Sedimentology*, Vol. 6, 247–266.

TURNER, C. 1973. Eastern England. 8–18 *in* A correlation of Quaternary deposits in the British Isles, MITCHELL, G F, and others. 1973. *Spec. Rep. Geol. Soc. London*, No. 4.

WARD, W H, BURLAND, J B, and GALLOIS, R W. 1968. Geotechnical assessment of a site at Mundford, Norfolk, for a large proton accelerator. *Geotechnique*, Vol. 18, 399–431.

WATT, A S. 1955. Stone stripes in Breckland, Norfolk. *Geol. Mag.*, Vol. 92, 173–174.

— PERRIN, R M, and WEST, R G. 1966. Patterned ground in Breckland: structure and composition. *J. Ecol.*, Vol. 54, 239–258.

WEST, R G. 1981. A contribution to the Pleistocene of Suffolk: an interglacial site at Sicklesmere, near Bury St Edmunds. 43–48 in *The Quaternary in Britain*. NEALE, J (editor). (Pergamon Press.)

— and DONNER, J J. 1956. The glaciations of East Anglia and the East Midlands: a differentiation based on stone orientation measurements of the tills. *Q. J. Geol. Soc. London*, Vol. 122, 69–91.

— and NORTON, P E P. 1974. The Icenian Crag of south-east Suffolk. *Philos. Trans. R. Soc. London*, B, Vol. 269, 1–28.

WHITAKER, W, BENNETT, F J, and BLAKE, J H. 1881. The geology of the neighbourhood of Stowmarket (explanation of Quarter-sheet 50 SW). *Mem. Geol. Surv. G.B.*

— and JUKES-BROWNE, A J. 1894. Borings at Culford, Winkfield, Ware and Cheshunt. *Q. J. Geol. Soc. London*, Vol. 50, 487–514.

— WOODWARD, H B, BENNETT, F J, SKERTCHLY, S B J, and JUKES-BROWNE, A J. 1891. The geology of parts of Cambridgeshire and Suffolk (Ely, Mildenhall, Thetford) (explanation of Sheet 51 NE, with part of 51 NW). *Mem. Geol. Surv. G.B.*

WILKINSON, I P. 1988. Ostracoda across the Albian/Cenomanian boundary in Cambridgeshire and western Suffolk, eastern England. 1229–1244 in Evolutionary biology of Ostracoda. HANAI, T, IKEYA, N, and ISHIZAKI, K (editors). *Proceedings of the Ninth International Symposium on Ostracoda.*

— and MORTER, A A. 1981. The biostratigraphical zonation of the East Anglian Gault by Ostracoda. 167–176 in *Microfossils from Recent and fossil shelf seas*. NEALE, J W, and BRASIER, M D (editors). (Chichester: Ellis Harwood Ltd, British Micropalaeontological Society.)

WILLIAMS, R B G. 1964. Fossil patterned ground in eastern England. *Biul. Peryglac.*, Vol. 14, 337–349.

— 1968. Some estimates of periglacial erosion in southern and eastern England. *Bull. Peryglac.*, Vol. 17, 311–335.

APPENDIX 1

List of Geological Survey photographs

Copies of these photographs may be seen in the library of the British Geological Survey, Keyworth, Nottingham NG12 5GG and at the BGS Information Desk at the Geological Museum, Exhibition Road, South Kensington, London SW7 2DE. They all belong to series A and may be supplied as black and white or colour prints and transparencies at a fixed tariff. The photographs were taken by H Dewey (5705 and 5706) and H J Evans (the remainder).

5705	Glacial Sand and Gravel, Warren Hill, near Mildenhall.
5706	Glacial Sand and Gravel, Warren Hill, near Mildenhall.
12808	General view of Boulder Clay terrain, Hawstead Place.
12809	Pit in poorly sorted clayey Glacial Sand and Gravel, North Hill Covert, Rushbrooke.
12810	Detail of poorly sorted clayey Glacial Sand and Gravel.
12811	First River Terrace Deposits overlying channel-fill silts, Lackford.
12812	Recumbent fold in Glacial Sand and Gravel, Ingham.
12813	Interbedded well-sorted and poorly sorted Glacial Sand and Gravel, Ingham.
12814	Laminated silts within sand and gravel, Ingham.
12815	Top Rock in the basal beds of the Upper Chalk, near Barrow Heath.
12816	Subsidence on housing estate, Bury St Edmunds.
12817	Subsidence on housing estate, Bury St Edmunds.
12818	Glacial Sand and Gravel overlying Boulder Clay, Cindron Hills, Tostock.
12819	Second River Terrace Deposits overlying channel-fill silts, Cavenham.
12820	Second River Terrace Deposits, Cavenham.
12821	Detail of sand and gravel of Second River Terrace Deposits, Cavenham.
12822	Cryoturbated contact of 'Cover Sand' and chalky Boulder Clay, Moreton Hall Development, Bury St Edmunds.
12823	Chalky Boulder Clay overlying Glacial Sand and Gravel, Fornham Park.
12824	Chalky Boulder Clay overlying contorted Glacial Sand and Gravel, Fornham Park.
12825	Chalky Boulder Clay overlying contorted Glacial Sand and Gravel, Fornham Park.
12826	Cryoturbated chalk-rich gravel within Head Gravel, Pakenham.
12830	Pit exposing Head Gravel, Pakenham.
12831	First River Terrace Deposits of River Lark, overlying Glacial Silt, Lackford.
12832	Glacial Sand and Gravel/Chalk contact, Ingham.
13036	Glacial Sand and Gravel overlying Chalk, Barton Mills.
13037	Detail of Glacial Sand and Gravel, Barton Mills.
13038	Solution pipe in redeposited chalk, filled with Glacial Sand and Gravel, Barton Mills.
13039	Glacial Sand and Gravel under possible flow till, Barton Mills.
13040	Detail of Glacial Sand and Gravel, Barton Mills.
13041	Method of working Middle Chalk for lime, Barton Mills.
13042	Woolpit Beds ('Brickearth'), Woolpit.
13043	Detail of Glacial and Gravel, Weatherhill Farm, Icklingham.
13044	Involutions in Chalk, Dairy Farm, Ixworth.
13045	Kesgrave Sands and Gravels, and Head, Burntfirs Plantation, Stanton.
13046	Kesgrave Sands and Gravels, and Head, Burntfirs Plantation, Stanton.
13047	Cryoturbations in the Upper Chalk, Stanton, 700 m SW of Wyken Hall.
13048	Cryoturbations in the Upper Chalk, Stanton, 700 m SW of Wyken Hall.
13049	Irregular Chalk surface underlying Glacial Sand and Gravel, Ingham.
13050	Irregular Chalk surface beneath Glacial Sand and Gravel, Ingham.
13051	Irregular Chalk surface beneath Glacial Sand and Gravel, Ingham.
13052	Lobate structure in Glacial Sand and Gravel beneath Boulder Clay, Ingham.
13053	Detail of calcrete, Ingham.
13054	Block of calcrete resting on irregular Chalk surface, Ingham.
13055	Cross-bedded outwash sands, Ingham.
13056	Cross-bedded outwash sands, Ingham.
13057	Cobble gravel channel fill, Ingham.
13058	Detail of sand and gravel, Weatherhill Farm, Icklingham.
13059	Boulder Clay, Barton Mills, Mildenhall.
13060	Dunes of Recent Blown Sand, Burntpin Plantation, Icklingham.
13061	Palaeosol within Recent Blown Sand, Burntpin Plantation, Icklingham.
13062	Sand and gravel of the Second Terrace of the River Lark, Cavenham.
13063	Ice-wedge cast within Second River Terrace Deposits, Cavenham.
13064	Cryoturbations of Cover Sand into Chalk, Kentford House Farm, Kentford.
13065	Possible interglacial silts exposed in Old Brickpit, Icklingham.
13977	Solution pipe on Chalk, Ingham.
13978	Ingham Sand and Gravel, Ingham.

APPENDIX 2

Stowlangtoft Borehole TL 96 NW/63
[9475 6882]

Stratigraphical borehole drilled by Drillsure Ltd for British Geological Survey in 1983. Abridged log.
Surface level 38 m above OD.

	Thickness m	Depth m
Mesozoic, Upper Cretaceous		
UPPER CHALK		
coranguinum Zone		
Open hole	6.45	6.45
Chalk, soft, white, with bands and patches of ochreous staining, 'finger' flints at 6.75; 'horned' flints at c.8.25	2.00	8.45
Core lost	3.72	12.17
Chalk, soft, white, blocky	0.35	12.52
Core lost	2.59	15.11
Chalk with small burrow-form flints at top	0.30	15.41
Core lost	0.91	16.32
Chalk, white, blocky, with ochreous stained bands; scattered small flint nodules, 0.6 m flint band at 16.42; scattered fish debris, trace fossils and *Platyceramus*; much bioturbation below 27.92; core lost 19.09 to 19.58; 23.72 to 23.96; 24.76 to 25. 27; 27.56 to 27.42	12.92	29.24
Core lost	2.37	31.61
Chalk, compact, white, with pale grey burrow fills; shells	1.68	33.29
Core lost	0.34	33.63
Chalk, very pale grey, with pale grey burrow fills; large and small flints; fairly compact; marly band 34.95 to 34.99; much burrowed below 37.10 with some microfaulting, hard gritty chalk 'nodules' at c.39.10	8.30	41.93
Core lost; approximate junction of *coranguinum* & *cortestudinarium* zones at 43.60 (resistivity log).	4.40	46.33
Chalk, very pale grey, with pale grey (N7) burrow fills; compact; flints; marly bands at c.46.73; 52.55 and 52.77; core lost 47.34 to 48.24; ?burrowed surface at 48.85	3.61	49.94
Core lost	1.01	50.95
Paler, harder chalk 52.60 to 52.70. Harder bed with burrowed top, 53.30 to 53.60. Chalk now becomes noticeable cyclic with grey marly burrowed chalk passing up into paler harder chalk with a burrowed upper surface. Band of flint nodules at 52.80, with *Inoceramus*. Harder bed with burrowed top 53.30 to 53.60	2.95	53.90
Chalk, fairly hard, whitish with grey burrow fills, cyclic, *Zoophycos* burrows. Burrowed surfaces on hard white chalk at 55.10. Flints and flint nodules at c.54.80 and c.55.00. Grey burrow fills with thin pyrite core in some cases. Flints, spiky and lobate forms at 56.15 to 56.23. Hardened burrowed surface at 56.65. Traces of sponges (in black pyrite) c.57.70. Hard nodules at c.56.70 and c.57.75; grey and marly below to hard surface at 58.11. Sponges at 58.40 with harder nodules. Chalk, very hard and gritty below, with nodules, sponge traces, large flint nodules 58.75 to 50.81	4.91	58.81
Chalk, cyclic as above, broken flints at top with hard nodules. Hard burrowed bed at 62.30. Black ovoid flints nodules 62.56 to 62.61, softer and greyer chalk below (base of *cortestudinarium* Zone 62.96)	4.15	62.96
'Top Rock' (top of *planus* Zone), very hard, with nodules and 'pebbles', pyrite traces and very small flints	0.49	63.45
Chalk, grey, cyclic, *Zoophycos* burrows, hard, burrowed, very marly and light olive-grey (5GY 6/1) to irregular contact at 64.00 with hard white burrowed chalk with spiky burrow-form flints 64.18 to 64.23. Continuing cyclic chalk with burrows	10.33	73.78
Chalk, strongly cyclic with rhythms of pale hard burrowed chalk passing down to more marly soft grey chalk. Shells (*Hyotissa semiplana*, *Spondylus sp.*, thin-shelled inoceramids, *Sternotaxis placenta*, *S. planus*) and echinoid debris, much burrowed throughout. Flints at 73.82, 77.60, 78.55, 77.40, 77.20 and 78.90	5.71	79.49
Chalk, as above, fairly hard and pale at top, with pale grey burrow fills, microfaults, becoming more marly below 80.00, to pale hard burrowed beds at 80.35, 81.82, 83.01 and 83.90. *Zoophycos* at c.80.50. Bivalves and echinoids. Small flints at c.80.55, 81.30, 81.40	5.41	84.90
?West Tofts Marl		
Marl, light olive-grey (5Y 6/1), finely laminated	0.10	85.00
Chalk, pale, hard, burrowed, becoming grey and marly below	0.27	85.27
?Chalk Rock		
Chalk, pale, very hard, with near vertical fissures, cyclic with other hard pale beds at 85.55 and 85.80	1.07	86.34
?top of Brandon Flint Series		
Flint, massive continuous bed, black with thin white cortex, irregular top and base (?'the Horns') up to	0.14	86.48
Chalk, cyclic, pale to light grey, with some very hard chalk nodules, small flints, many burrows. Pale hard tops of cycles at 86.55, 86.91, 87.19, 87.58, 88.52. *Inoceramus*, echinoids etc.	2.40	88.88
Flint, hard, regular band ?'Wall Stone'	0.11	88.99
Chalk, as above, very pale grey, burrowed, with harder lumps	0.64	89.63

88 APPENDIX 2

Description	Thickness	Depth
Flint, large, irregular nodules with flattish base up to	0.11	89.74
Chalk, cyclic as above, grey and marly to pale, hard top of cycle at c.90.00, burrow-form flints at 90.34. Ammonites 90.05, 90.15 *Scaphites geinitzii, Sciponoceras bohemicum, Yezoites [Otoscaphites] bladenensis.* Very hard nodules in part with 'reussianum' type of preservation of fossils as hollow moulds, irregular flint nodules at 90.50 to 90.61, partly hollow with small quartz crystals lining cavity	1.37	91.11
Chalk, pale, hard, nodular, core broken with grey burrow fills (with fish and carbonaceous debris)	3.12	94.23
Flint, massive flattish top and base (?'Floor Stone' of Grimes Graves)	0.15	94.38
Chalk, pale and hard with pale grey burrow fills, shell fragments, fish debris	1.64	96.02
?Grimes Graves Marl		
Marl, light olive-grey, highly listric with trace fossils (burrows) preserved on lower surface	0.12	96.14
Chalk, very pale grey with darker burrow fills, small 'tabular' flints c.97.00, small flints, fossils		

MIDDLE CHALK

Description	Thickness	Depth
Becoming grey and marly with chalk pebbles 98.70 to erosion surface at 99.00. Pale hard chalk below with small flints and irregular semi-tabular flint. More marly below 99.90, small brown phosphatic lumps and hard chalk pebbles. Fossils include echinoids ('*Hirudocidaris*' *hirudo, Gauthieria radiata*) bivalves (thin shelled inoceramids and *Spondylus spinosus*), brachiopods (*Orbirhynchia dispansa*), sponges	5.10	101.24
Chalk, much as above, but with fewer flints, generally cyclic with chalk pebbles in marly chalk above erosion surfaces; well-burrowed with darker burrow fills. Fossils include echinoids (*Gauthieria radiata, Sternotaxis planus*), bivalves (inoceramids and oysters), brachiopods (*Orbirhynchia dispansa*), sponges	5.64	106.88
Chalk, as above, cyclic, erosion surfaces at 107.35 and 109.12. Pebbles above surface yellow- and green-stained	2.70	109.58
'Twin Marls' (peak on resistivity curve)		
Marl, pale yellowish green, upper band, separated from lower band by pale marly chalk	0.22	109.80
Chalk, hard, whitish to 110.00, then more marly, with chalk pebbles	0.47	110.27
Chalk, grey and marly with chalk pebbles to erosion surface on harder pale chalk at 111.44; slight marly parting at 111.95 to 111.96. Fossils include bivalves *Inoceramus* ex gr. *lamarcki, I.* cf. *inaequivalvis, Plagiostoma sp., Syncyclonema sp.,* brachiopods (*Concinnithyris* or *Gibbithyris, Orbirhynchia sp., Terebratulina striatula, T. lata*), sponges and echinoids (*Sternotaxis planus*), small burrows. Microfaulting in harder chalk. Marly wisps in part	11.36	121.63
Mount Ephraim Marl (peak on resistivity log)		
Marl, light olive-grey (5Y 6/1), listric	0.10	121.73
Chalk, grey-white, burrowed, small burrow-form flints (up to 30 mm), much inoceramid shell debris and echinoid fragments	2.17	123.90
Chalk, slightly marly, grey-white, well-burrowed, compact; several steep slickensided fractures. Becoming greyer and more marly below 129.80 with slightly 'striped' appearance	6.22	130.12
Chalk, very pale grey, fairly hard with small spiky flints, well-burrowed, becoming more marly below 130.70, with chalk pebbles to erosion surface at 130.90. Paler, harder chalk below with marly wisps and microfaulting. Fossils include bivalves (*Inoceramus cuvierii*), brachiopods (*Orbirhynchia heberta, Terebratulina lata*), sponges, echinoids (*Sternotaxis planus*) and trails	5.34	135.46
Core lost (Pilgrims Walk Marl noted at c.137.00 on resistivity log)	3.80	139.26
Chalk, greyish white, fairly hard, well-burrowed, with marly wisps. Twin marly band at 139.92. Traces of shells below. Becoming more marly and grey from 141.80 to erosion surface with chalk pebbles at 141.92. Hard pale chalk below, with wispy marl band at 144.00. Many olive-grey 'styolitic' marly partings. Fossils include bivalves (*Inoceramus cuvierii*), brachiopods (*Terebratulina lata, Orbirhynchia sp.*) and echinoids (*Conulus*)	12.69	151.95
?Methwold Marl		
Marl, wispy band with 'augens' of chalk	0.10	152.05
Chalk, white, softish with harder nodules, traces of shell debris. Fossils include bivalves (*Mytiloides spp.*) and echinoids (*Conulus subrotundus*)	3.10	155.15
Melbourn Rock (155.15–163.25)		
Chalk, hard, gritty, nodular, with marly partings and wisps with much shell debris. Pale grey with whitish nodules enwrapped by greenish grey marl; some nodules green-coated. Fossils include bivalves and brachiopods. Chalk softer and less nodular from 156.50 to 157.00; pale, hard and nodular with marly wisps below; bivalves and gastropods	3.11	158.26
Chalk as above, pale, hard and gritty with occasional very pale grey marly bands with chalk pebbles; burrow-fills and marly wisps; shell fragments. Fossils include bivalves, brachiopods, fish. Strongly nodular band 163.00 to 163.10 with ochreous staining (?hard-ground)	4.99	163.25

LOWER CHALK
Plenus Marls (163.25–164.23)
Metoicoceras geslinianum Zone

Description	Thickness	Depth
Marl, greenish grey, finely laminated to 163.35, paler marly chalk interbedded in irregular wispy form to 163.45. Marly and greenish grey below, then becoming paler grey harder chalk with marl wisps and streaks	0.98	164.23

Calycoceras guerangeri Zone
Chalk, very pale yellowish grey, slightly

marly with pale grey-green burrow fills. Traces of shells etc with band of *Inoceramus pictus* at 164.80 to 164.90. Black carbonaceous debris at 170.35 within burrow fill   6.43   170.66

Chalk, as above, burrowed, some thin burrows pyritised c.171.53   1.15   171.81

Chalk, pale grey-white, slightly marly, pyritic trails and marly burrow fills, traces of fish debris and plant material c.172.25. Softer and more marly 172.45 to 172.50   2.79   174.60

Chalk, very pale grey-white, hard with rough conchoidal fracture, much shell debris, pyrite trails   0.73   175.33

Chalk, marly, with cyclic rhythms of varying clay content, very pale to medium grey. Paler, harder, calcareous beds with burrowed tops mark the top of cycles and pass downward into dark more marly chalk with pyrite trails etc. Microfaulting common. Fossils include brachiopods (*Concinnithyris?*), bivalves ('*Aequipecten*' *beaveri*), '*Inoceramus*' *atlanticus*, *Plagiostoma globosum*), echinoids, fish fragments and sponges   12.77   188.10

Totternhoe Stone (188.10–189.55)
Chalk, very hard, gritty, creamy and brownish white with pyrite trails, shell and fish debris, some silt grade quartz grains, well-indurated. Small brown phosphatic lumps from 189.10. Fossils include bivalves, brachiopods, fish, pyritised sponges   1.45   189.55

Chalk, marly, cyclic as above, well-burrowed, noticeably softer and more 'fissile' than chalk above Totternhoe Stone. Fossils include bivalves, brachiopods and sponges   7.97   197.52

Chalk, marly, pale greenish grey, cyclic, but less distinctly so than above. Rather uneven curved fracture. Band rich in *Orbirhynchia mantelliana*. Marly below 198.20, to hard burrowed surface at 199.70. Pale harder chalk below. Fossils include brachiopods, bivalves, fish, ?plants, ammonite fragments   7.13   204.65

Chalk, pale yellowish grey, marly, hard with trace of glauconite; bioturbated. Pyrite trails, fossils include ammonites (*Mantelliceras, Schloenbachia*), bivalves ('*Inoceramus*' *crippsi*, *Plicatula* ex gr. *radiola*, *Pseudolimea echinata*), brachiopods, plant debris, fish debris   1.65   206.30

Chalk, pale greenish grey, hard with darker marly burrow fills, scattered glauconite, small phosphatic lumps. Very gritty with shell debris below 208.00. Pyrite nodule at 208.73   3.70   210.00

Cambridge Greensand
Marl, calcareous, glauconitic, greenish grey, becoming darker green and more glauconitic downward. Burrowed surface at 210.32; scattered pale brown phosphatic nodules, highly bioturbated, few shells. Black phosphatic lumps above burrowed base   1.45   211.45

Gault
Mudstone, slightly silty, light olive-grey, smooth textured with pale pinkish brown phosphatic nodules and lumps (up to 10 mm). Scattered throughout, fine pyritised trails. Bivalves   2.05   213.50

Mudstone, smooth with fine burrows (up to 2 mm), scattered pale pinkish brown phosphatic nodules (up to 5 mm).   0.95   214.45

Mudstone, very smooth, greenish grey with pyritised trails and *Inoceramus* debris, slightly fissile with fine darker burrows. Fossils include bivalves, belemnites, ammonites (some phosphatised). Brownish phosphatic nodules   1.64   216.09

Mudstone, slightly paler grey, pale nodules, well-burrowed, pyritised trails, rough fracture, calcareous   0.61   216.70

Mudstone, smooth, pale greenish grey, bivalves and ammonites common, pale phosphatic nodules (up to 30 mm) at 217.30   1.00   217.70

Mudstone, calcareous, hard (cf. cementstone) with pyritised fossils; pale phosphatic nodules at 218.15   0.45   218.15

Mudstone, smooth, pale greenish grey, bivalves and belemnites. '*Inoceramus*' band 218.30 to 218.42. Small pale phosphatic nodules. Pyritised ammonites (small), corals, bivalves   0.55   218.70

Mudstone with *Birostrina sulcata*, ammonites, serpulids, darker burrows; intense *Chondrites* burrows. Small plant fragments, some local phosphatisation   0.80   219.50

Mudstone, pale grey (N7), silty texture with scattered fine shell and fish debris, phosphatic nodules, burrows, pyrite trails. Less silty below 220.00. Bivalves, ammonites, belemnites, scaphopods, ostracods   3.20   222.70

Mudstone, smooth, greenish grey, well-burrowed, with bivalves, ammonites, gastropods, orthocone nautiloid, ostracods; often pyritised; phosphatic nodules; strong band of phosphatic nodules with 'solid' fossils and green-coated pebbles at 223.16 to 223.20   1.00   223.70

Mudstone, slightly fissile, pale olive-grey with darker burrows. Fossils include bivalves, uncoiled ammonites; some phosphatic nodules   0.30   224.00

Mudstone, very smooth, pale greenish grey, with ammonites and bivalves. Band of phosphatic nodules at 224.28 (up to 30 mm)   0.28   224.28

Mudstone, darker, densely burrowed, with bivalves, ammonites and belemnites. Thin layer of pyritic, glauconitic clay at base with belemnites, resting with sharp unconformity on weathered surface of Palaeozoic rocks   0.66   224.94

Palaeozoic, Silurian

Ludfordian (Upper Ludlow)
Siltstone, medium-grained, greyish green (5GY 6/1) and greyish red (10R 4/2),

highly micaceous, hard, indurated. Yellowish carbonate mineral on cracks and in more porous layers. Interbedded with silty mudstone from 225.37 to 226.25; calcite veinlets on bedding planes	2.06	227.00
Sandstone, medium- to fine-grained, greyish red (10R 4/2), micaceous, fairly massive	0.21	227.21
Siltstone, fine- to medium-grained, reddish and greenish grey, with occasional interbedded mudstones alternating with fine-grained sandstone, greenish grey to Reddish grey, often micaceous and finely laminated. *Microsphaeridiorhynchus sp.* and *Orbiculoidea sp.* recorded at 234 m	9.65	236.86
Mudstone, silty with thin siltstone ribs, finely laminated, dip 30°. Fossils include *Lingula sp.* and *Orthonota rigida*	0.50	237.36
Siltstone, fine to coarse, reddish and brownish grey, interbedded with thin silty mudstones and alternating with sandstone, fine. Some bioturbation. Brachiopods, phacopid trilobites, crinoid columnals and molluscs, including bivalves, gastropods and orthocones, occur	12.69	250.05
Mudstone, silty, micaceous (N3–N4) with siltstone bands, bioturbation. Dip c.40°	1.31	251.36
Sandstone, very fine-grained, silty	0.52	251.88
Mudstone, silty, with laminated siltstone bands, bioturbated, loading structures, some red staining	2.72	254.60
Mudstone, silty, with laminated siltstone bands, bioturbated, loading structures, some red staining. Fossils include *Lingula sp.*, gastropods, *Nuculites sp.*, orthocones, crinoid columnals and *Londinia?*	2.72	254.60
Sandstone, very fine, silty micaceous laminated, alternating with siltstone with interbanded mudstone. Fossils, common at some levels, include *Craniops sp.*, *Palaeopecten* cf. *danbyi*, *Ptychopteria (Actinopteria) sp.*, gastropods, hyolithids, crinoid columnals, *Londinia?* and *Ceratiocaris sp.*	26.48	281.08
Breccia or cataclasite band, with dark subangular clasts in pale grey matrix, possibly a fault breccia. Inclined at 30°	0.02	281.10
Siltstone interbedded with mudstone as above. Dip 50°. Layers truncated by 'breccia' above. Quartz veinlets extend downward at high angles and along bedding laminae. Some disturbance of siltstone bands. Dip 55° at c.282.99	1.89	282.99
Mudstone with siltstone bands, dip 45°–50°, bioturbation, quartz veinlets, core much broken, dip 55°–60° below 285.52	3.21	286.20
Siltstone, laminated, interbanded with mudstone, bioturbated, quartz veinlets. Dip 50°	1.70	287.90
Breccia inclined at 60°	0.10	288.00
Mudstone, silty, highly sheared with quartz and iron-stained veinlets, interbanded with siltstone, medium to dark grey (N3–5), steeply dipping (60°–75°) with many quartz veinlets	7.65	295.65
Core not recovered	0.99	296.64

FOSSIL INDEX

No distinction is made here between positively determined genera, species and variants or examples doubtfully referred to it (i.e. with qualifications aff., cf. or ?, etc.).

Fossils identifiable at generic level only (e.g. *Bythoceratina spp.*) are listed after the named species.

Abies sp. 70
Acaste spp. 4, 30
Acesta sp. 9, 10
Acidota quadrata Zetterstedt 56
acritarchs 4, 76
Acroloxus lacustris (Linné) 69
Actactosia obtusa (J de C Sowerby) 17
A. sp. 19
Actinocamax primus Arkhangelsky 20
A. verus Miller 27, 29
A. sp. 27
Aegopinella pura (Alder) 69
'*Aequipecten*' *beaveri* (J Sowerby) 89
Agonum fuliginosum (Panzer) 56
Aleocharinae 56, 75
Alnus sp. 56
Amara sp. 75
Ambitisporites dilutus (Hoffmeister) Richardson & Lister 4
ammonites 8, 10, 14, 15, 19, 23, 25, 52, 88, 89
Amphidonte sp. 20
Anahoplites sp. 14
Ancylus fluviatilis Müller 69
Anisoceras sp. 11
Anisus leucostoma (Millet) 69, 70
A. vortex (Linné) 69
annelid 14
Anomia spp. 14, 17
Anotylus nitidulus (Gravenhorst) 75
A. rugosus (Fabricus) 75
Aphodius sp. 75
Apiculiretusispora sp. C 4
Apion sp. 75
Apodemus sylvaticus 61
Archaeozonotriletes chulus (Cramer) Richardson & Lister 4
A. divellomedium Chibrikova 4
A. dubius Richardson & Lister 4
Armiger crista Linné) 69, 76
Arpedium brachypterum (Gravenhorst) 56
asteroids 26
Atomaria mesomela (Herbst.) 75
Atreta nilssoni (Hagenow) 27
Aucellina coquandiana (d'Orbigny) 11
A. gryphaeoides (J de C Sowerby) 17, 19
A. uerpmanni Polutoff 17, 19
A. sp. 15, 17, 19

Bagous sp. 75
Bairdoppilata pseudoseptentrionalis Mertens 12

Balanus spp. 30, 57
Batavocythere gaultina (Kaye) 12, 13
Bathrotomaria sp. 26
Bathyomphalus contortus (Linné) 69
beetles 55, 75
belemnites 9, 13, 19, 20, 45, 52, 89
Bembidion assimile Gyllenhal 75
B. guttula (Fabricus) 56
Biplicatoria spp. 15, 17
Birostrina concentrica (Parkinson) 11, 14
B. concentrica gryphaeoides (J de C Sowerby) 11
B. subsulcata (Wiltshire) 11
B. sulcata (Parkinson) 11, 14, 15, 89
B. sp. 14
Bithynia tentaculata (Linné) 61, 69
bivalves 8, 9, 10, 11, 20, 23, 24, 50, 56, 57, 64, 87, 88, 89
Blethisa multipunctata (Linnaeus) 75
Boletobiinae 56
Bolivinoides strigillatus (Chapman) 29
bones 59, 64, 65, 67, 70
Boreaphilus henninigianus Sahlberg 56
Bos spp. 59, 64, 65, 70
Bourgueticrinus hureae (Valette) 29
B. sp. 22, 26, 27
brachiopods 4, 9, 15, 20, 23, 24, 27, 88, 89
bryozoans 27, 57
Buccella frigida (Cushman) 30
B. vicksburgensis (Cushman & Ellison) 30
Buccinum sp. 30
Bulimina elongata d'Orbigny 30
Bullapora 8
Byrrhus spp. 56, 75
Bythoceratina umbonata umbonata (Williamson) 12
B. spp. 19

Callihoplites spp. 11, 15
Cameroptychium campanulatum (T Smith) 26
C. planus 26
Camptonectes curvatus (Geinitz) 10
C. sp. 9
Candona albicans Brady 76
C. neglecta Sars 55, 56, 57, 76
Candonopsis sp. 76
Cantabrigites spp. 11
Capillithyris squamosa (Mantell) 20
Cardobairdia minuta (van Veen) 12
Carex sp. 56
Carpelimus sp. 75
Carychium minimum Müller 61, 69
C. tridentatum (Risso) 69, 75
Cassidulina obtusa Williamson 30
C. teretis Tappan 30
Cateretes pedicularis (Linnaeus) 56
Cepaea nemoralis (Linné) 69
Cerastoderma sp. 30
Ceratiocaris sp. 4
Ceratostreon rauliniana (d'Orbigny) 17
Cercyon melanocephalus (Linnaeus) 75
C. pygmaeus (Illiger) 75
C. sternalis (Sharp) 75
C. tristis (Illiger) 75
cervids 64, 70

Cervus spp. 48, 59, 65
Cetonia aurata (Linnaeus) 75
Chaetarthria seminulum (Herbst) 75
Chalenius sp. 75
Chlamys cretosa (Defrance) 27
C. opercularis (Linnaeus) 30
C. sp. 26
C. (Radulopecten) sp. 9
Chondrites sp. 10, 14, 15, 17, 22, 89
Cibicides beaumontianus (d'Orbigny) 28, 29
C. beaumontianus var. A Bailey (MS) 28
C. lobatulus (Walker & Jacob) 30, 57
C. lobatulus grossus Dam & Reinhold 30
C. ribbingi Brotzen 27, 29
C. sp. 28
'*Cidaris*' *perornata* Forbes 22, 27
'*Cirsocerithium*' *reussi* (Geinitz) 26
C. subspinosum (Deshayes) 14
C. sp. 14
Clithrocytheridea nana Triebel 12
Clivina collaris (Herbst) 75
C. fossor (Linnaeus) 75
coccoliths 13, 15
Cochlicopa lubrica (Müller) 61, 69
Coelostoma orbiculare (Fabricus) 75
Coleopterans 56
Concinnithyris subundata (J Sowerby) 20
C. spp. 21, 24, 26, 88, 89
Conulus albogalerus Leske 27, 29
C. subrotundus Mantell 21, 88
C. spp. 27, 88
corals 23, 24, 26, 89
Corbula gibba (Olivi) 30
Cordiceramus cordiformis (J Sowerby) 27
Cornicythereis bonnemai Triebel 12
C. cornueli (Deroo) 12, 13
C. lamplughi (Kaye) 12
C. larivourensis Damotte & Grosdidier 12
Coscinophragma sp. 21
Coscinopora sp. 26
Crania sp. 27
Craniops sp. 4
Craterastrer quinqueloba (Goldfuss) 27
Craticularia fittoni (Mantell) 26
Cremnoceramus erectus (Meek) 24, 26
C. rotundatus Tröger *non* Fiege 22, 24, 26
C. schloenbachi (Böhm) 24, 26
C. waltersdorfensis hannovrensis (Heinz) 24, 26
C. waltersdorfensis waltersdorfensis (Andert) 24, 26
Cretirhynchia cuneiformis Pettitt 26
C. plicatilis (J Sowerby) 29
C. subplicata (Mantell) 26, 27
C. sp. 27
Cretolamna appendiculata (Agassiz) 22
crinoid columnals 4, 14, 15, 57
Cryptopleurum minutum (Fabricus) 75
Cyclocypris laevis (Müller) 76
Cyclothyris sp. 26
Cypria ophthalmica (Jurine) 76
Cypridopsis aculeata (Costa) 76
Cythereis (C.) folkestonensis Kaye 12, 13, 15
C. (C.) hirsuta Damotte & Grosdidier 12

C. (C.) humilis Weaver 12
C. (C.) reticulata Jones & Hinde 12
C. (C.) thoerenensis Triebel 12
Cythereis (Rehacythereis) bemerodensis Bertram & Kemper 14, 19
C. (R.) luermannae hannoverana Bertram & Kemper 12, 13
C. (R.) luermannae luermannae Triebel 12
C. (R.) paranuda Weaver 12
C. (R.) sp. 12
Cytherella ovata (Roemer) 12
C. parallela (Reuss) 12
Cytherelloidea chapmani (Jones & Hinde) 12
C. kayei Weaver 12
C. knaptonensis Kaye 12
C. stricta (Jones & Hinde) 12, 13
Cytheropteron arguta Kaye 12
C. milbournei Kaye 12
C. nanissimum s.s. Damotte & Grosdidier 12
Cytilus siriceus (Forster) 75

Dereta sp. 15
Dicrorygma sp. 12
Dimorphoplites spp. 11
Ditrupa (Tetraditrupa) sp. 14
Dolocytheridea bosquetiana (Jones & Hinde) 12, 13
D. vinculum Wilkinson 12, 13
Donacia cinerea Herbst 75
D. sp. 75
Dryops sp. 75
dyad 4

Echinocorys gravesi Desor 23, 24, 26
E. scutatus elevatus Griffiths & Brydone 27
E. spp. 22, 27
echinoderms 9
echinoids 21, 22, 23, 24, 27, 87, 88, 89
eiffellithid 15
Eifellithus turriseiffelli (Deflandre) Reinhardt 15
Elephas primigenius Blumenbach 64, 65, 67
E. spp. 48, 70
Elmis aenea (Müller) 75
Elphidiella hannai (Cushman & Grant) 30, 57
Elphidium asklundi Brotzen 30
E. clavatum Cushman 57, 58
E. pseudolessoni Dam & Reinhold 30
Entolium laminosum (Mantell) 20
E. orbiculare Auctt 20
Eponides concinna Brotzen 28
Equus sp. 65
Eucythere solitaria Triebel 12
E. trigonalis (Jones & Hinde) 12
Eucytherura (Vesticytherura) multituberculata Gründel 12
Euhoplites inornatus Spath 14
E. spp. 11, 14
Eurete formosum Reid 26
E. spp. 26

Falciferella milbournei Casey 11
Filograna cincta (Goldfuss) 27
fish remains 10, 87, 88, 89
foraminifera 8, 9, 10, 21, 24, 27, 29, 33, 48, 57, 58
Freiastarte sp. 26

gastropods 14, 23, 24, 25, 57, 70, 88
Gauthieria radiata (Sorignet) 88
Gavelinella thalmanni (Brotzen) 28
G stelligera (Marie) 28, 29
Gibbithyris ellipsoidalis Sahni 27
G. subrotunda (J Sowerby) 22, 26
G. spp. 22, 26, 27, 88
Globigerinelloides bentonensis (Morrow) 15
Glomerula gordialis Schlotheim 27
Gonioteuthis westfalicagranulata (Stolley) 29
Grasirhynchia grasiana (d'Orbigny) 19
G. martini (Mantell) 20
Gryphaeostrea canaliculata (J Sowerby) 23, 26, 27, 29
Guettardiscyphia sp. 26
Gyraulus albus (Müller) 69
G. laevis 69
Gyrohypnus punctulatus (Paykul) 75

Habrocythere fragilis Triebel 12
Hamites spp. 11
Hechticythere speetonensis (Kaye) 12
Helophorus grandis Illiger 56
H. spp. 56, 75
Hemicytherura euglypha Kaye 12
Hibolites sp. 9
Hillendia sp. 26
Hippeutis complanatus (Linné) 69
Hippopotamus spp. 63, 65
Hirudocidaris hirudo (Sorignet) 26, 27, 88
Hoplites spp. 11, 14
Hybius sp. 75
Hydrobius fuscipes (Linnaeus) 75
Hydroporus sp. 75
Hydrothassa aucta (Fabricus) 75
hyolithid 4
Hyotissa semiplana (J de C Sowerby) 22, 23, 26, 87
Hysteroceras varicosum (J de C Sowerby) 15
H. spp. 11

Idiohamites alternatus (Mantell) 19
I. sp. 11
Ilyocypris gibba (Ramdohr) 55
Infracytheropteron obscura Kaye 12
inoceramids 13, 19, 20, 21, 22, 24, 25, 26, 27, 28, 29, 88
'*Inoceramus*' *anglicus* s.s. Woods 11, 14, 15
I. apicalis Woods 22
'*I.*' *atlanticus* (Heinz) 20, 89
'*I.*' *comancheanus* Cragin 19
'*I.*' *crippsi* Mantell 19, 89
'*I.*' *crippsi hoppenstedtensis* Tröger 19
'*I.*' *crippsi reachensis* Etheridge 19
I. cuvierii (J Sowerby) 21, 22, 88
I. etheridgei Woods 19
I. inaequivalvis Schlüter 22, 88
I. labiatus Schlotheim 22

I. lamarcki Parkinson 21, 22, 88
'*I.*' *lissa* (Seeley) 11, 15
I. longealatus Tröger 26
I. mytiloides (Mantell) 21
I. pictus J de C Sowerby 20, 89
I. virgatus Schlüter 19
I. websteri Mantell 26
I. websteri sensu Woods 22
I. spp. 26, 87, 89
Isocrinus granosus Valette 22
I. sp. 14
Isocythereis fissicostis fissicostis Triebel 12, 13
I. fissicostis gracilis Gründel 12
I. fortinodis fortinodis Triebel 12
I. fortinodis reticulata Gründel 12

Kingena concinna Owen 20
K. lima (Defrance) 27, 29
K. sp. 27
Kloedeniine 4

Laccobius sp. 75
Laminifera pauli 61
Lathrobium sp. 75
leaves 59
Leoniella carminae Cramer 4
'*Lepthoplites*' *spp.* 11
Leucophytia bidentata (Montagu) 69
Limnaea sp. 59
Limnobaris pilistriata (Stephens) 75
L. talbum (Linnaeus) 75
Limnocythere inopinata (Baird) 55, 56
Lingula sp. 4
Lingulogavelinella cf. *vombensis* (Brotzen) 28
Londinia sp. 4
Loxostomum eleyi (Cushman) 28
Lycopodium 70
Lyelliceras lyelli (d'Orbigny) 14
Lymnaea palustris (Müller) 69
L. peregra (Müller) 69
L. stagnalis (Linné) 69
L. truncatula (Müller) 61, 69, 76
L. sp. 69

Macrocypris siliqua (Jones) 12
M. simplex Chapman 12
Mammuthus spp. 64, 70
Mandocythere harrisiana (Jones) 12
Mantelliceras spp. 19, 89
Matronella corrigenda (Kaye) 12, 13
Megasterum obscurum (Marsham) 75
Meleagrinella sp. 9
Menetus dilatatus (Gould) 69
Metaclavites sp. 11
Metacypris cordata Brady & Robertson 57
Metopaster exsculptus Spencer 22
M. parkinsoni (Forbes) 27
M. uncatus (Forbes) 26
M. sp. 26
Micraster bucailli Parent 27
M. corbovis Forbes 21, 22, 23, 26
M. cortestudinarium (Goldfuss) 24, 26
M. gibbus (Lamarck) 27
M. leskei (Desmoulins) 23, 26

M. normanniae Bucaille   23, 26
M. spp.   26, 27
Micrhystridium penkridgensis Sarjeant & Strachan   76
M. stellatum Deflandre   4
miospores   4
Modestella geinitzi (Schloenbach)   20
Monticlarella carteri (Davidson)   17, 19
M. rectifrons (Pictet & Campiche)   19
Mortoniceras (*M.*) *spp.*   11
moss   55, 56
mouse   61
Moutonithyris dutempleana (d'Orbigny)   11, 15, 17
Multiplicisphaeridium asturiae (Cramer) Eisenack, Cramer & Diez   4
Murchisonia sp.   4
Mya arenaria Linnaeus   27
Myophorella sp.   9
Mytiloides dresdensis (Tröger)   24, 26
M. fiegei Tröger   26
M. incertus (Yabe)   26
M. labiatoidiformis Tröger   26
M. labiatus (Schlotheim)   22
M. lusatiae (Andert)   26
M. striatoconcentricus Gümbel   26
M. striatoconcentricus carpathicus Simionescu   26
M. spp.   21, 24, 26, 88

Neocythere (*Centrocythere*) *denticulata* Mertens   12
N. (*Neocythere*) *vanveenae* Mertens   12
N. (*N.*) *ventrocostata* Gründel   12
N. (*Physocythere*) *lingenensis* (Mertens)   12
N. (*P.*) *semiconcentrica* (Mertens)   12
N. (*P.*) *semilaeva* Kaye   12
N. (*P.*) *steghausi* (Mertens)   12
Neoflabellina suturalis suturalis (Cushman)   28
Neohibolites ernsti Spaeth   11
N. minimus minimus Miller   11, 15
N. oxycaudatus Spaeth   11
N. praeultimus Spaeth   11, 17, 19
N. sp.   15
Neomicrorbis crenatostriatus (Münster)   27
Nodosaria sp.   27
Notaris aethiops   56
Noterus clavicornis (Dejean)   75
Notiphilus sp.   75
Nucella lapillus (Linnaeus)   30
Nucula (*Pectinucula*) *pectinata* J Sowerby   14
Nuculites sp.   4
Nymphaster sp.   29

Ochthebius minimus (Fabricus)   56, 75
Olophrum fuscum (Gravenhorst)   56
Onchotrochus serpentinus Duncan   27
ophiuroids   26
Ophrystoma sp.   26
Oppilatala eoplanktonica (Eisenack) Dorning   4
Orbiculoidea sp.   4
Orbirhynchia compta Pettitt   21
O. cuvieri (d'Orbigny)   21
O. dispansa Pettitt   22, 88

O. heberti Pettitt   21, 88
O. mantelliana (J de C Sowerby)   19, 20, 89
O. pisiformis Pettitt   27
O. reedensis (Etheridge)   26
O. spp.   22, 24, 26, 27, 29, 88
Ornatothyris spp.   19
orthocone   89
Orthonota rigida (J de C Sowerby)   4
Osangularia cordieriana (d'Orbigny)   28
ostracods   4, 12, 13, 55, 56, 57, 76, 89
Ostrea cunabula Seeley   17
O. incurva Nilsson   26, 27
'*O.*' *papyracea* Sinzow   14
O. spp.   26, 45
Otiorhynchus nodosus (Müller)   56
Oxyloma pfeifferi (Rossmässler)   69
O. sarsi (Esmark)   69
Oxytoma seminudum (Dames)   20
oysters   8, 13, 15, 17, 20, 26, 27, 88

Palaeopecten danbyi (McCoy)   4
Paracypris wrothamensis Kaye   12
Paraplocia labyrinthica (Mantell)   26
Parasmilia sp.   26, 27
Parhabdolithus boletiformis Black   14
Parsimonia antiquata (J de C Sowerby)   26
Patrobus assimilis Chaudoir   56
P. septentrionis Dejean   56
Periaulax heberti (Barrois & Guerne)   26
Philonthus sp.   75
Phthanoloxoconcha icknieldensis (Weaver)   12
Phymosinion muricatum (F A Roemer)   26
P. sp.   26
Phymosoma sp.   27
Physia fontinalis (Linné)   69
Picea sp.   70
Pinus spp.   56, 70
Pisidium amnicum (Müller)   69
P. casertanum (Poli)   69
P. henslowanum (Sheppard)   69
P. milium Held   69
P. nitidum Jenyns   69
P. obtusale (Lamarck)   69
P. obtusale lapponicum (Clessin) Favre & Jayet   56, 64, 69, 70
P. pulchellum Jenyns   69
P. subtruncatum Malm   69
P. spp.   61, 69, 70, 75
Plagiostoma globosum J de C Sowerby   17, 19, 89
P. hoperi Mantell   27
P. sp.   88
Planileberis scrobicularis Weaver   12, 13, 15
Planolateralus dievarum (Cossmann)   26
Planorbarius corneus (Linné)   69
Planorbis carinatus (Müller)   69
P. planorbis (Linné)   69
P. sp.   59, 69
plants   10, 56, 61, 89
Platella icknieldensis Weaver   19
Plateumaris descolor (Panzer)   75
Platyceramus mantelli (Barrois)   24, 26, 27
P. spp.   24, 26, 27, 87
Platycythereis chapmani Kaye   12, 13
P. gaultina (Jones)   12
P. laminata Triebel   12, 13

Platystethus nodifrons (Mannerheim)   75
Plicatula barroisi Peron   22
P. radiola Lamarck   89
pollen   35, 56, 60, 63, 70
Pomatias elegans (Müller)   56
Pontocyprella harrisiana (Jones)   12
P. semiquadrata Kaye   12
Porcinolus murinus (Fabricus)   75
Porosphaera globularis (Phillips)   27
P. sessilis Brydone   27
P. sp.   22
Praebulimina reussi (Morrow)   28
Praelacazella wetherelli (Morris)   27
Prasocuris plellandrii (Linnaeus)   75
Prohysteroceras spp.   11
P. (*Goodhallites*) *sp.*   11
Proliserpula ampullacea (J de C Sowerby)   27
Protanisoceras sp.   14
Protelphidium anglicum Murray   57, 58
P. orbiculare (Brady)   57
Protochonetes sp.   4
Protocythere albae Damotte & Grosdidier   12, 13
P. lineata lineata (Chapman & Sherborn)   12, 13
P. lineata striata Gründel   12
'*proto-Eiffellithus*'   15
Pseudolimea echinata (Etheridge)   89
P. sp.   19
Pseudoperna sp.   27
Pterostichus minor (Gyllenhal)   75
P. nigrita (Paykul)   75
P. strenuus (Panzer)   75
Pterygocythereis (*Alatacythereis*) *sp.*   12
Ptychodus mammillaris Agassiz   26
Ptychopteria (*Actinopteria*) *sp.*   4
Pullenia bulloides (d'Orbigny)   30
Pupilla muscorum (Linné)   56, 61, 64, 69, 70
Pycnoglypta lurida Gyllenhal   56

Reussella kelleri Vasilenko   28
R. szajnochae praecursor de Klasz & Knipscheer   28, 29
Rhinoceros tichorhinus   64, 67
R. sp.   65
Rhizopoterion spp.   26, 27
Rhynchonella cuvieri d'Orbigny   21
rhynchonellids   8, 24
Rogerella sp.   27
Rotularia polygonalis (J de C Sowerby)   10

Saida nettgauensis Gründel   12
Saxocythere notera notera Gründel   12
S. notera senilis Kemper   12, 13
Scaphites geinitzii d'Orbigny   25, 88
scaphopods   23, 89
Schloenbachia spp.   19, 89
Schuleridea dimorphica Kaye   12
S. jonesiana (Bosquet)   12
Sciponoceras bohemicum (Fritsch)   25, 88
S. sp.   19
Selaginella spp.   56, 64, 70
Semenovites sp.   11
Serpula plana S Woodward   22
serpulids   8, 27, 45, 89

Simplocarea metallica Sturm 56
Sphaerium corneum (Linné) 69, 70, 75
S. sp. 61
Sphenoceramus cardissoides (Schlüter)/*pachti* (Arkhangelsky) 27
Spirorbis spp. 26, 27
Spisula sp. 30
Spondylus dutempleanus d'Orbigny 27
S. latus (J Sowerby)—*S. dutempleanus* 27
S. spinosus (J Sowerby) 22, 23, 26, 27, 88
S. spp. 27, 87
sponges 15, 23, 24, 25, 26, 27, 28, 87, 88, 89
Sporadoscinia alcyonoides (Mantell) 26
S. stellifera (Roemer) 26
S. sp. 26
spores 35, 56, 64
staphylinids 56
Stensioeina exsculpta exsculpta (Reuss) 28
S. granulata polonica Witwicka 27, 28, 29
Stenus spp. 56, 75
Sternotaxis placenta (Agassiz) 22, 23, 26, 87
S. plana (Mantell) 21, 22, 25, 87, 88
Stoliczkaia sp. 15
Stomatopora sp. 27
Stomohamites sp. 11
Succinea oblonga Draparnaud 56, 69, 70
S. putris (Linné) 69
S. sp. 69

succineids 56, 70
Suprionocyclus sp. 25
Syncyclonema sp. 88
Synolynthia subrotunda (Mantell) 26

Teichnichnus sp. 27
Temnocidaris (*Stereocidaris*) *sceptrifera* (Mantell) 26, 27
Tenea sp. 26
terebratulids 8, 24
Terebratulina lata Etheridge 21, 22, 88
T. nodulosa Etheridge 20
T. striatula (Mantell) 22, 26, 27, 88
T. sp. 15
Tethyoceramus humboldti (Eichwald) 24, 26
Thalassinoides sp. 19, 20, 23
Trachyporus sp. 75
Trechus quadristriatus (Schrank) 75
T. rivularis (Gyllenhal) 56
Trichia hispida (Linné) 69
T. striolata (Pfeiffer) 69
Trifarina angulosa (Williamson) 30
trilobites 4
Tritonophon trilobata (J de C Sowerby) 4
Tunisphaeridium tentaculaferum (Martin) Cramer 4
Turritella sp. 30
Tylocidaris clavigera (Mantell) 27

Uintacrinus spp. 24, 29

Vaginulinopsis scalariformis Prothault 28
Vallonia excentrica Sterki 69
V. pulchella (Müller) 61, 69, 75
Valvata cristata (Müller) 61, 69
V. macrostoma Mörch 69
V. piscinalis (Müller) 59, 69
ventriculids 26
Ventriculites sp. 26
vertebrates 70
vertiginids 61
Vertigo pygmaea (Draparnaud) 69, 75
Visbysphaera dilatispinosa (Downie) Lister 4
V. meson (Eisenack) Lister 4
Vitrea crystallina (Müller) 69
Viviparus contectus (Millet) 69
Volviceramus involutus (J de C Sowerby) 24, 26, 27
V. spp. 24, 26, 27

wood 10, 56, 59, 60

Xantholinus longiventris Heer 75

Yezoites [*Otoscaphites*] *bladenensis* (Schlüter) 25, 88

Zonitoides excavatus (Alder) 69
Z. nitidus (Müller) 61, 69
Zoophycos 23, 87

GENERAL INDEX

Page numbers in italics refer to illustrations

A45 road 23, 24, 25, 26, 42
Aalenian 8
Acanthoceras jukesbrownei Zone 16, 20
A. rhotomagense Zone 16, 20
Acutistriatum Band 9
Albian 10, 14
Allerød Chronozone 56
Alluvium 35, 68, 74–76
Ampton 62
Anahoplites intermedius Subzone 12, 14
A. picteti-rich band 11
Anglian 35, 40, 55, 58, 60, 72
Anglian Till 36, 48
Anglian Water Authority 81
'Anomia Beds' 14
Anomia-rich band 11
Aptian 9
Ash Carr 68
Ashley 47, 50, 66
athleta Zone 9
Aucellina coquandiana-rich band 11
Avenue Farm 22
Aycliff Borehole 14
Aylesbury 14

Badwell Ash 35, 36
Bailey, H W 27, 29
Baileypool Bridge 27, 41
Baker, O 58
Ballingdon Grove brickpit 58
Bangrove Wood 41
Barber Green Factory 27
Bardwell 27, 37, 38, 39, 40, 41, 65, 70, 76, 79
Bardwell Mill 49
Barham Sands and Gravels 35, 36, 37, 43, 47, 54
Barnfield Pit 61
Barnwell 'Hard Band' 11, 15
Barrois' Sponge Bed (Kent) 27
Barrow 26, 43, 50
Barrow Heath 25, 26, 81, 86
Barton Bottom 52
Barton Mere 52, 63
Barton Mill 44, 45, 48, 50, 55, 62, 64, 80, 81, 86
Barton Stud 49
basement 2, 6, 7
Bathonian 8
Battlies Green 52
Beck Bridge 81
Beeches Pit 61
Beestonian 37
'Belemnite Beds' 15
Bernersfield Farm 72
Beyton 30, 32, 41, 51, 54
Beyton By-pass 32, 37, 41, 51, 63

Beyton council house well 32
Beyton School 32
Birostrina concentrica-rich band 11
B. concentrica grypaeoides-rich band 11
B. sulcata-rich band 11
Black Bourn 38, 39, 40, 41, 47, 48, 49, 51, 53, 54, 63, 65, 70, 75–76, 76–77, 79
Black Bourn valley 57
Black Hill 38, 62
Blackthorpe 63
Blisworth Limestone 8, 9
'Blown Sand' 70, 86
Botanic Garden 67
Botesdale 37
Boulder Clay 35, 38, 40, 41, 42, 44, 45, 46, 47–51, 52, 53, 54, 55, 56, 57, 58, 59, 60, 61, 62, 63, 67, 70, 72, 73, 74, 75, 76, 78, 79, 81, 86
Bradfield Combust 46, 53, 62, 75
Bradfield Combust Hall 50
Bradfield Pumping Station 31
Bradfield St Clare 31, 51
Bradfield St George 30, 31, 51, 53, 75, 82
Brakey Pin 50, 73
Bramerton 30, 58
Brandon 23, 24
Brandon Flint Series 16, 18, 21, 22, 23, 24, 87
'Brassil' 20
Breckland 70, 71, 74
Breckland Tills 36
brevispina Subzone 8
Brewster's Farm 41
brick-clay 80–81
'Brickearth' 48, 57, 58, 59, 81, 86
Brick Kiln Plantation 52
brick pits 67
Bridge Farm 41, 51, 54, 62, 63, 68, 75, 76
Bridgham 4
British Sugar Corporation 81
Broadgrass Green 63, 76
Brush Hills 45
Bull Bridge 40, 47, 70, 76
Bullhead Bed 2, 30
Bullock's Lodge 26
Bull Road 41, 53
Bunbury Arms 63
Bunker's Barn 50, 56
Burgate 37
Burnham Chalk Formation 21
Burntfirs Plantation 34, 37, 86
Burntpin Plantation 86
Burwell Rock 19
Bury 42
Bury Lane 37
Bury St Edmunds 5, 6, 24, 26, 36, 43, 52, 54, 57, 62, 63, 64, 67, 68, 75, 76, 80, 81, 82, 86
Bury St Edmunds airfield 73
Bury St Edmunds Golf Course 27
Bury St Edmunds Hospital 27, 46
Bury St Edmunds old barracks 42, 50, 57
Bury St Edmunds Record Office 80

Bury–Thetford railway 52

Cage Grove 46
calcareous tufa 68, 76
calcrete 49
Callihoplites auritus Subzone 12, 15
Calloviense Zone 9
Calycoceras guerangeri Zone 16, 20, 88–89
Cambridge Borehole 5
Cambridge (188) district 9, 15, 19, 20, 54, 61, 66
Cambridge Greensand 13, 15, 16–19, 89
Cargate 53
Carstone 9, 10
Cattishall 73
Cavenham 22, 50, 55, 56, 57, 63, *64*, 67, 86
Cavenham Church 50
Cavenham Mill 56
Cavenham pit 55, 56, 67, 68
Cenomanian 20
Chalk 16–29, 41, 42, 44, 45, 46, 47, 48, 49, 50, 55, 56, 57, 61, 62, 63, 66, 67, *71*, 72, 73, 74, 75, 76, 79, 80, 81, 86, 87–89
Chalk Hill 22, 45, 50, 62
Chalk Marl 16, 19, 20
Chalk, reconstituted 40, 68
Chalk Rock 16, 17, 18, 20, 21, 22, 23, 24, 25, 26, 87
Chalky Boulder Clay 36, *38*, 41, 47
Chapelhill Farm 31
Chedburgh 30, 46, 48, 50
Chedburgh Airfield 30
Chelford Interstadial 56
Chelmsford 37
Chestnut Holdings 33
Chestnuts 32
Chevington 52
Cibicides ex gr. *beaumontianus* Zone 27, 28
Cindron Hills 86
Cindron Wood 54
Clare 13
Clare Borehole 4
clay mineralogy 48
Clopton Green 47
Clopton Hall 32
Cobb's Hall 30
Cock and Bull Farm 65
Cocks Green 31, 46
Coniacian 24, 27
Coniacian-Santonian boundary 24, 27
Conulus-rich horizon 27
Conyer's Green 43, 49, 52
Coope, G R 55, 56
Copy Farm 42
Cornbrash 9
Coronatum Zone 9
Cottenham Well 14
Cover Sand 3, 35, 49, 50, 52, 57, 60, 61, 66, 70–74, 79–80, 86
Crag 30–34, 36, 37, 47, 63, 72, 78, 79, 81
Crag, mineral composition 33, 34
Crag sand, size distribution 31

Crane Bridge 58
Cranmore Bridge 58
Cranmore Bridge pit 59
Crawley Hall 33
Cromerian interglacial 35, 37
Cromerian palaeosol 36
Crossways 59
cryoturbation 35, 60, 63, *71*, 80, 86
Culford 42, 45
Culford Borehole 4, 8, 9, 13, 81
Culford Heath 62, 72
Cythereis (Cythereis) folkestonensis Subzone 12, 15
Cythereis (Rehacythereis) luermannae hannoverana Zone 12, 13, 19
Cythereis (Rehacythereis) luermannae luermannae/Neocythere (Neocythere) ventrocostata Zone 12, 13

Dairy Farm 27, 86
Dairy Hall 41
Dairy Wood 50
Dalham 24, 25, 26, 46, 50
Dane Hill 66
davoei Zone 8
'Dead-Lime' 22, 24
Denham 36, 46, 62
Denham Castle 79
densiplicatum Zone 9
'dentatus nodule Bed' 14
Dentatus nodules 11
Desnage Lodge 24
Devensian 35, 40, 55, 56, 57, 60, 63, 70, 72
Devonian 4, 5, 6
Dimorphoplites-rich band 11
Dipoloceras cristatum Subzone 12, 14
Diss 36, 39
Dixon's Covert 49, 67
Downton Series 4
Drift-filled channels 38–43
Drinkstone 54, 63, 79
Drinkstone council houses 32
Drinkstone Green 32, 47, 51, 54
Drinkstone Park 32, 47
Drinkstone, The Moat 51
Ducksluice Farm 49

East Barton 63, 74
Easton Bavents 58
Economic Geology 78–82
Eldohouse Farm 46, 73
Elmswell 51, 71, 72
Elmswell New Hall 33, 47
Elmswell, St John's Church 54
Ely–Ouse Borehole 1a 8, 9, 10, 13, 14, 20, 21
  2 10, 12, 13, 14, 15, 19, 20, 21, 22
  3 14, 20
  4 10, 13, 14, 15, 20, 72
  5 10, 14, 15, 20
  6 9, 10, 13, 14, 17, 19, 20
  7 14, 15, 19, 20
  8 13, 14, 19, 20
  9 10, 14, 15, 20
  11 12, 13, 14
  23 13

Entolium orbiculare-rich band 11
Eriswell 8, 9, 13, 14, 15
Eriswell Borehole 5, 7, 8, 19, 20
Estuarine Series 8
Euhoplites alphalautus-rich band 11
Euhoplites lautus Zone 12, 14
Euhoplites loricatus Zone 12
Euhoplites meandrinus Subzone 12, 14
Euhoplites nitidus Subzone 12, 14
Euston 24
Exogyra Beds 15
Eye 34
Eye (190) district 77

False Chalk Rock 23, 25
Felsham 31, 43, 51
Felsham House 32
Felsham Rectory 31
Fir Wood 37, 49
First Pipe-Clay 23, 24, 25
First River Terrace Deposits 65, 67, 68, 70, 74, 79, 86
Flandrian 35, 60
Flempton 46, 47, 50, 56, 57, 67, 73, 75
Flempton Hall 26
Floor Stone 23, 24, 88
Folly Grove 72
Fornham All Saints 67
Fornham Park *44*, 467, 49, 86
Fornham St Genevieve gravel pit 24, 26, 43, 46, 75
Fornham St Martin 42, 49, 52, 57, 60, 61, 63, 67, 73
Fornham St Martin Church 42
Four Ashes Borehole 4, 13, 21, 22
Fourth River Terrace Deposits 64, 65, 66, 67, 79
Foxmould 15
Fox Spinney 49
Freckenham 6, 20
Freecroft Wood 63
Friar's Hall 32

Gault 2, 10–15, 89
'gaults' 49, 70
Gravelinella cristata Zone 28, 29
Gazeley 42, 50
Gedding 31, 51
Gedding Hall 32
Gedding House 32
George Inn, Stanton 27
Gipping 63
Gipping Till 36, 47, 71
Glacial Loam 54
Glacial Sand and Gravel 41, 50, 61, 63, 64, 67, 68, 70, 73, 75, 76, 79, 81, 86
Glacial Silt 35, 38, 40, 48, 49, 50, 53, 54–57, 60, 67, 68, 79, 80
Glassfield Road 37
Glebe Farm 68
Glen 80
Globigerinelloides rowei Zone 28, 29
grain size 30
Grange Farm 56, 75
Grantham Formation 8
Great Barton 41, 46, 49, 52, 54, 57, 62, 63, 74

Great Barton Church 74
Great Green 47, 51
Great Livermere 39, 45, 49, 54, 62, 63
Great Ouse River Division 81
Great Queach 27
Great Saxham 30, 50
Great Welnetham Church 50
Great Welnetham Windmill 62
Green Farm 47
Greenway House 31
Grime's Graves 23, 88
Grime's Graves Marl 18, 23, 24, 88
Grimstone End 39, 40, 41, 49, 51, 63, 65, 70, 79
Grindle Pit 61, 67
'gulls' 70

Haddenham Axis 9
Hall Farm 52, 67
Hall Heath 46
Hardwick Heath 46
Hare Farm 31
Haughley Park Sands and Gravels 2, 35, 36, 52, 54
Hawstead 39, 50, 62, 64
Hawstead Green 42, 68
Hawstead Hall 42, 50, 68
Hawstead House 50
Hawstead Place 86
Head *36*, 61, 62, 63, 73, 86
Head and Head Gravel 35, 61–63, 79, 86
Head Gravel 60, 62, 63, 68
Heath Farm 46, 49
heavy minerals 30
Hengrave 42, 43, 56, 64, 67, 75
Hengrave Hall 57
Hengrave Park 57, 73
Hepworth 49
Herringswell 66, 67, 76
Herringswell Church 66
Herringswell Manor 62
Hessett 32, 47, 51, 53, 79
Hessett Church 51
Higham 23, 25, 46
Higham railway cutting 25, 26
High Barn Hazel 32
High Hall 33
High Lodge 44, 48
Hill Farm 32, 33
Hitchin 61
Holaster subglobosus Zone 20
Hollybush Farm 32
Holmes, S C A 48
holton 37
Home Farm 46
Honington 38, 39, 41, 62, 65, 70, 72, 73
Honington Airfield 49, 62
Hoplites dentatus Zone 12, 14
Hoplites spathi Subzone 12, 14
'Horns' 87
Horringer 43, 48
Horringer Court 24, 27
Horringer Court galleries 80
Horringer Hall 46
Howe's chalk pit 45

Hoxnian Interglacial   35, 36, 48, 55, 60, 61, 80
'hummocky ground'   61, 62
Hunston   36, 41, 51, 53, 54, 57, 63, 76
Hunston Green   51
Hunston Hall   51, 53
Hunston Lodge   33
Hysteroceras orbignyi Zone   12, 14, 15
Hysteroceras varicosum Subzone   12, 15

ibex Zone   8
ice wedge casts   35, *64*, 86
Icklingham   2, 22, 23, 24, 35, 44, 48, 49, 56, 60, 64, 72, 86
Icklingham Church   61
Ickworth Park   50
Ingham   8, 38, 45, 49, 54, 79, 86
Ingham Borehole   42
Ingham Dairy   57
Ingham Farm   49
Ingham Folly   *43*
Ingham gravel pit   27, 49
Ingham Sand and Gravel   2, 35, 36, *38*, 43, 45, 79, 86
Inoceramid Bed   2, 14
'Inoceramus Beds'   19, 20
Inoceramus labiatus Zone   21
'*inoceramus lissa*'-rich band   11
Ipswich (207) district   30
Ipswichian   35, 60
Isle of Thanet   24
Isocythereis fissicostis fissicostis ostracod Subzone   12, 14
Ixworth   24, 27, 39, 40, 49, 53, 65, 70, 76, 81, 86
Ixworth Thorpe   41, 76

Jacqueline Close   27, *80*
jamesoni Subzone   8
jamesoni Zone   8
jason Zone   9
'Jukes-Browne Bed 7'   20
Jurassic   8–9

Kellaways Beds   9
Kennett   38, 54, 55, 56, 66
Kennett Church   42, 54, 55, 65, 66
Kennett Hall   65, 66, 67, 75
Kennett, River   38, 46, 54, 64, 65, 66, 81
Kennett valley   55, 62, 64–67, 75
Kentford   6, 38, 50, 64, 65, *71*, 79, 81, 86
Kentford channel   40
Kentford Church   65, 66, 75
Kentford Heath   66
Kentford Home Farm   86
Kesgrave Sands and Gravels   2, 33, 34, 35, *36*, 37, 38, 43, 47, 79, 86
Kettlebaston Fault   30
Kiln Farm   33
Kiln Meadow   33
Kiln Wood   33, 37
Kingsburyhill Wood   75
King's Forest   45, 72
Kingshall Street   30

Lackford   39, 42, 54, 55, 56, 57, 63, 64, 68, 75, 79, 86
Lackford Bridge pit   56
Lackford Church   56
Lackford Manor House   56
Lackford Pit   68
Lacustrine Deposits   35
Lady Katherine's Wood   48
Lakenheath Borehole   4, 5, 7, 9
Langham   33, 47, 49, 75
Larke, River   22, 38, 39, 40, 46, 48, 50, 52, 54, 56, 62, 64, 67, 75, 76, 79, 81
Lark valley   39, 40, 41, 42, 46, 55, 61, 62, 63–64, 67–70, 75, 76
late Albian   14
Leighton Buzzard–Woburn area   9
Lias   8
Lidgate   22
Limekiln Plantation   44
Lingheath   23
Link Wood   51, 53
Linnet, River   76
Linnet valley   62
Little Haugh Hall   40, 47, 51
Little Horringer Hall   46
Little Saxham   50
Little Welnetham   52, 53
Little Welnetham Church   53
Livermere   75, 76
Livermere Heath   38
Livermere Park   57
Livermere Thicks   49
Loch Lomond stadial   56
Lodge Farm   73
London Clay   30
London Platform   1, 2, 4, 8, 13
Lower Albian   10
Lower Aptian   9
Lower Chalk   16–19, 88–89
Lower Chalky Boulder Clay   36
Lower Coniacian   24
Lower Cretaceous   9–15
Lower Devonian   4, 5, 6
Lower Estuarine Series   8
Lower Gault   13, 14
Lower Glacial Sand and Gravel   35, *43*–47, 51, 52, 53, 54
Lower Green   66
Lower Greensand   9–10, 81
Lower Lias   8
Lower London Tertiaries   30
Lower Orbirhynchia Band   19
Lower Oxford Clay   9
Lower Pliensbachian   8
Lower Wood   32
Lowestoft Till   36, 47
Low Green   46, 50
Low Wood   53
Loxostomum eleyi Zone   27, 28
Ludfordian Stage   4, 89–90
Ludham   58
Ludlow Series   4, 89–90
luermannae-hannoverana Zone   15
luermannae-ventrocostata ostracod Zone   14, 15
luridum Subzone   8

Luton–Cambridge Basin   6
Lyelliceras lyelli Subzone   12, 14

Maldon Till   36
mammillatum Zone   10
Manor Farm   41, 50, 74
Mantelliceras dixoni Zone   16, 19
Mantelliceras mantelli Zone   16, 19
Mantelliceras saxbii Subzone   19
mariae Zone   9
Markham, R   30
Marly Drift   36
Marsupites testudinarius Zone   16, 22
masseanum Subzone   8
Matronella corrigenda Subzone   12, 14
Maulkin's Hall   41, 49, 51
Melbourn Rock   16, 18, 20, 21, 22, 88
Methwold Marl   18, 88
Metoicoceras geslinianum Zone   16, 20, 88
Mickle Mere   41
Micraster coranguinum Zone   16, 17, 18, 22, 24, 26, 27, 29, 87
Micraster cortestudinarium Zone   16, 17, 18, 22, 24, 26, 27, 87
mid-Cenomanian nonsequence   20
Middle Cenomanian   20
Middle Chalk   20–22, 61, 66, 80, 81, 86, 88
Middle Oxford Clay   9
Middle Oxfordian   9
Middle Pleistocene   58
Mildenhall   5, 6, 8, 13, 20, 21, 22, 42, 48, 64, 70, 81, 82, 86
Mildenhall brickyard   48, 55, 68
Mildenhall Golf Course   68
Mildenhall Second Upper School   68
Mildenhall Upper School   68
Mildenhall Warren   68
Millfield Wood   53
Mill Hill   63
Milton borrow-pit   15
Milton Brachiopod Band   11, 15
Miocene   2
Mitchel Head   22
Moat Farm   31
Monkspark Wood   53
Moreton Hall   46
Moreton Hall Development   86
Mortoniceras inflatum Zone   12
Mortoniceras perinflatum Subzone   19
Mortoniceras rostratum Subzone   12, 15, 19
Moulton   25, 82
Moulton Bridge   64, 65, 66
Mount Ephraim Marl   18, 21, 88
Mundford   21
Mytiloides labiatus s.l. Zone   16, 17, 18, 21

Nar Valley   58
Needham Hall   42
Neocardioceras juddii Zone   16, 21
Neohibolites-rich bed   11
Neostlingoceras carcitanense Subzone   19
Nether Hall   41
'Nettleton Stone'   18, 20
Newe House   41

New Hall   51
Newhall Covert   74
Newmarket   6
Newmarket Road quarry   21
niobe Subzone   14
North Common   40, 41
North Downs   21
North Hill Covert   52, 86
North Sea   48
Norton   33, 39, 40, 47, 51, 53, 54, 55, 57, 63, 65, 70, 76, 79
Norton Wood   47
Norwich   36
Norwich Crag   30
Nowton   50
Nowton Court   42, 46, 60
Nowton Lodge Farm   42
Nowton Park   62

Oak's Kiln   60
Old Hall   39, 41, 49, 51, 53
Old Hall Farm   47, 76
'*Ostrea*' *papyracea*-rich band   11
O. vesiculosa Beds   15
Ousden   46, 47, 50, 65, 66
Oxford Clay   9

Pakenham   38, 39, 40, 47, 50, 51, 52, 53, 63, 74, 76, 86
Pakenham Church   47
Pakenham Fen   41, 42, 47, 49, 51, 63, 68, 70, 77
palaeosol   35
Palaeozoic   2, 4, 6, 7, 89
'Paradoxica Bed'   19
Park Farm   50, 67
Pastonian   37
patterned ground   49, 70, 72, 74
Peat   35, 68, 76–77
Pilgrim's Walk Marl   18, 88
Pinfold End   62, 75
Pipeclay (1st)   23, 24, 25
  (2nd)   23, 24, 25
  (3rd)   23, 24, 25
Pitcher's Green   31
Planileberis scrobicularis Subzone   12
Platyceramus horizon   29
Plenus Marls   16, 18, 20, 89
Plumpton House   75
Porcellaneous Beds   19
post-Pastonian   37
Potash Farm   34
Pre-Anglian   35
Precambrian   4, 5
Přídolí Series   4
Protocythere albae/bosquetiana   12, 14
Protocythere albae/Dolocytheridea (P.) vinculum Zone   12, 13
Pseudobrecciated band   11

Quaker's Farm   32

Rampart Field   44
Rattlesden   32, 51, 54, 63
Rattlesden School   32
red beds of uncertain age   7
Red Chalk   15

Red Crag   30, 32
Rede Hall   50
redeposited chalk   41
Red Lodge   80
Reid, R E H   26
Richardson, J B   4
Risby   26, 73
Risby Church   73
Risby Heath   22
Risby Poor's Heath   23, 24, 25, 50, 62, 73
River Terrace Deposits   35, 63–70, 79
Robert's Bridge   22
Rose and Crown Well, Stanton   38
Rougham   70
Rougham Green   31, 51
Rougham Green Almshouses   31
Rougham Green Old Hall   31
Rougham Green Old Rectory   31
Rougham Place   32
Rough and Smooth Blacks Flints   22, 23, 24, 25
Rushbrooke   30, 31, 50, 73, 81, 82, 86
Rushbrooke Hall   31

St Botolph's Bridge   76
St Ives Sand and Gravel Co.   32
Sandringham Sands   71
Santonian   27
Sapiston   38, 49, 76
Saxham   30
Saxocythere notera senilis Subzone   12, 13, 14
Second Pipe-Clay   23, 24, 25
Second River Terrace Deposits   64, 65, 66, 67, 68, 70, 79, 86
Seend Ironstone   9, 10
Seven Mile Bridge   26, 66
Sheep Lane   41
Sicklesmere   2, 31, 35, 42, 48, 60, 61, 62, 63, 64, 67, 75, 76
Sieveking, G de G   48
Silurian   4, 5, 89–90
Siluro-Devonian   4, 9
Siveter, D J   4
Slades Covert   62
Smith, D B   8
Snail, River   64
Snail valley   64
Soham Axis   9
Soham Borehole   5, 6, 8, 9
sol lessivé   37
Southgate brickyard   46
Southgate Bridge   67
South Wood   67
Springhill Covert   62
Stanton   16, 27, 30, 33, 36, 37, 38, 43, 47, 49, 53, 79, 86
Stanton Chare   41, 49
Stanton Street   53
Starston Till   47
Stensioeina exsculpta Biozone   27
S. granulata perfecta Biozone   29
S. granulata polonica Biozone   27
Sternotaxis plana Zone   16, 17, 18, 22, 23, 24, 26, 87
Stoliczkaia dispar Zone   12, 15, 17, 19

Stonecross Green   75
Stowlangtoft   30, 36, 37, 39, 40, 41, 42, 47, 48, 51, 53, 65, 70, 73, 76
Stowlangtoft Borehole   4, 8, 13, 18, 19, 20, 21, 22, 23, 24, 25, 26, 87–90
Stowlangtoft chalk pit   18, 27, 28, 33, 37, 74
Stowlangtoft Church   53
Stowlangtoft Hall   41
Street Farm   40, 47
Stretham Axis   9
subdelaruei Subzone   14
Subprionocyclus neptuni Zone   23
Sudbury   48, 58
Sudbury (206) district   30
Suffolk Whites   57, 81
Sugar Beet Factory   26
Swanscombe   61

Taylor, B J   56
Temple Bridge   76
Temple Weir   81
tenuiserratum Zone   9
Terebratulina lata Zone   16, 17, 18, 21, 22
Thalassinoides burrows   20
Thames (proto)   2, 35
Thanet Beds   2, 30
'Thanet Sand'   32
The Holmes   62
Thelnetham   49
'The Mottled Bed'   14
The Plains   62
Thetford district   13, 21, 23, 24
Thetford Heath   71, 74
Thetford Museum   27
Third Pipe-Clay   23, 24, 25
Third River Terrace Deposits   65, 66, 67, 70, 79
Thurston   16, 32, 37, 41, 63
Thurston Grange Hotel   41
Thurston House   32
Thurston Planch   63
Thurston Station   32
Ticehurst House   32
Till — see Boulder Clay
Timworth   38, 46, 52, 67, 75
Timworth Church   76
Timworth Farm   68
Timworth Green   52, 61, 63, 73
Timworth Hall   52, 62
Timworth Long Court   52
Tollgate Bridge   75
Tooley, M J   56
Toppings Flint   23, 24
Top Rock   16, 17, 18, 23–24, 25, 26, 86, 87
Tostock   32, 36, 37, 51, 52, 54, 71, 72, 76, 79, 86
Tostock council house   32
Tostock gravel pit   47
Tostock House   32, 54
Tostock Place   32, 54
Totternhoe   20
Totternhoe Stone   16, 18, 19–20, 89
Triassic strata   6, 7–8
Troston   38, 39, 40, 45, 48, 49, 62
Troston Borehole   41

Troston Hall 49
Troston Heath 62
Troston Mount 62
Tuddenham 22, 42, 54, 55, 63, 64, 65, 66, 68, 76, 79
Tuddenham Heath 42, 64, 70
tufa 61, 68, 76
tunnel-valleys 38, 54, 60
Turonian 21
Turrilites costatus ammonite Subzone 20
Twelve Acre Plantation 33
Twin Marls 18, 22, 88

Uintacrinus socialis Zone 16, 17, 18, 22, 24, 27, 29
Upper Aptian 9
Upper Cenomanian 20
Upper Chalk 21, 22–29, 62, 79, 81, 86, 87–88
Upper Chalky Boulder Clay 36
Upper Crust Flint 23, 24
Upper Estuarine Series 8
Upper Gault 13, 14
Upper Glacial Sand and Gravel 35, 47, 49, 51, 52–54, 58, 59
Upper Ludlow 4, 89–90
Upper *Orbirhynchia mantelliana* Band 20
Upper Oxford Clay 9
Upper Silurian 4, 5, 89–90

Upper Town 41, 63
Upware Axis 9

valdani Subzone 8
'*Volviceramus*-Belt' 18, 24, 26, 27

Wall Stone 23, 24, 25, 87
Walsham-le-Willows 34
Wangford 37
Warren Belt 44
Warren Hill 48, 86
Watermill Farm 47
water supply 81
Watinoceras coloradoense Zone 21
Wattisfield 37
Weatherhill Farm 22, 44, 49, 86
Westfield Farm 49, 57
Westland Green Member 35
Westleton Beds 37
Westley 27, 46, 50
Westley Bottom 73
West Row 20
West Stow 40, 49, 67, 75, 82
West Tofts Marl 18, 23, 26, 87
West Walton Beds 9
Whepstead 30, 52, 62, 75
Whitaker's 3-inch Flint Band 27
Whitefield House 32

Willowmere Spinney 24
Windermere Interstadial 56
Winery, Risby Poor's Heath 23, 25
Woburn Sands 9, 10
Wolstonian 36, 52, 60
Woodcock Covert 68
Woodlands 66
Woodstreet Farm 29, 34, 41, 49, 51
Woolpit 32, 33, 36, 37, 39, 40, 47, 48, 51, 54, 57, 59, 65, 70, 71, 72, 78, 79, 86
Woolpit Beds 3, 35, 36, 57–59, 80, 81, 86
Woolpit No. 1 Borehole 58
No. 2 Borehole 58
No. 3 Borehole 30, 31, 33, 57, 58
Woolpit brickworks 33, *58*, 81
Woolpit By-pass 74
Woolpit Church 59
Woolpit Green 33, 51, 53, 54
Woolpit Green searchlight station 33
Woolpit Whites 57, 81
Worlington 21, 64, 68
Wyken Hall 37, 86
Wyken Wood 24, 29, 34, 37
Wymer, J 70

Younger Cover Sand 72

BRITISH GEOLOGICAL SURVEY

Keyworth, Nottingham NG12 5GG
(06077) 6111

Murchison House, West Mains Road,
Edinburgh EH9 3LA   031-667 1000

London Information Office, Natural History Museum
Earth Galleries, Exhibition Road, London SW7 2DE
071-589 4090

The full range of Survey publications is available through the Sales Desks at Keyworth, Murchison House, Edinburgh, and at the BGS London Information Office in the Natural History Museum, Earth Galleries. The adjacent bookshop stocks the more popular books for sale over the counter. Most BGS books and reports are listed in HMSO's Sectional List 45, and can be bought from HMSO and through HMSO agents and retailers. Maps are listed in the BGS Map Catalogue and the Ordnance Survey's Trade Catalogue, and can be bought from Ordnance Survey agents as well as from BGS.

The British Geological Survey carries out the geological survey of Great Britain and Northern Ireland (the latter as an agency service for the government of Northern Ireland), and of the surrounding continental shelf, as well as its basic research projects. It also undertakes programmes of British technical aid in geology in developing countries as arranged by the Overseas Development Administration.

The British Geological Survey is a component body of the Natural Environment Research Council.

Maps and diagrams in this book use topography based on Ordnance Survey mapping

HMSO

HMSO publications are available from:

HMSO Publications Centre
(Mail and telephone orders)
PO Box 276, London SW8 5DT
Telephone orders 071-873 9090
General enquiries 071-873 0011
Queueing system in operation for both numbers

HMSO Bookshops
49 High Holborn, London WC1V 6HB
  071-873 0011 (Counter service only)
258 Broad Street, Birmingham B1 2HE
  021-643 3740
Southey House, 33 Wine Street, Bristol BS1 2BQ
  (0272) 264306
9 Princess Street, Manchester M60 8AS
  061-834 7201
80 Chichester Street, Belfast BT1 4JY
  (0232) 238451
71 Lothian Road, Edinburgh EH3 9AZ
  031-228 4181

HMSO's Accredited Agents
(see Yellow Pages)

And through good booksellers